WORDSWORTH'S INFLUENCE ON SHELLEY

Wordsworth's Influence on Shelley

A Study of Poetic Authority

G. KIM BLANK

Assistant Professor of English
University of Victoria, Canada

St. Martin's Press   New York

© G. Kim Blank 1988

All rights reserved. For information, write:
Scholarly & Reference Division,
St. Martin's Press, Inc., 175 Fifth Avenue, New York, NY 10010

First published in the United States of America in 1988

Printed in Hong Kong

ISBN 0–312–01179–2

Library of Congress Cataloging-in-Publication Data
Blank, G. Kim, 1952–
Wordsworth's influence on Shelley.
Bibliography: p.
Includes index.
1. Shelley, Percy Bysshe, 1792–1822—Criticism and
interpretation.   2. Wordsworth, William, 1770–1850—
Influence—Shelley.   3. Shelley, Percy Bysshe, 1792–1822—
Contemporaries.   4. Wordsworth, William, 1770–1850, in
fiction, drama, poetry, etc.   5. Influence (Literary, artistic,
etc.) I. Title.
PR5433.B5   1987   821'.7   87–13058
ISBN 0–312–01179–2

For Gloria, Danny, and Kirk

True poetic history is the story of how poets as poets have suffered other poets

                        Harold Bloom

In honoured poverty thy voice did weave
Songs consecrate to truth and liberty, –
Deserting these, thou leavest me to grieve,
Thus having been, that thou shouldst cease to be.

                Shelley, 'To Wordsworth'

Contents

	Preface	ix
	A Note on the Text	xii
Part I	**Foundations**	
	Introduction	3
1	Shelley's Scene of Influence	8
2	A New Presence	26
3	'Proteus Wordsworth'	45
Part II	**Speculations**	
	Introduction	81
4	Poets, Princes and Fallen Figures	86
5	The Maniac Poet	113
6	Shelley Unbound	132
7	Righting Wordsworth	159
8	The Wind of Inspiration	193
	Epilogue	221
	Notes	226
	Index	240

Preface

To study the influence of one poet on another is to attempt to study a process, or at least the various outcomes of a process. Some might argue that it is an impossible task simply because of the complexity involved, that studying influence not only means working on a number of levels where complicated information is available, but also that *one* influence can never be singled out as *the* influence. Influence, they could argue, works by combinations and accumulation: one effect comes about not just as a point in an infinite chain of causes, but as the result of a number of causes working at once. There is also the rather troubling reminder that to study the influence of one poet on another is to interpret one poet's interpretation of another.

Admittedly, the study of the influence of just one poet on another is an act of exclusion, of disacknowledging other influences; but though this is necessary, it is also temporary: the influenced poet is closed down to other influences in order to negotiate and evaluate one aspect of his poetry or poetical being. On the other hand, we could abandon the study of influence between two poets altogether and concern ourselves with the less problematical job of comparison. But this would not solve the problem of influence, only deny that it exists, that poets influence each other at all. It would only serve to disacknowledge a fundamental truth of literary history: writers are concerned with other writers. The trouble, of course, is determining the effect this 'concern' has on the act of creation. At any rate, comparison is necessarily a mode of examination in studying influence. From the beginning one can only acknowledge the inherent complexity and pitfalls of the task, and hope to do justice to the specific problem by admitting that it is part of the much greater problem of not just how art comes to being, but of how art can be studied.

In this book I want to consider three interrelated things: first, that Percy Bysshe Shelley was very concerned with being influenced, with the problems of literary influence (especially contemporary influence: the spirit of the age); second, that Shelley's work is often involved with the production of poetry and the figure of the poet coming-into-being; and third, that Shelley was troubled by and knowledgeable about Wordsworth, the issues and problems Wordsworth and his poetry raised, to the extent that throughout his career as a poet he was continually compelled to poetically address his older contemporary. I want to prove what many critics have intuited: that Wordsworth is the single most important influence on Shelley's poetic development.

The study falls into two parts. Part I examines Shelley's awareness of influence and his familiarity with Wordsworth. It also evaluates Shelley's poetry which is actually about Wordsworth. The evidence in this first part forms the foundations for the second part of the study. Part II moves between being tentative and being speculative, attempting to cope with the subtleties of what takes place when one poet and his poetry come under the influence of another. In choosing which poems to examine, my aim has been selective rather than exhaustive. In shape, sound and sense there are hundreds of phrases and lines in Shelley that unmistakably bear the mark of Wordsworth's influence. I have by-passed many of these. Instead, in Part II I selected those poems and passages which in more sustained and engaging ways witness Shelley contending with Wordsworthian problems and poet-figures.

I see my study as complementing those of Richard Cronin (*Shelley's Poetic Thoughts*, 1981) and Angela Leighton (*Shelley and the Sublime*, 1984). What I think we are pointing to in Shelley's work is a self-consciousness of poetry itself, a kind of creative reflexiveness. Shelley's poems are often about themselves as works of literature, and thus their subject matter is related to aspects of poetry and the formulation of poetry: poetic language, poetic form, composition, inspiration, influence, and the figure of the poet. They are allegories of writing poetry. This is not to say that Shelley's work lacks connections with the real world or with pragmatic concerns, but that his work has a manifestly literary side that is only now beginning to be understood. It is hoped that this present work contributes to this understanding.

I would like to acknowledge three bodies for their financial assistance at various stages in completing this study: the University of Southampton, the Committee of Vice-Chancellors and Principals of the Universities of the United Kingdom, and the Social Sciences and

Humanities Research Council of Canada. I would like to thank Isobel Armstrong for her encouragement and advice throughout the early stages of this study. But I am especially grateful to Derek Attridge for acting as my acknowledged legislator. I also thank my wife, Tara, for giving me her support throughout this project. And I must mention my beautiful daughter Acia, whose birth and growth coincided so happily with this project.

Portions of this study have appeared in *The Wordsworth Circle*, *Philological Quarterly*, and *English Studies in Africa*.

G. K. B.

Windhoek,
SWA/Namibia

A Note on the Text

Unless indicated otherwise, all quotations from Shelley's poems, his prefaces to the poems, and Mary Shelley's notes to his poems, are from *Shelley: Poetical Works*, edited by Thomas Hutchinson and corrected by G. M. Matthews (Oxford University Press, 1970). All quotations and dating of Shelley's letters are from *The Letters of Percy Bysshe Shelley*, edited by Frederick L. Jones (2 vols, Oxford University Press, 1964; hereafter abbreviated as *Letters*). The texts of Shelley's essays *A Defence of Poetry* and *On Life* and *On Love* are taken from *Shelley's Poetry and Prose*, edited by Donald Reiman and Sharon B. Powers (New York: W. W. Norton, 1977). All other quotations from Shelley's prose are from *Shelley's Prose; or The Trumpet of a Prophecy*, ed. David Lee Clark (1954; revised edn, Albuquerque, N.M.: University of New Mexico Press, 1966). Quotations from Wordsworth's poems and Preface to the *Lyrical Ballads* (1880 and 1802) are from the edition of R. L. Brett and A. R. Jones (1963; rev. edn, London: Methuen, 1965). All other quotations from Wordsworth's poems are from *Wordsworth: Poetical Works*, edited by Thomas Hutchinson and revised by Ernest de Selincourt (Oxford University Press, 1936).

Part I
Foundations

Introduction

Wordsworth and Shelley have often been compared in passing. Recall, for example, Francis Thompson's comments in *Shelley* (1909). Thompson claimed that Shelley and Wordsworth are, respectively, analogous to the Nightingale and Stock-dove in Wordsworth's poem of that name of 1807:

> O Nightingale! thou surely art
> A creature of a 'fiery heart':–
> These notes of thine – they pierce and pierce;
> Tumultuous harmony and fierce!
> Thou sing'st as if the God of wine
> Had helped thee to a Valentine;
> A song in mockery and despite
> Of shades, and dews, and silent night;
> And steady bliss, and all the loves
> Now sleeping in these peaceful groves.
>
> I heard a Stock-dove sing or say
> His homely tale, this very day;
> His voice was buried among trees,
> Yet to be come-at by the breeze:
> He did not cease; but cooed – and cooed;
> And somewhat pensively he wooed:
> He sang of love, with quiet blending,
> Slow to begin, and never ending;
> Of serious faith, and inward glee;
> That was the song – the song for me!

These descriptions coincide neatly with the popular views of 'pensive' Wordsworth and 'fierce' and unsettled Shelley, though Shelley might have preferred to be a high-flying skylark. As another example, recall F. R. Leavis's comparison of the two poets in *Revaluation* (1936), where the clarity and soundness of Wordsworth's poetry is judged to be superior to the opaqueness and confusion in Shelley:

Shelley's 'weak grasp upon the actual' as opposed to 'the sureness with which Wordsworth grasps the world of common perception'.[1]

Leavis's comparison itself appears more in touch with the 'actual' than Thompson's, although it might be argued that both contribute to stereotypical views inherited from the Victorians: Leavis from the condemnations of Shelley by Matthew Arnold;[2] Thompson from the rather flowery biographies that also appeared at the time.[3] But what both Leavis and Thompson have done is to compare the two poets on just one level. Neither critic approaches the problem of 'Wordsworth and Shelley' with both historical and psychological premises which would establish a relationship between contemporaries – one older, one younger – working at rather close quarters.

It is somewhat surprising that there is no detailed study of this poetic relationship. If it were the case that we were studying the influence of a major poet on a minor poet, or a minor on a major, we might expect some gaps in the literature. But this is not the case. Wordsworth and Shelley are both acknowledged to be major figures. Thus while there are a number of studies tracing the influence of each on a number of other poets, the history and nature of the relationship between Wordsworth and Shelley has not been considered in detail. What I hope to establish is that Wordsworth was constantly (and creatively) on Shelley's mind, so much so that the claim might be made that Wordsworth is the single most important poetic influence on Shelley.

Since identification, mastery and power will play important parts in the scene of influence I wish to direct, and since the double-bind over originality/imitation is especially relevant to the Romantics, it is a psychoanalytical model which at times proves to be helpful in approach – specifically, the structure of the Oedipal situation. (And here Harold Bloom's work on influence is acknowledged.) Yet because this study is not always dealing with personalities but with poetry too, a statement must be formulated which can account for both the poetry and the personalities and the relationship between them. What I want to offer is this: *Shelley's problematic identification with the figurative authority of Wordsworth*. By this I mean two interdependent things: first, that Shelley was influenced by the figure of authority (the *authoritative* poet) named William Wordsworth; second, that Shelley was influenced by the originating poetic authority in Wordsworth's figurative language, metaphors and tropes: Wordsworth's *authorial* presence. My reason for formulating a double pun on the figure/author relationship is to emphasise the dualistic, ambiguous representation Wordsworth was for Shelley. It is hoped that this way of formulating the problem expresses this difficulty not through any semantic trickery, but by enunciating the problem in its most precise form. The emphasis on *figure* is especially important. In Wordsworth's own poetry his presence (as poet-speaker) is frequently the most powerful if not most potent and perplexing image. In other words, the figure of the poet in Wordsworth's poetry is necessarily a figurative presence, a figure of speech, if you will. Thus what Shelley confronts in Wordsworth's poetry is often Wordsworth's own poetic (authorial/authoritative/figurative) presence.

Wordsworth was not only seen by other poets as a precursor, as a sort of father figure, but also saw himself in that role of a guiding influence. 'Every great Poet is a Teacher,' he wrote to Sir George Beaumont in 1808; 'I wish either to be considered as a Teacher, or as nothing.'[4] It is a matter of opinion whether his progenitorial and pedagogical motivation was a kind of poetic altruism or a self-deification deriving from a fear of death. Perhaps they are the same thing, in that for Wordsworth 'immortality' (poetic endurance) is always at stake. But there is little doubt that he was conscious of leaving an inheritance, his own story to be taken up and retold. Shelley not only saw the potential in this inheritance, but attempted to poetically actualise it as well. These following lines from Wordsworth enumerate that will and inheritance, and I propose that it is Shelley, more than anyone else, who becomes Wordsworth's 'second self':

> Therefore, although it be a history
> Homely and rude, I will relate the same
> For the delight of a few natural hearts,
> And with yet fonder feeling, for the sake
> Of youthful Poets, who among these Hills
> Will be my second self when I am gone.
> (*Michael*, 34–9)

Because in Shelley's eyes Wordsworth could go no further, and because it is especially the Solitary of *The Excursion* who often represents the inadequacies and unresolved problems facing the older poet, Shelley's project is to take the Solitary/Wordsworth through a series of poetic trials, akin to and ranging from the ceremonies of baptism (the rights of admission to Wordsworth's sublime) to exorcism (possessed by the 'spirit' of Wordsworth,

Shelley must free himself from Wordsworth). The former can be found in Shelley's earliest poetry, in some of the poems of the Esdaile Notebook; the latter, Shelley freeing himself and proclaiming himself a poet, is evident in some of the poems written in his *annus mirabilis*, from autumn 1818 to early 1820.

The question is: to what extent, and in what ways, are Shelley's heroes (and his poems) determined and prefigured by Wordsworth (and Wordsworthian problems)? And by 'Wordsworth' I mean Shelley's Wordsworth, that complicated entity who is man and poet, contemporary yet predecessor, who is to be praised, pitied and scorned; I mean the complicated entity always to be emulated and subverted; a figure of Oedipal complexity. Might it then be suggested that Shelley 'killed' Wordsworth, his father figure, in order to marry the same Muse to which Wordsworth was wed? Could it be said that Shelley sought to engage the source of Wordsworth's own inspiration? The answer is yes. Shelley's poetry about Wordsworth portrays the older poet as if he were dead. This figurative death allows Shelley to hold on to the early Wordsworth (eulogising him), to punish him for his poetic and personal failings, and to inherit the place of the dead leader. Because the hostile component of the Oedipal complex dictates that the son has wishful thoughts of killing the father whom he also imitates, there are (repressed) manifestations of this in Shelley's poetry: Shelley figuratively killing Wordsworth in a Wordsworthian mode. In other words, those poems of Shelley where this poetic parricide takes place are some of his most Wordsworthian poems. But for Shelley 'Wordsworth' is not now a man and now a poet, now a good poet and now a bad poet, now to be followed and now to be avoided: he is at all times all these figures, all these situations; and Shelley is never certain of how quite to distinguish them. His poetry tries to work this out. Further, besides being a historical individual, 'Wordsworth' for Shelley is also a force representing the burden of the past, the given of the poetic tradition and its language: 'Wordsworth' as a style of expression that Shelley must contend with and surpass.

From the invocation to *Alastor* (1816), which is Shelley's first sustained Wordsworthian trial, and which marks the beginning of his mature poetry, Shelley waits as Wordsworth's progeny on the threshold of usurping his predecessor's life-giving inspiration: he appeals to Wordsworth's own Muse:

> I wait thy breath, Great Parent, that my strain

> May modulate with murmurs of the air,
> And motions of the forest and the sea,
> And voice of living beings, and woven hymns
> Of night and day, and the deep heart of man.

It is difficult to find anywhere else in Shelley where a nurturing figure is held in such reverent and anxious deferral, and anywhere else where Shelley or any other poet sounds so much like young Wordsworth.

1
Shelley's Scene of Influence

Harold Bloom says that 'all poets, weak and strong, agree in denying any share in the anxiety of influence'.[1] I am surprised Bloom says this; for Bloom is (using his own poetic lexicon) a 'strong' and 'deep' reader of Shelley. As I hope to show, Shelley acknowledges his anxiety over influence and uses it as a source of poetic strength. In short, this chapter examines the development of Shelley's idea of poetic influence, noting that Shelley often uses aspects of Wordsworth's Preface to the *Lyrical Ballads* as a foil in the formulation of his argument.

I

In the Preface to *The Revolt of Islam* (1818) Shelley begins a discussion of influence by declining rivalry with his contemporaries, yet at the same time claiming originality:

> I do not presume to enter into competition with our greatest contemporary Poets. Yet I am unwilling to tread in the footsteps of any who have preceded me. I have sought to avoid the imitation of any style or language of versification peculiar to the original minds of which it is the character; designing that, even if what I have produced be worthless, it should still be properly my own. Nor have I permitted any system relating to mere words to divert the attention of the reader, from whatever interest I may have succeeded in creating, to my own ingenuity in contriving to disgust them according to the rules of criticism. I have simply clothed my thoughts in what appeared to me the most obvious and appropriate language. A person familiar with nature, and with the most celebrated productions of the human mind, can scarcely err in following the instinct, with respect to selection of language, produced by that familiarity.

There is something uneasy and unconvincing here. Shelley mentions his contemporaries by way of avoiding them, or 'any who have preceded' him. The value of his work, he claims, is apparently secondary to the fact that at least the work is his own. His poem just doesn't naturally happen to be original; it is, Shelley states, his design and intention to be unique. But by setting himself up like this Shelley is of course drawing attention to his work *relative* to the influences he disclaims – namely, to those 'greatest contemporary Poets'. By way of exclusion, then, Shelley has actually included himself in competition with his peers. One paragraph later he realises he cannot avoid resemblance with those sharing the age with him.

But for the moment, how does Shelley believe he can achieve originality in his poetry? In the second half of the above passage he says he can by employing a language which comes by being 'familiar with nature', by 'following the instinct . . . produced by that familiarity'. This recalls Wordsworth's idea (in the Preface to the *Lyrical Ballads*) that poetry must be the natural language of men:

> There will also be found in these volumes little of what is usually called poetic diction; I have taken as much pains to avoid it as others ordinarily take to produce it; this I have done for the reason already alleged, to bring my language near to the language of men, and further, because the pleasure which I have proposed to myself to impart is of a kind very different from that which is supposed by many persons to be the proper object of poetry.

Wordsworth too is claiming originality in his poetic language, as well as in the type of 'pleasure' he is imparting to his readers. Shelley, following Wordsworth, in fact uses the same term as his great contemporary – 'avoid' – to indicate the conscious desire to evade conventional poetic language. But whereas Wordsworth claims his originality on the basis of using language *copied* from a source that seems to be outside of himself and not normally considered poetic (he also writes, 'I have proposed to myself to imitate, and, as far as is possible, to adopt the very language of men'), Shelley believes his originality in poetic language comes about by following his instincts, what comes most naturally to himself. On this basis Shelley's language appears to have a more personal source than Wordsworth's. But we cannot forget the other 'familiar' source that Shelley says he is following, what he calls 'the most celebrated productions of the human mind'. Shelley must be referring to works of art created by those he wishes to emulate – those, we must think, like Wordsworth.

So what background does Shelley believe a poet should possess, and what about Shelley's own personal background? The young and obviously aspiring poet goes on to talk about his 'accidental education', and to give a rather dramatic catalogue of his personal experiences, his familiarity with nature and solitude, his wanderings through mountains and fields. At the same time he has seen the 'visible ravages of tyranny and war'. He also 'conversed with living men of genius', and has passionately enjoyed Greek and Roman poetry, as well as contemporary Italian and English works. These, together with readings of 'the Poets and the Historians and the Metaphysicians', and along with his experience of the beautiful and majestic 'scenery of earth', he calls the

> common sources of those elements which it is the province of the Poet to embody and combine. Yet the experience and the feelings to which I refer do not in themselves constitute men Poets, but only prepares them to be the auditors of those who are. How far I shall be found to possess that more essential attribute of Poetry, the power of awakening in others sensations like those which animate my own bosom, is that which, to speak sincerely, I know not; and which, with an acquiescent and contented spirit, I expect to be taught by the effect which I shall produce upon those whom I now address.

What the poet must do is 'embody and combine' both literary and personal influences. Yet this is still not enough; this just qualifies someone to be an 'auditor' of poetry. To be a Poet, Shelley says, is to have 'the power of awakening in others sensations like those which animate my own bosom'. In one sense this again calls back to what Wordsworth says in the Preface to the *Lyrical Ballads*, that 'The Poet writes under one restriction only, that of the necessity of giving immediate pleasure to a human Being possessed of that information which may be expected from him.' But there is a difference between what Shelley sees as the relationship between a Poet and his reader and what Wordsworth sees is proper to that relationship. Shelley's emphasis on that 'more essential attribute of Poetry' is to share the immediacy of his experience with his reader through his poetry, to have his reader relating, as it were, on the same level. He wants his reader to take part in that which motivates and inspires him.

Wordsworth, by comparison, sees the Poet's position in this relationship as removed from that which he described in his poetry and the response he elicits. While Wordsworth's stated purposes are to describe, imitate and illustrate, Shelley's purpose is to awaken and affect his reader. Wordsworth hopes that his Preface to *Lyrical Ballads* has 'assisted' his reader in understanding and enjoying his poetry. But there is another, more interesting way of putting one of the differences between the two poets: Wordsworth desires that his Poet comes down to the common reader; Shelley desires that his reader comes up to the uncommon Poet.

One significant difference between the two poets becomes noticeable here, and it has to do with what they believe the subject matter or experience of poetry is or should be. Wordsworth holds that his poetry translates and enhances real life, making 'the incidents of common life interesting'. Shelley, on the other hand, believes his poetry to be about the experience of poetry, not necessarily real life. The effect he often wishes his poetry to create is the same effect it had on him while creating it. In this sense Shelley's poetry is bound to be reflexive and self-referential, in what might be called an ironic mode. It may constantly undercut and question its own formulations. For this reason Shelley's poems frequently end on a note of irresolution and disaffirmation. This is another way of saying that Shelley has a sceptical strain, something which readers have always felt to be present in his arguments.[2] But what I want to suggest here, and to substantiate later in readings of some of Shelley's poems, is that this scepticism is related to a scepticism of poetry itself, the problematical truth that poetry can only ever seek out its own precariousness, and what strong poetry displays is never more than a changing potential, yet never less. A part of this is, in short, a scepticism of Wordsworth's mode of poetry that is founded on a rhetoric of resolution and affirmation.

Shelley continues to discuss influence in the Preface to *The Revolt of Islam*, but now his arguments are more sharply focused. He realises that there is an *anxiety* hanging over the poet, a desire to *escape* influence but an inability to do so:

> I have avoided, as I have said before, the imitation of any contemporary style. But there must be a resemblance, which does not depend upon their own will, between all the writers of any particular age. They cannot escape from subjection to a common influence which arises out of an infinite combination of circumstances

belonging to the times in which they live; though each is in a degree the author of the very influence by which his being is thus pervaded.

Shelley concludes that 'points of resemblance' between writers are the ineluctable result of the times: 'And this is an influence which neither the meanest scribbler nor the sublimest genius of any era can escape; and which I have not attempted to escape.' Originality, then, is always a relative term, never an absolute. And it is especially a relative term for those who share the 'common' and 'inevitable influence' of their era. But the poet is both a product and producer of his age, and in this realisation he can rest a little more easily. After all, the poet has little choice in this matter. It is, Shelley says, beyond his will.

Two points must be underlined here and following. First, Shelley's concern with influences is mainly with contemporary influence. The voices of the past do not, for Shelley, speak as loudly as those of the present. Second, note the implication of the terms Shelley uses in describing influence: *avoidance*, *subjection* and *escape*. All of these conjure up a scene where a struggle takes place between an artist who is striving for individual creativity and external forces existing beyond his control. The result of this struggle, which above appeared as a contradiction in Shelley's argument, is a form of submission: from this, Shelley says, 'I have not attempted to escape'. But, as I shall point out, this submission has positive consequences: the submission is, Shelley holds, not a form of restriction, of containing or constraining, but rather the predicament becomes a source of liberation and inspiration. When Shelley began his argument by saying 'I do not presume to enter into competition with our greatest contemporary Poets', he is now in effect admitting that it cannot be helped. He has entered into competition with those very writers who have influenced him. And this, Shelley finds, is a source of inspiration.

II

The reasoning on influence and originality that Shelley developed in the Preface to *The Revolt of Islam* continues a few years later in the Preface to *Prometheus Unbound* (1820). But instead of working towards a conclusion where the problematics of these issues are rationalised,

Shelley is now confident enough to begin with a statement of artistic freedom and creative revisionism:

> The Greek tragic writers, in selecting as their subject any portion of their national history or mythology, employed in their treatment of it a certain arbitrary discretion. They by no means conceived themselves bound to adhere to the common interpretation or to imitate in story as in title their rivals and predecessors. Such a system would have amounted to a resignation of those claims to preference over their competitors which incited the composition. The Agamemnonian story was exhibited on the Athenian theatre with as many variations as dramas.

> I have presumed to employ a similar licence.

Shelley feels here no compulsion to retell histories or myths as they were originally told. He feels writers should intentionally, even capriciously *reinterpret* the stories they tell; and so, as Shelley goes on to explain, *Prometheus Unbound* becomes his poetic (creative) revision of Aeschylus' story.

Shelley has no problem in managing influence from the past. However, he once more admits that he finds contending with contemporaries, with the *Zeitgeist*, more difficult. He writes about how 'the study of contemporary writings may have tinged my composition':

> It is impossible that any one who inhabits the same age with such writers as those who stand in the foremost ranks of our own, can conscientiously assure himself that his language and tone of thought may not have been modified by the study of the productions of those extraordinary intellects. It is true, that, not the spirit of their genius, but the forms in which it has manifested itself, are due less to the peculiarities of their own minds than to the peculiarity of the moral and intellectual condition of the minds among which they have been produced. Thus a number of writers possess the form, whilst they want the spirit of those whom, it is alleged, they imitate; because the former is the endowment of the age in which they live, and the latter must be the uncommunicated lightning of their own mind. . . .

> The great writers of our own age are, we have reason to suppose, the companions and forerunners of some unimagined change in our social condition or the opinions which cement it. The cloud of

mind is discharging its collected lightning, and the equilibrium between institutions and opinions is now restoring, or is about to be restored.

As to imitation, poetry is a mimetic art. It creates, but it creates by combination and representation. . . . A poet is the combined product of such internal powers as modify the nature of others; and of such external influences as excite and sustain these powers; he is not one, but both. Every man's mind is, in this respect, modified by all the objects of nature and art; by every word and every suggestion which he ever admitted to act upon his consciousness; it is the mirror upon which all forms are reflected, and in which they compose one form. Poets, not otherwise than philosophers, painters, sculptors, and musicians, are, in one sense, the creators, and, in another, the creations, of their age. From this subjection the loftiest do not escape.

As in the Preface to *The Revolt of Islam*, Shelley again acknowledges the impossibility of *escaping* contemporary influence. A poet is a part of the influence which he partakes, a creation of that which he creates. Wordsworth too was aware of this relationship, although in some ways he denies influence by making it more a pedagogical act of will: as he wrote to Lady Beaumont in May 1807, 'every great and original writer, in proportion as he is great or original, must himself create the taste by which he is to be relished; he must teach the art by which he is to be seen'. Behind Wordsworth's reasoning is this: the stronger the poet, the less he is influenced and the more he influences. Then again, we know that Wordsworth always wanted to be remembered as a teacher, not a pupil.

But what would be the result of a poet deciding that he is no longer going to partake of the influence of his age? Shelley answers in the Preface to *Prometheus Unbound*:

> He might as wisely and as easily determine that his mind should no longer be the mirror of all that is lovely in the visible universe, as exclude from his contemplation the beautiful which exists in the writings of a great contemporary. The pretence of doing it would be a presumption in any but the greatest; the effect, even in him, would be strained, unnatural, and ineffectual.

So any doubts the poet has about being original outside of a contemporary context can only lead to inferior poetry. Shelley bluntly dispels the myth (indeed, it is a Romantic myth) of the isolated artist working without any outside contact. In short, the poet *must* be influenced to be successful.

Shelley shows in these passages a remarkable concern about how influence works on writers – or at least on himself. He sees the poet as a medium through which things pass. But the image of a medium is too simplistic, as well as too benign or passive. The poet does not just let things pass through him unchanged. He combines one influence with others passing through him. In this process the poet is thus an active agent, himself also changing. His 'consciousness' is in a constant state of modification, and itself is a constant modifier. Shelley holds that *everything* acts not just upon the poet's mind, but on 'Every man's mind' – every object in 'nature and art' and 'every word and suggestion' modifies the mind, and what the mind produces. In the case of the poet this is, of course, poetry. The only way that this flux can be coped with by the mind (as mirror-lens) is by reflecting and focusing it as 'one form'. But what remains singularly important and unique in Shelley's argument is that the greatest originality goes hand-in-hand with the greatest openness to influence. Working between and with these forces of influence, himself a force of influence, the poet composes his poetry.

For Shelley the formal aspects of poetry inevitably follow contemporary style or conventions. But there is more to what makes a 'great writer'. He must, as Shelley says, not only be an *influenced* factor but an *influencing* one as well. Holding on to inspiration and producing poetry remains a precarious task, as precarious as the way in which this process can be described. Thus the metaphor of the creative poet's mind first evolves in the Preface to *Prometheus Unbound* as one of a lightning storm, where charged particles collect in a cloud and then, upon reaching a critical moment, discharge into momentary flashes of brilliance or illumination. What new influences or changes will come into being cannot be apprehended in advance, and it is the unpredictable results of these new combinations that excite Shelley so much. This is what he wants to share with his reader – new relationships. But even the cloud and lightning analogy can for Shelley only partly express the properties of the poet's influential being. Shelley retains the metaphor of light, but he also invokes an all-collecting and all-reflecting mirror as an analogue for the mind. Shelley's mode of description might be commented on here, as it is, in fact, an example of the very process he is describing. That is, here in Shelley's writing about the workings of creative expression he does what he says the poetic mind must do: just as he moved from an image of clouds and lightning to an image of a mirror, the poet in an attempt to express his inspiration must be constantly shifting and adapting; the creative act must be an act of seeking out, exploration and moving on. Poetry, like the poet himself, is an object of modification. It is this tropological restlessness, this seeking out and moving on in his metaphorical constructions, that characterises some of Shelley's greatest poetry. It is also where it is most likely to fail by over-searching, over-reaching. Shelley cannot, in composing poetry, hold or sustain a single image before it fades away or becomes another image. His poetry is, to borrow and extend just a part of one of Wordsworth's most famous phrases, the spontaneous overflow of powerful images, one overflowing into another. The opening section of *Mont Blanc* is a perfect example of this.

It must be admitted, then, that Shelley's images in this passage from the Preface to *Prometheus Unbound* are not consistent. One image seems, only by loose association, to lead to another. But this is not saying that he is using an extended metaphor. After all, a mirror is not the natural extension we might make from lightning. The distinction Shelley makes between the two is important: he knows that the way one part of contemporary influence touches him is analogous to mirroring (imitating); but he intuits that it also works in a more sublime or supernatural mode ('uncommunicated lightning'). But the image he uses – that is, the idea of mind-as-light – does not join the two. What Shelley is doing is exploring an *associative relationship* along different poetic avenues; he is discovering the limits of his imagination through exploiting the metaphor and the figurative capabilities of the language. Shelley may be resorting to such a strategy because he is figuratively engaged with a paradox which apparently stands beyond rational explanation, namely, that originality is synonymous with openness to influence. In poems when this metaphorical shifting comes into play we might predict that Shelley is also attempting to cope with something that lingers just beyond explanation or logical thinking. How does one express the ineffable, describe the indescribable? Influence seems to be, for Shelley, one of these things: it happens – Shelley knows it happens. The problem, as always, is how to enunciate it, how to (as Shelley might put it) mirror it in language. We can therefore look forward to readings of some of Shelley's poems as works which not only exhibit influences but are also about being influenced.

After all this, we discover what may be an important clue as to why Shelley in the Preface to *Prometheus Unbound* is so intent on discussing influence and imitation. The clue is that the parts of the Preface are in fact a reply to an anonymous reviewer's charge made in *The Quarterly Review*, April 1819, that Shelley is 'an unsparing imitator; and he draws largely on the rich stores of another mountain poet'. Moreover, the reviewer goes on to say, Shelley misreads and perverts the work of this poet.

The 'mountain poet' of whom Shelley is 'an unsparing imitator' is of course Wordsworth. This is what prompted Shelley to begin his discussion of influence with 'One word is due in candour to the degree in which the study of contemporary writings may have tinged my composition, for such has been a topic of censure with regard to poems far more popular.' And after having reasoned that all writers are inescapably predisposed to the influence of their contemporaries, the similarities 'between Homer and Hesiod, between Aeschylus and Euripides, between Virgil and Horace, between Dante and Petrarch, between Shakespeare and Fletcher, between Dryden and Pope' being examples of 'a generic resemblance', Shelley ends his argument by neatly turning the accusation to advantage: 'If this similarity be the result of imitation, I am willing to confess that I have imitated.'

What Shelley achieves in these passages from the prefaces to *The Revolt of Islam* and *Prometheus Unbound* is a sort of freedom. Paradoxically, by demonstrating the impossibility of originality and the unavoidability of imitation, Shelley perhaps frees himself from the repressiveness of these twin stiflers which act as one overwhelming force. He has made anxious confinement the necessary condition of poetic emancipation. But here again I must contend with Harold Bloom: 'if any poet knows too well what causes his poem, then he cannot write it, or at least will write it badly.'[3] But from what we have so far seen it must be agreed that Shelley has a substantial understanding of the issues in question. Shelley says in the Preface to *Prometheus Unbound* that 'one great poet is a masterpiece of nature which another not only ought to study but must study'. One poet generates poetry by knowing well (therefore being influenced by) another's poetry. And certainly the product in question here, *Prometheus Unbound*, is not written 'badly'. Bloom's statement might be countered with one made by André Gide: the French writer could be referring to Shelley when he says, 'we see great minds never fearing influences, but on the contrary seeking them with a sort of eagerness like the eagerness of *being*'.[4] In these terms Shelley is definitely an eager seeker.

But Shelley was not always so positive in accepting influence. In the fragment essay *Speculations on Metaphysics* (?1815–16) he notes:

> We do not attend sufficiently to what passes within ourselves. We combine words, combined a thousand times before. In our mind we assume entire opinions; and in the expression of those opinions, entire phrases, when we would philosophise. Our whole style of expression and sentiment is infected with the tritest plagiarisms. Our words are dead, our thoughts cold and borrowed.[5]

There is obviously a great deal of despair in these words. Whereas in the prefaces to *The Revolt of Islam* and *Prometheus Unbound* Shelley appears to have reasoned influence as a source of strength, here originality (a creative or positive use of influence) is said to be virtually impossible. Language, the chief mode of influence in this case, is more than just a sort of prison-house – it is a charnel-house. One thing, however, remains the same: Shelley holds that the human mind cannot but help being extraordinarily receptive to all that it encounters. In another extreme moment, this time in his fragmentary essay *On Life* (1819), Shelley could say this: 'Mind . . . cannot create, it can only perceive'. For the poet, the problem is whether or not this is a benefit or a burden. Again, as in the Preface to *Prometheus Unbound* where Shelley says 'every word and suggestion' modifies the mind, his argument is extreme, but now he expresses the negative potential of influence. It is not hard, then, to understand why his poetic language works so hard to find new combinations, new forms of expression. A poet less aware of this restricting effect would perhaps strive less to use influence as a positive force.

III

Compared to the prefaces cited, Shelley presents influence as a rather more benign force in the *Defence of Poetry*, perhaps because the *Defence* is intended as a general statement about poetry (in response to Thomas Peacock's *The Four Ages of Poetry*), while the prefaces are more personal defences. Nonetheless, while composing the *Defence* early in 1821, Shelley still insists upon the dynamic nature of a poem: a poem is open to the past, contains the present, and runs into the future. A poem is permanent, yet mutable; but more than that, it is expansive:

> A great Poem is a fountain for ever overflowing with the waters of wisdom and delight; and after one person and one age has exhausted all its divine effluence which their peculiar relations enable them to share, another and yet another succeeds, and new relations are ever developed, the source of an unforeseen and an unconceived delight.

The poem as an overflowing fountain is here Shelley's model of poetic influence, of literary history. All poets share, so to speak, the same water, adding to it as they take their portion. A great poem does not remain unto itself. It eternally goes beyond its own limits, becoming the material for other poems of other ages as it encounters and interacts with new relations. In Shelley's model, then, the struggle for originality gives way to participation in this overflowing. The selfish gives into the selfless. Of course the image of a poem as an object flowing into a poet itself suggests the word 'in-influence' (in-flowing). Because the poet takes from and adds to this forever-flowing fountain, Shelley is also able to claim in the *Defence* that 'A Poet participates in the eternal'.

In attempting to analyse Shelley's view of influence working on the poet, I stated above that he sees the poet as an active medium through which influences pass, the poet himself contributing to what is produced by the incoming influences. In the second paragraph of the *Defence* Shelley finds another image of this, his most powerful:

> Man is an instrument over which a series of external and internal impressions are driven, like the alternations of an ever-changing wind over an Aeolian lyre, which move it by their motion to every-changing melody. But there is a principle within the human being, and perhaps within all sentient beings, which acts otherwise than in the lyre, and produces not melody, alone, but harmony, by an internal adjustment of the sounds or motions thus excited to the impressions which excite them. It is as if the lyre could accommodate its chords to the motions of that which strikes them, in a determined proportion of sound; even as the musician can accommodate his voice to the sound of the lyre. A

child at play by itself will express its delight by its voice and motions; and every inflexion of tone and every gesture will bear exact relation to a corresponding antitype in the pleasurable impressions which awakened it; it will be the reflected image of that impression; and as the lyre trembles and sounds after the wind has died away, so the child seeks, by prolonging in its voice and motions the duration of the effect, to prolong also a consciousness of the cause. In relation to the objects which delight a child, these expressions are, what poetry is to higher objects.

There is no mistaking here that Shelley sees influence as a determining factor in man's being. Man is primarily a creature susceptible to being influenced. He is impressionable, hypersensitive and predisposed to affectability. The metaphor Shelley uses here as an analogue of man's receptivity to influence, that of an Aeolian lyre (wind harp), makes man an instrument that is 'played' by 'internal and external impressions'.[6] The dynamic winds of influence passing through man allow him to produce not just 'melody', but 'harmony' as well. Why Shelley adds 'harmony' to the resulting sound is to once more give man a participatory function in the dynamic process of influence; and by participating he can, within the limits of his own creative potential, himself adjust or determine the external forces. Without this control, harmony (and, implicitly, originality) cannot be achieved. We would be too open to influence, and never ourselves.

In the second half of the Aeolian lyre passage Shelley uses the analogy of a 'child at play with itself' to suggest how he believes influence is sustained. Shelley's example requires some very deliberate explication. A child experiences delight, and the delight is expressed by corresponding sounds and movements. The experience of delight can be called the cause or primary action; the resulting sounds and movements can be called the effect or secondary action. The actual experience of delight, Shelley implies, is temporary. It passes away, just as the wind dies away after having passed through the wind harp. But the harp continues its motions (as reverberations), just as the child does when the delight (primary action) has passed. The original delight, in this analogy, is equivalent to the wind's influence on the lyre *as it is blowing*. By the child's secondary action (his expression of delight) the primary action (the experience of delight) can be prolonged.

Shelley's example in this passage tells us a few more things about his idea of influence, anticipating the famous 'fading coal' image found later in the *Defence*. He moves towards clearing up the distinction between influence (the experience of delight) and the production of poetry (the expression of delight). The first instigates the second, but by the second the first is sustained. But by saying the first is sustained by the second it is not meant that the influence remains unaltered: it must be remembered that in Shelley's scene of influence the later poet himself adds his own harmonising influence – in that moment of inspiration he *combines* with the influence, and in this way he hopes positively to contend with the influence. This, then, is what the poet searches for, that elusive instant of inspiration. And this, as I will argue in the second part of this study, is the problem some of Shelley's poems address, where Shelley's speakers and protagonists work towards being successful poets by pursuing figures of inspiration.

For Shelley, the poet gives and receives, influencing as well as being influenced. In some ways these are almost indistinguishable, for the poet takes part in a process that is rather more cyclical than linear, with the motion of the process falling back upon itself. In the *Defence* he describes the poet's hyper-sensitive state like this:

> Those in whom it [a 'faculty of approximation to the beautiful'] exists in excess are poets, in the most universal sense of the word; and the pleasure resulting from the manner in which they express the influence of society or nature upon their own minds, communicates itself to others, and gathers a sort of reduplication from that community.

Just as Wordsworth in the Preface says that poets differ from other men 'only in degree', so Shelley says that poets have not different qualities but an 'excess' in particular qualities. Once more the complexity of Shelley's logic is guarded by its dense expression. The cyclical process begins (but it doesn't really begin at any one point in the process) with 'the influence of society or nature' upon the poet's mind, which the poet expresses; the 'manner' of this expression leads to the poet's 'pleasure', which itself must be a part of the poetry or expression; and this 'communicates itself to others', those, presumably, who read the poetry; following, the 'pleasure' in the poetry 'gathers a sort of reduplication from that community' composed of readers. The connection making this process of influence cyclical is that the 'community' itself, which is influenced by 'pleasure' given by the poet, apparently influenced the poet in the first place. This, perhaps, is what Shelley means by 'reduplication': the taking-out of what was put in, the putting-in of what was taken out. Of course this is not a closed or static system of one-way influence. Shelley held that circumstances (society, nature, relations) change, and so the cyclical model is a spiralling one as well.

As in the Preface to *Prometheus Unbound*, Shelley in the *Defence* once more resorts to analogies of light in an attempt to convey what his poem is like and how the poet's mind creatively responds to influence. He says poetry 'is ever still the light of life', giving it the figurative status of leadership, knowledge and even worship. More important, Shelley gives his most famous account of the power and precariousness of influence in its relationship to the production of poetry:

> Poetry is not like reasoning, a power to be exerted according to the determination of the will. A man cannot say, 'I will compose poetry.' The greatest poet even cannot say it: for the mind in creation is as a fading coal which some invisible influence, like an inconstant wind, awakens to transitory brightness: this power arises from within, like the colour of a flower which fades and changes as it is developed, and the conscious portions of our natures are unprophetic either of its approach or its departure. Could this influence be durable in its original purity and force, it is impossible to predict the greatness of the results: but when composition begins, inspiration is already on the decline, and the most glorious poetry that has ever been communicated to the world is probably a feeble shadow of the original conception of the poet.

Shelley's imagery here is as restless and searching as ever. He moves from coals to flowers to shadows. But what he is trying to put his finger on (his pen to) is a particular inadequacy in the poet's retention of inspiration as he attempts to manifest it in his poetry. First of all, the poet cannot help but be influenced; but the inspiration the influence gives to the mind fades with the dissipation of the influence, and cannot be put into a form that conveys its original impact. Unfortunately, influence works on the poet in an inconstant and unforeseeable way: the poet can never know when influence will awake him to creativity or, for that matter, when it actually leaves him. In this sense influence is 'bigger' than the poet, exerting more force on him than he can exert on it. To use Shelley's own image, influence overshadows the individual poet.

Shelley's view of how even the 'greatest poet' cannot say 'I will compose poetry' is in fact formulated as a counter-statement to Wordsworth (in the Preface to the *Lyrical Ballads*) where the older poet talks about the 'mood' in which 'successful composition can begin':

> I have said that Poetry is the spontaneous overflow of powerful feelings: it takes its origin from emotion recollected in tranquillity: the emotion is contemplated till by a species of reaction the tranquillity gradually disappears, and an emotion, similar to that which was before the subject of contemplation, is gradually produced, and does itself actually exist in the mind. In this mood successful composition generally begins, and in a mood similar to this it is carried on; but the emotion, of whatever kind and in whatever degree, from various causes is qualified by various pleasures, so that in describing any passions whatsoever, which are voluntarily described, the mind will upon the whole be in a state of enjoyment.

Wordsworth suggests that the inspiration behind poetry seems to originate in the poet's own emotions 'recollected in tranquillity'. The emotion is 'contemplated' until the 'tranquillity' vanishes, and then the poet recovers a 'similar' emotion and maintains it through the 'successful' composition of his poetry. Wordsworth's style of inspiration, unlike Shelley's, is constant, recoverable and durable. It can be recreated and held. While Shelley's creative act is haphazard and unpremeditated, Wordsworth's is deliberate, a process whereby in effect Wordsworth can say, 'I will compose poetry'. What is most difficult to reconcile or account for in Wordsworth's formulation of the creation of poetry is the apparent spontaneousness of the act with its calculated and schematic procedure. Some of Wordsworth's greatest poetry is just on this subject, taking memory and recollection as the mode of poetic experience, and permanence (immortality) as the state to be achieved. The differences between the two poets serve to show that Shelley was (at least more visibly) anxious regarding the source of, and therefore the subject matter of, his poetry. It can be suggested that Wordsworth, through the production of his poetry, attempts to confirm the mind's relationship to itself as a form of confidence, or more strongly, a faith that holds things together. Shelley, on the other hand, is troubled by the mind's capacity to hold, and by its relationship to things not itself, things that influence it. At this point in his poetics Shelley was certain of his uncertainty, but tried, nevertheless, in some of his poetry, to follow up Wordsworth's programme of solipsistic creativity.[7]

But what is the goal of a poet, and where does his poem stand in relation to previous poems? Shelley gives us a radical answer to this in the *Defence*. He talks of 'that great poem, which all poets, like the co-operating thoughts of one great mind, have built up since the beginning of the world'. The radical answer, then, is that there are no individual poems, that all poems come to form 'that great poem'. Shelley has in mind here a sort of transcendental intertextuality: all poems are 'built' *into* other poems, becoming the material of that greater construction. Once more Shelley is clear in expressing the idea that poets necessarily participate in a larger project beyond their own immediate concerns.

Images of light continue in the *Defence*, once more used to illuminate a discussion of influence. 'Poetry', says Shelley, 'is a mirror which makes beautiful that which is distorted'. In other words, poetry not only reflects the subject but also unifies it in the process of making it 'beautiful'. And in the penultimate passage of the *Defence* he writes:

> It is impossible to read the compositions of the most celebrated writers of the present day without being startled with the electric life which burns within their words. They measure the circumference and sound the depths of human nature with a comprehensive and all-penetrating spirit, and they are themselves perhaps the most sincerely astonished at its manifestations, for it is less their spirit than the spirit of the age. Poets are the hierophants of an unapprehended inspiration, the mirrors of the gigantic shadows which futurity casts upon the present, the words which express what they understand not; the trumpets which sing to battle, and feel not what they inspire: the influence which is moved not, but moves. Poets are the unacknowledged legislators of the World.

Poets deal with and are even used by forces greater than themselves, with forces not directly initiating from themselves; yet in doing so they explore the dimensions of 'human nature'. Their own creativity is merely that which enables them to partake of and reflect that greater 'spirit' which moves through the age. But more than that, by taking up that 'spirit of the age' they (great poets) increase the power of the spirit. When Shelley says that poets are 'legislators', he means it not in the sense of law-givers; he means that poets are utilitarian media through which influences are channelled or negotiated. They are not so much figures of authority, but of dissemination. Here we can look forward to the poet of the *Ode to the West Wind* who wants the wind to 'Scatter . . . my words among mankind!'.

We cannot help but recognise particular aspects of Shelley's thinking about influence that have already been underlined. But it does seem that now Shelley is more specific in calling influence a collection of energies from individuals which in turn forms one greater energy – the whole is greater than its parts, and yet the parts take from the whole they constitute. It is difficult to think of any other major poet who develops such an enthusiastic yet selfless portrayal of the positive values of his contemporaries. Of course this is another way of saying that it is difficult to think of any other original poet who so badly not only wanted to be influential, but to be influenced as well. Shelley finds that the human condition is determined by influences, and as a poet he finds it impossible *not* to be influenced by the writers of his own age. Unlike many of his contemporaries, Shelley was proud to be living at this particular time, if perhaps just a little intimidated or awed by the potential he saw in this 'new birth'.

Shelley is a poet who is very concerned with being a part of his *own* time, with taking part in his *own* time. 'When I consider the vivid energy to which the minds of men are awakened in this age of ours', Shelley wrote to Charles Ollier late in 1819, 'ought I not to congratulate myself that I am a contemporary with names which are great, or will be great, or ought to be great?' (*Letters*, II, p. 164). And once more in the *Defence*: 'we live among such philosophers and poets as surpass beyond comparison any who have appeared since the last national struggle for civil and religious liberty'. Shelley's relationship with his contemporaries is surely one of the most important aspects of his poetics, and this relationship, virtually ignored in studies of Shelley's development, must be the moving force behind a great deal of his poetry. Unfortunately, neither did Shelley's peers fully appreciate or recognise this great theme; the claim that still lingers is that Shelley overshot the mark. Regardless, it was Shelley's desire to make the effort in his own way, which was, he realised, always relative to the ways of others. Shelley himself was an unacknowledged legislator, a spirit of the age of which he himself took part in creating.

2
A New Presence

Thomas Medwin, Shelley's cousin, records that in 1809 Shelley was uninterested in Wordsworth's poetry: 'Wordsworth's writings were at that time by no means to his taste. It was not sufficiently refined to enjoy his simplicity, he wanted something more exciting.'[1] Yet by the summer of 1816, while Shelley was in Switzerland associating with Byron, Medwin notes that Wordsworth was one of Shelley's 'favourites'.[2] Somewhere between these two dates Shelley began to become more concerned with Wordsworth, and more appreciative of his poetry.

I

In the autumn of 1811, a few months after his elopement with and marriage to Harriet Westbrook, we find Shelley at Keswick, the centre of the Lake District, home of the then notorious Lake Poets. This last fact (and to a lesser degree Shelley's attempt to protect his young bride from the amorous advances of his friend Thomas Jefferson Hogg) may very well have been the underlying reason for this stay there, for Shelley was never one to shy away from introducing himself to the famous. Perhaps Shelley was also seeking some paternal guidance, since he had just quarrelled with his father and they had mutually rejected any allegiance to each other. Shelley's father could not accept his son's expulsion from Oxford (in March 1811) and the political and moral attitudes the young Shelley had advertised. Wordsworth, Coleridge, De Quincey, Southey and Professor John Wilson ('Christopher North') were all either close by or had very recently been in the area. It was from Keswick that Shelley also took it upon himself to write to William Godwin, who was in a few years to become his father-in-law. That the landscape of the Lake District may have been secondary to Shelley's reasons for his stay there is implied by Shelley himself: in a letter to Elizabeth Hitchener (14 November 1811) he writes that the 'scenery here is awfully beautiful – our window commands a view of two lakes, and the giant mountains which confine them, but the object most interesting to my feelings is Southey's habitation' (*Letters*, I, p.183). But his meetings with Southey, who was his favourite poet at least until 1809, were to prove to be important in an indirect and unanticipated way.

In December 1811, while planning *Queen Mab*, Shelley mentioned to Miss Hitchener that he was hoping to see the three most important poets of the older generation. On 10(?) December he wrote: 'I told you of a strange man [William Calvert] I met the other day. I am going to see him. I shall also see Southey, Wordsworth & Coleridge there. I shall then give you a picture of them' (*Letters*, I, p. 201). Five days later he wrote again, saying that 'Southey has changed. I shall see him soon, and I shall reproach him of [for] his tergiversation – He to whom Bigotry Tyranny and Law was hateful has become the votary of these Idols, in a form the most disgusting' (*Letters*, I, p.208).[3] In this same letter Shelley mentions Wordsworth, 'a quondam associate of Southey'. He praises Wordsworth for retaining, as he put it, 'the integrity of his independence, but his poverty is such that he is frequently obliged to beg for a shirt to his back' ('honoured poverty' Shelley later called it in his sonnet *To Wordsworth*). The older poet was not, however, quite so badly off as Shelley may have wanted him to be.

By or around about the new year Shelley had actually met Southey at William Calvert's house, Greta Bank, and subsequently he had a number of meetings with him at Southey's own home, Greta Hall. (Southey's household must have appeared to be a rather interesting one for young Shelley. Greta Hall was originally Coleridge's home, or at least it was until 1804 when he left for Malta. In 1803 Southey arrived for a visit and ended up staying. There he lived with his wife and wife's sister, the latter being the estranged wife of Coleridge. But Mrs Southey's other sister also lived there: she was the surviving wife of the poet Robert Lovell.) Shelley reported in a letter to Miss Hitchener on 2 January 1812 that he had 'some conversation' with Southey over the meaning of God (*Letters*, I, p.215). But more significant for us, apparently from memory, Shelley in this letter transcribed about one half of Wordsworth's *A Poet's Epitaph* (1800) for Elizabeth (I quote the first two and last two and one-half stanzas of what he wrote and put in brackets Wordsworth's correct version):

> Art thou a statesman? in the van
> Of Public business born [train'd] and bred. –

> First learn to love one living man
>   Then mayest thou think upon the dead.
>
> Art thou a lawyer . . . come not nigh
> [A Lawyer art thou? – draw not nigh]
>   Go carry to some other place
> The hardness of thy coward eye
>   The falsehood of thy sallow face.
>
>   . . .
>
> But who is He with modest looks
>   And clad in homely russett brown [?]
> Who [He] murmurs near the running brooks
>   A music sweeter than their own.
>
>   . . .
>
> And you must love him, ere to you
>   He will seem worthy of your love.
>
> All [The] outward shews of sky & earth
> Of sea [hill] & valley he hath viewed
> And impulses of deeper birth
>   Have come to him in solitude.

Shelley comments on the lines: 'I have transcribed a piece of Wordsworth's poetry. – It may give you some idea of the Man – how expressively keen are the first stanzas. I shall see this man soon' (*Letters*, I, pp. 217–18). It must be assumed that Southey had shown Shelley (and/or read to him) the 1800 *Lyrical Ballads*. But we are at least certain that at this time Shelley was coming into close contact with some of Wordsworth's work.

This, then, is the first real indication we have of the impact of Wordsworth's poetry on Shelley. As opposed to his feelings regarding Wordsworth in 1809, Shelley is now obviously excited, and he now appears to be appreciative of the poetry. Shelley very much wants to meet Wordsworth. Perhaps too William Calvert (along with Southey) inspired Shelley's new interest in Wordsworth, as Calvert's relationship with Wordsworth dated back to 1793. The Calverts became Shelley's closest acquaintances at Keswick, and it is certainly probable that Calvert was keen to mediate Wordsworth's influence. (It was just a few years earlier in the autumn of 1809 at Keswick that Calvert, along with Southey, Coleridge, and Wordsworth, as well as one of

Wordsworth's old schoolfellows, were all busying themselves in protest against England's treaty with France. Calvert's brother was Wordsworth's benefactor.) The poem that Shelley took trouble enough to repeat is noteworthy in that it takes up the figure of the solitary poet as the subject of eulogy. And as I shall show later, it is this figure, moulded into the figure of the Solitary of *The Excursion*, who in part becomes Shelley's formulation of the Wordsworthian poet-figure from *Alastor* onwards.

Five days after writing out Wordsworth's *A Poet's Epitaph* Shelley again wrote to Miss Hitchener. He describes his further discussions with Southey about the separation of politics and morals, Shelley naturally arguing for their inseparability. Southey apparently had the rather annoying habit of dismissing Shelley's arguments by saying, 'Ah, when you are as old as I am you will think with me.' Shelley was upset by Southey's narrow mindedness; he was upset when he thought of what Southey 'might have been'. He ends by saying, 'Wordsworth & Coleridge I have yet to see' (*Letters*, I, p.223).

There is something ominous in the last sentence, something of the feeling one-down-and-two-to-go, as if Shelley felt the inevitability of becoming disappointed by Coleridge and Wordsworth as well. One can only wonder what would have happened had Shelley succeeded in meeting Coleridge or Wordsworth on this occasion. Twenty years later Coleridge wondered too:

> Poor Shelley, it is a pity I often think that I never met with him. I could have done him good. He went to Keswick on purpose to see me and unfortunately fell in with Southey instead. There could have been nothing so unfortunate. Southey had no understanding for a toleration of such principles as Shelley's. . . . I have often bitterly regretted in my heart of hearts that I never did meet with Shelley.[4]

Well, although Coleridge would have liked to have thought otherwise, Shelley did not really go to Keswick just to see him; but there is probably some truth to Coleridge's opinion that his views would have been closer to Shelley's than Southey's actually were. De Quincey, who was just a few miles away in Grasmere, also expressed some regret in having missed Shelley, as he says his 'library, which, being rich in the wickedest of German speculations, would naturally have been more to Shelley's taste than the Spanish library of Southey'. He also adds that he would have introduced Shelley to Wordsworth.[5]

Shelley left Keswick for Dublin on 2 February 1812, his aim being to deliver his *Address to the Irish People* in order to convert them to atheism – for their own good, of course. Southey recorded the visit of the ebullient young poet with some egotistical nostalgia: 'Here is a man at Keswick, who acts upon me as my own ghost would do. He is just what I was in 1794. . . . He is brimful and overflowing with everything good and generous.'[6]

The scene, then, had really been set for Shelley to meet Wordsworth: there he was in the Lake District, already associating with two of Wordsworth's closest friends and being exposed to Wordsworth's poetry; he was young enough to be impressionable and old enough to form his own judgements. But the opportunity went by. Wordsworth passed through Keswick later that year. How should it be put – that Shelley left too early, or that Wordsworth came too late? However whimsical one might get in speculating on the outcome of such a meeting, I think it might have been something of a letdown. Wordsworth was not particularly known for being accommodating, and Shelley wasn't respectfully passive in such circumstances. At any rate, Shelley would have probably followed the pattern of infatuation followed by resentment that he had already set in his relationships with other figures of authority: with Captain Pilfold (his uncle), Southey and later with Godwin. Perhaps it was better that they did not meet, for it left Shelley to creatively work out his relationship through the dynamics of poetry.

II

The first glimmerings of the influence of Wordsworth's poetry on Shelley's verse can be found in poems written in the first half of 1812, poems drafted into what is now called the *Esdaile Notebook* (after Shelley's daughter by Harriet Westbrook, Ianthe, married into the Edward Jeffries Esdaile family in 1837; the family remained custodians of the *Notebook* until 1962).

Significantly, in the same letter written from Keswick in which Shelley expressed his disillusionment with Southey and his hope to see Wordsworth and Coleridge (7 January 1812), Shelley also wrote to Miss Hitchener: 'I now send you some Poetry – the subject is not fictitious; it is the overflowings of the mind this morning' (*Letters*, I, p. 223). The poem, which can be found in the *Esdaile Notebook* in a revised and expanded version (we know it under the title of *A Tale of*

Society as It Is: From Facts, 1811), both in style and sentiment clearly follows the tales of loss, separation and death in the *Lyrical Ballads*;[7] and his description of the poem as 'overflowings of the mind' simulates Wordsworth's Preface where 'all good poetry' is said to be 'the spontaneous overflow of powerful feelings'. Shelley has obviously become stimulated by Wordsworth's work.

The subject of the poem is a poor and crippled old woman. But even though her 'natural powers' have decayed, she still manages to express the 'soul's imperishable energy' (7).[8] In her 'silent misery', 'unparticipated solitude' and 'unspeaking sorrow' (6, 25, 31) her only hope is to be reunited with her long-lost son (who, perhaps not incidentally, happens to be named William). One clear June evening upon a moor her hope is realised, but her son, returned from war and exposure to tyranny, is a wasted form. Charity is not sufficient to support the two. Because their pride is stronger than their humility, they perish under the 'law's stern slavery . . . With which law loves to rend the poor man's soul' (75–6). In the *Esdaile Notebook* version (in the letter the poem is seven stanzas; in the *Notebook* it is ten) the suggestion is that William is eventually reduced to being a beggar (97–108), and the speaker points to a 'spot', the grave where the old lady rests, and asks that 'a blessing' be left there (118–20).

In the letter to Elizabeth Hitchener, Shelley prefaced his poem with these words: 'The facts are real; that recorded in the last fragment of a stanza is literally true. – The poor man said: – None of my family ever came *to parish*, and I wd. starve first. I am a poor man but could never hold my head up after that' (*Letters*, I, pp. 223–4). And after the poem he added: 'Think of the Poetry which I have inserted as a picture of my feelings not a specimen of my art' (*Letters*, I, p. 226). Shelley's priority is apparently to give a true account of destitute people in an uncaring society. Nevertheless, his concern is that Miss Hitchener knows that he has a sympathetic response to human suffering and social injustices, and that his poem is not necessarily to be taken as an example of his poetry.

The obvious is hardly worth stating – how much the circumstances, characterisations, sentiment and uncluttered style in this 'Tale of Society' owe to Wordsworth's tales from the *Lyrical Ballads*, to such poems as *The Female Vagrant, The Thorn, The Idiot Boy, The Mad Mother, The Complaint of a Forsaken Indian Woman, The Old Cumberland Beggar* and *Michael*. Having said that Shelley's motivation behind the poem is to expose and implicitly comment on the misery of a certain class of people in society, we are naturally drawn to make a comparison with Wordsworth's comments on his intentions in the *Lyrical Ballads*. What we find is that Wordsworth's aim is not necessarily to expose particular injustices or suffering, but, as he says in the Preface, to use 'the incidents of common life' in order to develop a particular mode of poetic expression, what he calls 'a plainer and more emphatic language'. Shelley is using Wordsworth's style as a means, not as an end in itself. It would not be forcing the issue to say that parts of Shelley's poem are Wordsworthian in diction, tone and imagery:

> The same kind light feeds every living thing
> That spreads its blossoms to the breath of spring,
> But who feeds thee, unhappy wanderer?
> (89–91)

But nowhere in the *Lyrical Ballads* would we find such unchecked vehemence as in the lines directly following these:

> With the fat slaves, who from the rich man's board
> Lick the fallen crumbs thou scantily dost share
> And mutterest for the gift a heartless prayer,
> The flowers fade not thus. Thou must poorly die.
> The changeful year feeds them. The tyrant, man, feeds thee.
> (92–6)

The aggressive style of expression in its abrupt impetuosity reminds us more of the hotspur in some of Shakespeare's characters. But this is still not Shelleyan verse.

Worth noting is that after this point Shelley never returns so explicitly to the theme of the sufferer in humble or destitute circumstances for the subject of his poetry. It is as if Shelley had begun with aspects of Wordsworth's own poetic beginnings, only to leave them.

The *Esdaile Notebook* contains a few other poems which suggeest this new presence in Shelley. For example, the poem *Written on a Beautiful Day of Spring* (in all likelihood Spring 1812) takes us back to Wordsworth's *Lines Written in Early Spring* (1798), if not in theme, at least in the circumstances of composition, but *To Harriet* ('It is not blasphemy'), probably written in the summer of 1812 when Shelley was in Devon, has a stronger, more deliberate Wordsworthian connection. The poem, addressed to his young wife, has obvious hangovers from *Tintern Abbey*:

> . . . will not thy glowing cheek,
> Glowing with soft suffusion, rest on mine
> And breathe magnetic sweetness thro' the frame
> Of my corporeal nature, thro' the soul
> Now knit with these fine fibres?
> (*To Harriet*, 13–17)

> Until, the breath of this corporeal frame,
> And even the motion of our human blood
> Almost suspended, we are laid asleep
> In body, and become a living soul. . .
> (*Tintern Abbey*, 44–7)

> . . . the frigid intercourse
> Of common souls lives but a summer's day . . .
> (*To Harriet*, 27–8)

> . . . The dreary intercourse of daily life. . .
> (*Tintern Abbey*, 132)

There is even some circumstantial evidence to suggest that Shelley either passed by or stopped at Tintern Abbey in the last week of June 1812. Coach routes from Rhayader in Wales (where close by at Nantgwillt Shelley tried unsuccessfully to set up a commune after returning from Ireland) show that Shelley would have been close to Tintern Abbey as he made his way to Devon. On his way South he planned to stay at Chepstow on the mouth of the river Wye (*Letters*, I, p. 308), and Tintern Abbey is just a few miles out of town.

More important than these verbal repetitions and external circumstances, *To Harriet* in part takes up the same problem as *Tintern Abbey* – the problem of retention-but-change, of, in Wordsworth's phrases in his poem, 'tranquil restoration' and 'Abundant recompence' (31, 89). Shelley's poem begins by expressing the hope that earthly (or bodily) feelings will be 'More perfectly' (2) expressed in Heaven. There is some hint of a passionate *vs* platonic incompatibility. Young Shelley thanks Harriet for bringing him back from the solitary and 'gloomy path' (6). Their love, their union, will not be affected by mortal concerns. When time passes and earthly passions become 'tempered' (33), their love will not be hardened or diminished by the familiarity the years are supposed to bring. They will remain as they were, as circumstances once were – deeply committed, unchanged. Time will not erase or weaken their bond. Shelley seems, however, somewhat cool or restrained in his feelings towards his new wife – he calls their love 'holy friendship' (42–3). As K. N. Cameron has commented, it is 'a curiously low-keyed poem for a young husband to write to a young wife, especially a husband capable of such intensity as Shelley'.[9] But then perhaps *To Harriet* is not so much a love poem but a more personalised address to the workings of that 'Dark Flood of Time'(58) Shelley hopes to resist in his poetry.

We know very well the crucial passage in *Tintern Abbey* where Wordsworth looks to the future as something that will be fortified against loss:

> . . . and in after years,
> When these wild ecstasies shall be matured
> Into a sober pleasure, when thy mind
> Shall be a mansion for all lovely forms,
> Thy memory be as a dwelling-place
> For all sweet sounds and harmonies; Oh! then,
> If solitude, or fear, or pain, or grief,
> Should be thy portion, with what healing thoughts
> Of tender joy wilt thou remember me,
> And these my exhortations!
>
> (138–47)

By the end of *Tintern Abbey* Wordsworth's fear of change, which is at root a fear of death, is overcome, if only through the knowledge that his words will survive. This is not so much a fear of forgetting, but of being forgotten. Wordsworth anticipates that through memory his past and present feelings will counteract any future despondency. Loss becomes a gain. The language and sentiment clearly persist in Shelley's poem:

> Nor when age
> Has tempered these wild extacies, and given
> A soberer tinge to the luxurious glow
> Which blazing on devotion's pinnacle
> Makes virtuous passion supersede the power
> Of reason, nor when life's aestival sun

> To deeper manhood shall have ripened me,
> Nor when some years have added judgement's store
> To all thy woman sweetness, all the fire
> Which throbs in thine enthusiast heart, not then
> Shall holy friendship (for what other name
> May love like ours assume?) not even then
> Shall custom so corrupt, or the cold forms
> Of this desolate world so harden us
> As when we think of the dear love that binds
> Our souls in soft communion, while we know
> Each other's thoughts and feelings, can we say
> Unblushingly a heartless compliment,
> Praise, hate or love with the unthinking world
> Or dare to cut the unrelaxing nerve
> That knits our love to Virtue – can those eyes
> Beaming with mildest radiance on my heart
> To purify its purity e'er bend
> To soothe its vice or consecrate its fears?
> Never, thou second self! is confidence
> So vain in virtue that I learn to doubt
> The mirror even of Truth?
>
> (32–58)[10]

Shelley's words are clearly an adaptation of Wordsworth's account of the process of retrospection and reconciliation, the process of absence triumphing over presence, or memory overriding direct experience. Moreover, these words offer a subtle challenge to Wordsworth's version of this process. The point of contention is the sufficiency of recovery that can be achieved by commemoration. Wordsworth posits a temporal gap which is to be closed (in his own terms, to be restored, recompensed, healed); Shelley refuses to posit this gap because to do so would be to admit a loss, because it would in some sense negate what *is* and what *has been*. Shelley, at the end of the poem, says that he would rather sleep forever than have to resign himself:

> If I wake no more
> My life more actual living will contain
> Than some grey veteran's of the world's cold school
> Whose listless hours unprofitably roll
> By one enthusiast feeling unredeemed.

> Virtue and Love! unbending Fortitude,
> Freedom, Devotedness and Purity –
> That life my Spirit consecrates to you.
>   (65–72)

In the same way Wordsworth in his poem ends by inscribing on Dorothy's memory his presence, a presence that will live on when he has gone, Shelley too, if he were to live no more, passes what he feels are the values of his life to Harriet. Shelley, after Wordsworth, is using the female closest to him as a safeguard against oblivion and as an agent of self-preservation. We wonder too if that 'grey veteran' Shelley mentions is a generalised or particular figure. Perhaps it is Wordsworth who, in Shelley's view, has resigned himself to emotional or poetic inactivity, and who has given in to the future without actually confronting it.

Another poem in the *Esdaile Notebook*, *The Retrospect*, also contains obvious repetitions from Wordsworth, this time from the opening of the *Intimations Ode*:

> A scene which wildered fancy viewed
> In the soul's coldest solitude,
> With that same scene when peaceful love
> Flings rapture's colour o'er the grove,
> When mountain, meadow, wood and stream
> With unalloying glory gleam
> And to the spirit's ear and eye
> Are unison and harmony.
>   (*Retrospect*, 15–22)

> There was a time when meadow, grove, and stream,
> The earth, and every common sight,
>   To me did seem
>   Apparelled in celestial light,
> The glory and the freshness of a dream.
>   (*Intimations Ode*, 1–5)

But more significant, Shelley's poem is in some ways again modelled after *Tintern Abbey*. We know about the compositional circumstances behind Wordsworth's poem, that it was occasioned upon revisiting Tintern Abbey on the banks of the river Wye while travelling with his sister, Dorothy. Here, partly through his sister's reflective presence, Wordsworth formulates a mode of creative retrospection which he hopes will strengthen the future:

> . . . in thy voice I catch
> The language of my former heart, and read
> My former pleasures in the shooting lights
> Of thy wild eyes. Oh! yet a little while
> May I behold in thee what I was once,
> My dear, dear Sister!
> (117–22)

Through her, Wordsworth goes on to say, he and his memories will live on. The background to Shelley's poem follows a remarkably similar pattern. His poem was occasioned upon revisiting the estate of his cousin (Thomas Grove), Cwm Elan, in June 1812, a beautiful area through which the river Elan flows. The first time Shelley visited his cousin had been the previous summer, but then Shelley was alone and had been taken ill, probably as a result of exhaustion and depression after his dealings with his father over expulsion from Oxford and money matters. Shelley hardly enjoyed his stay: he was bored and lonely (*Letters*, I, pp. 118, 122, 129). But when Shelley returned the following summer he was with Harriet (and Eliza, her older sister). Because of Harriet's presence Shelley is now, like Wordsworth through Dorothy in *Tintern Abbey*, able to achieve a form of recovery – indeed, a dazzling metamorphosis:

> How changed since nature's summer form
> Had last the power my grief to charm,
> Since last ye soothed my spirit's sadness –
> Strange chaos of a mingled madness!
> Changed! – not the loathsome worm that fed
> In the dark mansions of the dead,
> Now soaring thro' the fields of air
> And gathering purest nectar there,
> A butterfly whose million hues
> The dazzled eye of wonder views,
> Long lingering on a work so strange,
> Has undergone so bright a change!
> (132–43)

Shelley's whole being is transformed, even more so than the worm feeding off a corpse which becomes a butterfly feeding off nectar. Accompanying this imagery which moves from death to life, Shelley accordingly suggests a movement from confinement to freedom, decay to regeneration, darkness to light, from low to high – these figurative differences express the positive dimensions of Shelley's change.

Up until this remarkable transformation Shelley says that he has experienced a solitary and dispirited restlessness. At the beginning of the poem he states, quite conventionally, that he is going to compare the past thoughts and experiences with those of the present, his past disconsolateness with the 'peaceful love' (17) he now feels. He follows by recalling his efforts to alleviate his 'overwhelming woe' (28) by wandering at night because during the day 'even tears refused to flow' (38). Again, one thinks of the opening of *Tintern Abbey*: just as Wordsworth says he again can 'hear' the 'waters' of the Wye with their 'sweet inland murmur' contributing to 'Thoughts of more deep seclusion', so Shelley, probably referring to the River Elan, says he can 'hear' the 'unremitting roar' from 'the wild brook's shore' until the 'ideal flow' is over-run by an 'overwhelming woe' (25–8); and just as Wordsworth says, 'I again repose / Here, under this dark sycamore', so Shelley recalls how he would 'stretch my languid frame / Beneath the wild-woods' gloomiest shade' (39–40). In effect, then, Shelley is also hearing *Tintern Abbey*'s flow and is channelling through his own poem, and he is striking Wordsworth's own poetic pose of contemplation.

Shelley claims his despondency was neither the result of 'unrequited love' (49) nor the result of apathy or pride. Early he learned to scorn not just conventions but moral constraints as well. No support was to be found in any corner, only a 'friendless solitude' (85). Others he had contact with could not share or communicate their feelings; neither could they perceive the paradoxes and 'mysteries' of our being, of 'How little yet how great we are' (98–103). The famous too could only offer fashionable superficialities, but never friendship. Just as Wordsworth in *Tintern Abbey* describes how he was moved by the hills, mountains, rivers and streams, looking for 'the thing he loved' (66–73), Shelley too says the mountains, vales, rocks, streams, woods and meadows have all witnessed his searching in the past for some object that would appease his enigmatic yearning (112–27). He asks these 'varied beauties' if it is not true that they have witnessed the signs of 'unuttered pain / That froze my heart and burned my brain?' (128–31). It is at this point that

Shelley describes the metamorphosis in his outlook and spirit through Harriet's presence. Yet once more, as in *To Harriet*, the reference to his relationship with her is rather cool, calling it in the last part of the poem 'ardent friendship' (158). (Shelley's notion of love here may, however, have been partly influenced by Platonic ideals.) Shelley wants to celebrate his new state and his emancipation from the past. But he ends the poem condemning and making inferior another sort of thinking, perhaps another sort of poet and poetry:

> The gloomiest retrospects that bind
> With crowns of thorn the bleeding mind,
> The prospects of most doubtful hue
> That rise on Fancy's shuddering view,
> Are gilt by the reviving ray
> Which thou has flung upon my day.
>
> (163–8)

Those who look to the past, who magnify it through their imagination, do so with dubious results. Like Wordsworth, Shelley wants to escape the past, or at least somehow turn it to advantage. Wordsworth's 'boyish days' (74) are not, however, so full of distress. They become a source for retrospection, a measure for the present and future.

The Retrospect loosely uses aspects of *Tintern Abbey* as a model, but it departs from it in three important ways. First, Shelley's poem is the history of a change; Wordsworth's poem traces a process of thought, the history of a history. Second, Shelley's poem is dramatic and celebratory; Wordsworth's poem is deductively reasoned and congratulatory. Finally, in *The Retrospect* something lacking is found, discovered; in *Tintern Abbey* something lacked is created, invented.

The River Elan, we might note, flows into the Wye. So Shelley's poem flows, so to speak, into Wordsworth's. As in his model of influence, the lesser poem is consumed by that greater flow. But this is certainly as coincidental as it is poetically fitting.

In sum, what can be seen in these early poems is Shelley's growing familiarity with Wordsworth's verse, with the moment of his turning to Wordsworth coming with his stay at Keswick. Even these first explorations led Shelley to discover the regions of both his and Wordsworth's limitations and inadequacies. However, he shows that he is still neither strong nor confident enough to challenge Wordsworth more directly, but this, as we shall see in later chapters, is to come.

Late in 1812, about a year after having written out Wordsworth's *A Poet's Epitaph*, and a few months after composing *To Harriet* and *The Retrospect*, we find Shelley in North Wales working for the Tremadoc Embankment scheme in order to raise funds for the repair of the partially collapsed sea-wall. At the same time he was, under Godwin's guidance, diligently engaged in a programme of study. (Shelley met Godwin for the first time early in October 1812.) Godwin wrote to Shelley on 10 December telling him that he must, as a 'true student', be 'surrounded with a sort of entrenchment and breastwork of books' (*Letters*, I, pp. 340–1). Indeed, Shelley responded immediately (on 17 and 24 December) by making three orders to two different London booksellers (*Letters*, I, pp. 340–5). He asked for works by more than sixty writers, and if the orders were filled, Shelley would have received well over 150 volumes! Godwin also told Shelley on 10 December that, '*You* have what appears to me a false taste in poetry. You love a perpetual sparkle and glittering, such as are to be found in Darwin, and Southey, and Scott, and Campbell.' After receiving Godwin's comments he included in one of his orders, 'Wordsworth's Poems, 4 vols', which would have been the two-volume *Lyrical Ballads* (1800) and the 1807 *Poems in Two Volumes* (*Letters*, I, p. 345).

III

The period between 1812 and publication of the *Alastor* volume in 1816 was a crucial one for Shelley's developing interest in Wordsworth. Besides being a time of great personal change – his separation from Harriet and subsequent elopement with Mary Godwin – it was for Shelley a time of reading and thinking. During those few years the event which stands out for this present study – an event which in its ramifications will later be examined in some detail – is Shelley's disappointment with *The Excursion*, which he read just a few weeks after its publication in August 1814. Perhaps, too, Wordsworth's acceptance of patronage in being appointed the Stamp-Distributor for Westmorland in March 1813 added to Shelley's feeling that the older poet had, like Southey, fallen from the grace of revolution to the servility of the status quo. Later I will also point out how *To Wordsworth*, written in either 1814 or 1815, partly expresses that fall, how Shelley identified with and venerated one part of Wordsworth, yet was now forced to express his disappointment over Wordsworth: more than anything else, the sonnet is the first important poetic indicator of Shelley's deep concern with Wordsworth, and how the older poet became a problem for Shelley. In later poems, from *Alastor* through to *Prometheus Unbound*, we continue to see Shelley's various formulations of that problem, the way that Shelley through his poetry attempts to disentangle himself from this troubling identification with his predecessor.

There is also some anecdotal evidence of the continuing and growing presence of Wordsworth in Shelley's thoughts during the period from 1814–16. Medwin tells us that in 1814 Shelley actually mimicked the action of Wordsworth's *The Blind Highland Boy* (1807) by sailing a washtub in a pool near his house.[11] Claire Clairmont noted in her *Journal*, 5 October 1814, that one evening Shelley read out Wordsworth's *The Mad Mother*.[12] And Peacock records 'discoursing of Wordsworth' with Shelley one winter evening in 1814 when 'suddenly' Shelley asked, 'Do you think Wordsworth could have written such poetry, if he had ever had dealings with moneylenders?'[13]

In Shelley's prose written between 1812–15 there is also some passing evidence of his growing familiarity with Wordsworth. In *A Refutation of Deism* he misquotes the dimensions of the apparent grave in Wordsworth's *The Thorn*; and in the fragment essay *A Treatise on Morals* he directly quotes two lines from *Tintern Abbey*.

Slight though these incidents may be, this evidence nonetheless indicates that Wordsworth was on Shelley's mind at this time, and the example of the money lenders especially shows that Shelley identified with Wordsworth, or at least was drawn to make a comparison between himself and an older poet whose poetry he respected.

In his letters in following years Shelley continued to mention Wordsworth. He was apparently willing to uphold the older poet's qualities against those of other poets. On one social occasion in the winter of 1817 he defended Wordsworth's superiority over the Scottish poet Thomas Campbell. But Shelley's mentioning of Wordsworth (at least on the evidence we have left to us) was almost always to Peacock, perhaps because Shelley felt Peacock to be (as he described him to Hunt in December 1816) 'an amiable man of great learning, considerable taste, an enemy to every shape of tyranny & superstitious imposture' (*Letters*, I, p. 518), and therefore someone who would share his divided view of Wordsworth.[14] For example, on 15 May 1816, Shelley writes to Peacock from Geneva:

> So long as man is such as he now is, the experience of which I speak will never teach him to despise the country of his birth. Far otherwise, – like Wordsworth he will never know what love subsisted between himself and it, until absence shall have made its beauty heartfelt. Our Poets and our Philosophers our mountains & our lakes, the rural lanes and fields which are ours so especially, are ties which unless I become utterly senseless can never be broken asunder. These and the memory of them if I never should return, these and the affections of the mind with which having once been united they are inseparably united, will make the name of England, my country dear to me forever, even if I should permanently return to it no more. (*Letters*, I, p. 475)

This passage expresses an aspect of the sentiment of departure from *Tintern Abbey*, but it more obviously derives from Wordsworth's

> I travelled among unknown men,
> In lands beyond the sea;
> Nor, England! did I know till then
> What love I bore to thee.
> (1807)

This was also the summer during which Shelley became close friends with Lord Byron. Byron too remembered Shelley's enthusiasm for Wordsworth's poetry: 'Shelley, when I was in Switzerland, used to dose me with Wordsworth physic even to nausea; and I do remember then reading some things of his with pleasure.'[15] That Shelley would go so far as to continually inundate Byron with the older poet's work can only indicate just how highly Shelley held Wordsworth in 1816. The benefits for Byron's poetry which appear in Canto III of *Childe Harold* are certainly the result of Shelley convincing Byron of Wordsworth's merit.

But Shelley's ambivalence towards Wordsworth continued. After *The Excursion* he could never totally accept the older poet. On 23 January 1817 Benjamin Robert Haydon recorded in his *Diary* Shelley's condemnation of a passage in *The Excursion* where Wordsworth describes the 'beauty of the shining trout as they lay after being caught'.[16] And after dining one evening with Shelley at Godwin's, the entry under 6 November 1817 in Henry Crabb Robinson's *Diary* records how 'abusive' he was towards Southey. Robinson adds that 'Shelley spoke of Wordsworth with less bitterness, but with an insinuation of his insincerity, etc. The passage about baptism in *The Excursion*, it is not easy to defend.'[17]

Shelley also continued to use Wordsworth's poetry, in passing, to comment on various circumstances. Describing the climate of Italy to Peacock in a letter of 17(?) December 1818, Shelley slightly misquotes a few lines from Wordsworth's *Lines Written at a Small Distance from My House* (1798): 'The weather is usually like what Wordsworth calls the "first fine [mild] day of March", sometimes very much warmer, though perhaps it wants that "each minute sweeter than before" which gives an intoxicating sweetness to the awakening of the earth from its winter's sleep in England' (*Letters*, II, pp. 60–1). From Livorno, 6 July 1819, upon the sighting of a comet, Shelley refers in passing to two lines of Wordsworth's *To the Small Celandine* (1807) where a comet is also mentioned (*Letters*, II, p. 100). On 12 July 1820 from Leghorn, the first two lines of Wordsworth's *Thoughts of a Briton on the Subjugation of Switzerland* (1807) are applied to Peacock's personal situation (*Letters*, II, p. 212). And Shelley writes to Marianne Hunt from Bagni di Pisa, 29 October 1820, noting that Keat's style in his latest volume of poems is of that sort 'fashionable among those who fancy that they are imitating Hunt and Wordsworth' (*Letters*, II, p. 239).[18]

But the most revealing insight into Shelley's regard for Wordsworth came in response to information about Wordsworth which Shelley had received from Peacock. On 5 July 1818 Peacock wrote:

> Wordsworth has published an *Address to the Freeholders* [of Westmorland], in which he says they ought not to choose so poor a man as Brougham, riches being the only guarantees of political integrity. He goes farther than this, and actually asserts that the Commons ought to be chosen by the Peers. Now there is a pretty rascal for you. Southey and the whole gang are supporting the Lowthers, *per fas et nefas*, and seem inclined to hold out a yet more flagrant specimen of the degree of moral degradation to which self-sellers can fall under the dominion of seat-sellers. The example will not be without its use. Of course, during the election, Wordsworth dines every day at Lord Lonsdale's.[19]

And twenty days later Shelley replied from Bagni di Lucca:

> What a beastly and pitiful wretch that Wordsworth! That such a man should be such a poet! I can compare him with no one but

Simonides, that flatterer of the Sicilian tyrants, and at the same time the most natural and tender of lyric poets. (*Letters*, II, p. 26)

What becomes clear by this response is that Shelley finds it painfully difficult to reconcile the older poet's political activity with his earlier poetical activity, the older man with the younger poet. In this same letter, just a few paragraphs above, Shelley describes a bathing pool in terms of Wordsworth's description of the 'little pond' in *The Thorn* (1798). One hates to resort to over-simplistic evaluations of one person's regard for another, but it now begins to become clear that Shelley suffered a love/hate relationship with his precursor.

The documentary evidence cited in this chapter clearly shows that Wordsworth was of continuing importance to Shelley. We saw how very keen he was to meet Wordsworth. There is also in some of his early poems an undeniable familiarity with Wordsworth's poetry, and this familiarity continued for years after in his off-handed allusions to Wordsworth's poetry. Combined with the evidence in the previous chapter which clearly shows Shelley's great concern with contemporary influence and his desire to be a part of this influence, I can now, in the final chapter to Part I, examine Shelley's poetry which constitutes further direct evidence of the importance of Wordsworth, but which will also show something of the complexity of Shelley's poetic response to his elder.

3
'Proteus Wordsworth'

Shelley's cousin Thomas Medwin at one point attempts to summarise Shelley's estimation of Wordsworth:

> No one was more sensible to the merits of Wordsworth than himself, but he no longer, as proved by his sonnet [*To Wordsworth*], looked upon him as his ideal. He was still an enthusiastic admirer of his early productions, and particularly of his inimitable lines in blank verse to his sister, which satiate with excess of sweetness [*Tintern Abbey*]; but these, he said, were written in the golden time of his genius, and he held with Byron, as Nursery Rhymes, the Idiot Boy, and many others. *The Excursion* I never heard him mention; and he thought that Wordsworth had left no perfect specimen of an Ode, – that he always broke down when he attempted one.[1]

Medwin notes here that Shelley admired Wordsworth's early poetry – the insinuation being that he disliked Wordsworth's later poetry. It is interesting that Shelley apparently thought that Wordsworth's odes were lacking, the implication being that the older poet could not follow through his own formulations, and that his odes express some kind of inadequate compromise and show a poetic weakness. We can look forward, then, to Shelley in his own poetry attempting to reformulate those inadequacies and complete that lack. This reference made by Medwin to *The Excursion* is also an interesting one in that there appears to be some expectation in this non-mentioning, as if Shelley *should* have mentioned something about the poem. We know, however, that Shelley made a number of references to *The Excursion*, and we know that he was disappointed with it. In her *Journal*, dated Wednesday, 14 September 1814, Mary Shelley unceremoniously records Wordsworth's subservience to mediocrity: 'Shelley . . . brings home Wordsworth's *Excursion*, of which we read a part, much disappointed. He is a slave.'[2]

At this time Shelley had not yet written most of the poems found in his first volume of poems, *Alastor; or, The Spirit of Solitude: and Other Poems* (1816). In other words, it is significant that virtually all of

Shelley's major poetry comes after his apparent disappointment with Wordsworth, and specifically with *The Excursion*. Thus, noting that before reading *The Excursion* Shelley's estimate of Wordsworth was so high, and remembering how keen he was to meet him, it would be possible to read some of Shelley's poetry in the light of, or as a reaction to, what Shelley thought to be Wordsworth's failure.

This chapter surveys and examines those portions of Shelley's poetry which are (or with good reason appear to be) specifically about Wordsworth. Shelley's idea of Wordsworth is determined not only by the distinction he makes between Wordsworth the man and Wordsworth the poet ('That such a *man* should be such a *poet!*'), but also by the further distinction he makes between Wordsworth the 'tender' lyric poet and Wordsworth the failing poet, a distinction determined mainly by time. It is this latter ambivalence which defines Shelley's idea of Wordsworth while simultaneously leading him to reject the older poet's influence: Wordsworth as a problem for Shelley. Two further characteristics of Shelley's poetry about Wordsworth will be pointed out and discussed: first, that Shelley often writes in a Wordsworthian way about Wordsworth; and second, that Shelley expresses aspects of his ambivalence towards Wordsworth in imagery of death.

I

Medwin said that in *To Wordsworth* Shelley realised the merits of the older poet, but he ceased to hold him as his 'ideal'. The poem, published in the *Alastor* volume, begins by acknowledging the validity of Wordsworth's poetic endeavour, referring directly to Wordsworth's *Intimations Ode* – 'The things which I have seen I now can see no more' (9). Shelley, the poet-speaker, sympathises:

> Poet of Nature, thou hast wept to know
> That things depart which never may return:
> Childhood and youth, friendship and love's first glow,
> Have fled like sweet dreams, leaving thee to mourn.
> These common woes I feel.
>
> (1–5)

Shelley too mourns the departure of youth and youth's special powers of perception, this loss and separation, and in doing so identifies with Wordsworth. Shelley's sympathy and praise continue, but not before foreshadowing a dissimilarity and rejection expressed at the end of the poem:

> One loss is mine
> Which thou too feel'st, yet I alone deplore.
> (5–6)

Here the sympathy includes hints of an uneasiness. The 'loss' is both Shelley's and Wordsworth's, but now, and significantly, Shelley separates from Wordsworth (and surpasses him) by having to *'alone* deplore' the 'loss' which Wordsworth only 'feel'st'. That is, both Wordsworth and Shelley *feel* the 'loss', but Shelley 'alone' and independent of Wordsworth *deplores* it. Shelley, by deploring, expresses a greater depth of feeling. This is at once an assimilation, extension, and rejection of both Wordsworth and Wordsworthian sentiment.

The praise goes on:

> Thou wert as a lone star, whose light did shine
> On some frail bark in winter's midnight roar:
> Thou hast like to a rock-built refuge stood
> Above the blind and battling multitude:
> In honoured poverty thy voice did weave
> Song consecrate to truth and liberty . . .
> (7–12)

Shelley metaphorically attributes brilliance, strength, and permanence to Wordsworth, as well as an accompanying elevated position and isolation: the star must be above, but it is a 'lone star', and the 'refuge' stands 'Above', thus away from the 'multitude'. Being so, Wordsworth's poems did sing forth 'truth and liberty'. The implication is that Shelley is that 'frail bark' under the guiding beacon of influence ('light' of the 'star') of Wordsworth, similarly alone before 'winter's midnight roar' as Wordsworth was before the 'battling multitude'. Shelley's use of a solitary star to represent a precursor poet seems to derive from Wordsworth's sonnet to his most important precursor, Milton (1807): 'Thy soul was like a Star, and dwelt apart'. The parallel imagery hints that Wordsworth is to Shelley as Milton is to Wordsworth. Shelley in this ratio must have imagined himself as next in line. The image used by both Shelley and Wordsworth to represent a precursor – that is, as a star – is fitting in terms of influence in its astrological significance: 'influence' proper is the description given to the flow of ethereal fluid from stars and planets affecting the behaviour of individuals. Shelley and Wordsworth were surely conscious of this metaphor of influence, so each in his way is making an imagistic acknowledgement of indebtedness to his respective forerunner.

Finally, what was foreshadowed in lines 5–6 is made more explicit in the couplet ending the sonnet:

> Deserting these, thou leavest me to grieve,
> Thus having been, that thou shouldst cease to be.

Shelley's separation is completed by negating Wordsworth's existence. With Wordsworth ceasing to be what he has been, Shelley grieves the loss. Having before considered himself alone *with* Wordsworth, he now views himself alone *without* Wordsworth.

Shelley addressing Wordsworth in this way seems to have been taken from his translation of Guido Cavalcanti's sonnet to Dante (?1815). Cavalcanti was from a well-known Florentine family, but he was exiled from his home city for opposing an oppressive faction governing at that time. In his poem he addresses Dante, once his best friend. *To Wordsworth* actually contains six direct borrowings from the translation, including 'weep' and 'grieve'. The implication is, of course, Shelley's identification with Cavalcanti's break with Dante – one strong poet breaking away from another, as Shelley is attempting to break away from Wordsworth.

The manner in which Shelley expresses his separation from and loss of Wordsworth in *To Wordsworth* is strongly elegiac: there is praise, but the language of the poem rings of a funeral oration: Wordsworth is referred to as existing in the past, and Shelley has 'woes' and is left to 'grieve' because Wordsworth 'shouldst cease to be' as he has been. Shelley is saying that Wordsworth has changed, and the eulogistic tone reflects what that change meant to Shelley. The poem falls back upon itself at this point with the irony that the line 'That things depart which never may return' refers not just to Wordsworth's *Intimations Ode*, but to both Wordsworth and his creativity as Shelley sees them. Shelley accordingly suffers a Wordsworthian loss of Wordsworth. He has inherited Wordsworth's stance of solitude and loss by rejecting Wordsworth. Wordsworth has become a figure for those things which he himself poetically subverted: absence, mutability and impermanence.

Shelley sympathises with the Wordsworth who struggles with the separation of past from present as voiced, for example, in the *Intimations Ode*, but he laments the Wordsworth who deserts the ideals of 'truth and liberty', which suggest the hope of the French Revolution. But beyond this, would Shelley also condemn Wordsworth for feeling a connecting relationship with his environment – moreover, for idealising his relationship with nature? For there is evidence in another poem in the 1816 volume that Shelley in a fashion celebrates or praises perceptual separation, implying that he would be sceptical of Wordworth's connecting and internalising imagination which harmonises not only past, present and future, but also subject and object. The poem I have in mind here is *Oh! There Are Spirits of the Air*, which Mary Shelley records in her 'Notes on the Early Poems' as being 'addressed in idea to Coleridge, whom he never knew'. The figure in this poem has, like the former Wordsworth in *To Wordsworth*, 'turned from men [his] lonely feet' (6); but he has been left rejected and unanswered by the voices of nature: 'they / Cast, like a worthless boon, thy love away' (7–12).

The importance of these lines – 'worthless boon' echoing 'sordid boon' from Wordsworth's *The World Is Too Much With Us* – is that they are a direct challenge to the Nature Wordsworth is correspondent with, a Nature which is perceived as constant and responsive and where strength can be found to fortify the mind. Shelley's lines counter the logic of permanence expressed in the *Intimations Ode*:

> Though nothing can bring back the hour
> Of splendour in the grass, of glory in the flower;
>   We will grieve not, rather find
>   Strength in what remains behind;
>   In the primal sympathy,
>   Which having been must ever be.
>   (181–6)

In Shelley's poem 'The glory of the moon is dead', and the 'soul' is 'changed to a foul fiend through misery' (27–30). For Wordsworth, because of his compensating mode of recollection, immediate loss of 'glory' does not lead to grieving; for Shelley it does. Shelley ends his poem by directing this figure, regardless of his perceptual cul-de-sac, to 'Be as thou art' (35). Shelley has more than a sympathetic affinity with this figure, with the cleavage and dejection he goes through, but does not feel at all the same about the reconciling 'philosophic mind' (*Intimations Ode*, 190) of Wordsworth. Of the latter's idealism Shelley is sceptical, but a total pessimism is withheld.

We must consider too the argument made that the title piece of the 1816 volume, *Alastor* itself, is a response to Wordsworth; specifically, that *Alastor* is about the decline of youthful genius – Wordsworth's genius, that is.[3] But this conclusion cannot be drawn quite so glibly. *Alastor* is an important and deceptively complex poem, to be examined carefully beyond its visionary quest theme. It was, after all, as Shelley (sounding Wordsworthian) told Southey, his 'first serious attempt to interest the best feelings of the human heart' (*Letters*, I, p. 462).

Over the years *Alastor*'s complexity has led interpreters to disagree on both the poem's meaning and merit. The arguments over the poem's meaning set up a clash between autobiographical and allegorical readings; the arguments over the poem's merit centre around the issue of *Alastor*'s consistency or confusion, thematically and structurally. Those involved on both sides in the first clash make the same mistake in attempting to impose various reductive certainties on the poem, thus limiting its scope. Little is gained (except perhaps in the way of interesting sidelines) by noting that the hero of the poem is, like Shelley, a young, sensitive, vegetarian poet leaving his cold home; or that just as the poet dies, Shelley was, as Mary tells us in her 'Note' on the poem, at the time of composing *Alastor* told by a physician that 'he was dying rapidly of a consumption'; or the even riskier suggestion that the situation in *Alastor* derived from the repressed attraction Shelley had for Claire Clairmont while on his trip, with Mary, to the Continent in 1814–15.[4] And although Shelley himself tells us in the Preface to the poem that '*Alastor* may be considered as allegorical of one of the most interesting situations of the human mind', it is impossible to reduce that 'situation' to any simple, clear or single representation, just as it is impossible to confine the Poet to one identifiable figure. The arguments over the poem's merit are at least a little more interesting in that they expose one of the most problematic aspects of *Alastor*. Perhaps attempting to confirm Leavis's strong words about the confusion and insubstantiality in Shelley's poetry, critics have argued that the relationship between the Preface, the invocation (1–49) and the actual story of the Poet is disordered and contradictory; that Shelley says one thing and does another; that *Alastor* is confused because Shelley was confused.[5] But inevitably other interpreters of the poem rescued *Alastor* by finding it has some type of thematic unity.[6]

Can we, however, ignore those aspects of *Alastor* – its tension between the Narrator's attitude and the Poet's action, its simultaneous allusions to Shelley's own life and its direct quotations of and overt references to Wordsworth's poetry[7] – which give it the appearance of structural faults and thematic uncertainty without attempting to bring them together or clarify them? What is, for example, the relationship between the Narrator and the Poet? And is this parallel with the relationship between Shelley and Wordsworth? Most of the answers to these last two questions, especially the complexity in the cross-identifications, will be reserved for the following chapter.

But let me start here with a simple axiom: *Alastor* is about a particular kind of poetic failure, or the failure of a poet. A Narrator (invoking Wordsworthian inspiration) tells the story of a young 'Poet' who has an encounter with a vision, whereafter he seeks the vision, but only to go to an early grave. This account of the plot opens up the poem to further possible readings. Two points can be combined here, one already stated and the other implied: first, the inconsistency in the poem, the changing attitude of the Narrator towards the Poet;[8] second, as a corollary to the first point, the fact that the Narrator is *not* the Poet. The combination of these points suggests that perhaps the inconsistency of the poem – the Poet punished (by the Narrator) for his solipsistic and misanthropic attitude, yet eulogised (by the Narrator) in the end of the poem – may not be inconsistency at all. Rather, this may be a form of ambivalence where the Poet in his failure is portrayed as an object both of condemnation and sympathy; or else it could be suggested that the Poet is a composite figure, originating partly in Shelley's autobiography and partly by a different (fictional?) figure (I say different because it seems evident that Shelley neither held the self-indulgent attitude of the Poet as stated in the Preface, nor had he experienced the Poet's fall); or, more simply, it could be said that the Poet is a single figure who changed. All three of these possibilities point in greater or lesser degrees to Wordsworth, as we know Shelley both sympathised with yet condemned the changed and fallen Wordsworth – the Wordsworth who experienced, in Shelley's opinion, poetic failure.

Since the way to Wordsworth's presence behind *Alastor* has already been pointed out,[9] critics now note more confidently the older poet's effect on Shelley's poem, as, for example, in the argument that *Alastor* can be seen as a reinterpretation of Wordsworthian narrative,[10] or that *Alaṣtor* challenges Wordsworth's transcendental imagination.[11] But it is Harold Bloom who takes this furthest, noting that Shelley's poetry from *Alastor* onwards is *against* Wordsworth,[12] especially against the older poet's naturalism and natural religion.[13] As stated, my purpose here in describing aspects of *Alastor* is to note how far it fits with Shelley's poetry which is more explicitly on Wordsworth.

The reading that takes Wordsworth as the prototype of the Poet has been criticised, but often only to the extent of replacing Wordsworth with alternatives – for example, Coleridge and Rousseau.[14] But there is something more to be said for a reading of *Alastor* with the *idea* of Wordsworth in mind or, more precisely, with the idea of *Alastor* as addressing itself to the problem which Wordsworth and his poetry posed for Shelley, especially considering what is expressed in *To Wordsworth*. Also, more revealing than just a matching of the hero of the poem with Shelley's contemporaries, or reading *Alastor* as an autobiographical artefact or a poem confined to the limitations of an allegorical interpretation, is seeing the Poet of *Alastor: Or the Spirit of Solitude* in some ways as Shelley's version of *The Excursion*'s Solitary.[15] If *The Excursion* marks a turning-point in Shelley's idea of Wordsworth, the Solitary, being the most remarkable feature in that poem, must figure importantly in Shelley's disappointment. It is the Solitary who turns away from his fellow man, who denies responsibility except to himself, and it may be the Solitary whom Shelley has in mind when in the Preface to *Alastor* he mentions the Poet's 'self-centred seclusion'. Shelley thus takes one of Wordsworth's most enigmatic figures, one that must have both perplexed and stimulated him greatly, and through the Poet's death makes his comment on the limitations of such a figure. Simultaneously, the irresistible association of the Solitary with Wordsworth gives us Shelley's comment on the limitations of the older poet. Yet we find that not only is the Poet a Wordsworthian figure, but that the Narrator himself is exposed as a Wordsworthian poet in the invocation. In this light *Alastor* presents with an extraordinary situation: it is a serious poem about a failing poet in the mode of that poet. I say 'serious' because otherwise we would have to read *Alastor* as a burlesque on Wordsworth. Shelley, I think, takes Wordsworth seriously in his poem; but, as I shall point out, even in *Peter Bell the Third*, where the mode of expressing his dissatisfaction with Wordsworth is satire, there is an underlying earnestness in his intention. On a rhetorical level this is high irony; on a psychological level this is a step towards abreaction. However we take it, it reflects Shelley's deep concern with Wordsworth.

Shelley's crucial disappointment with Wordsworth that came after his reading of *The Excursion* is to a great extent based on his feeling that Wordsworth suffered from a loss of creativity; more precisely, Shelley felt Wordsworth's perception had become unrewardingly self-centred, an elegant yet destructive form of solipsism. This can be seen in Shelley's poem. When the Poet of *Alastor* has his 'vision' of a 'veiled maid' and follows her to his destruction, she is essentially a reflection of the Poet: 'Her voice was like the voice of his own soul', and she too is a poet (149–61). In the Preface this is paraphrased as the Poet thirsting 'for intercourse with an intelligence similar to itself'. After this vision – and it can be taken that the Poet's vision is an analogue of Shelley's idea of Wordsworth's self-centred perception – Nature in itself no longer holds the Poet's interest, or at least there is a failure to see as he has seen. As he gazes on 'the empty scene' around he wonders where the colours and sounds of nature have gone, 'The mystery and majesty of earth / The joy, the exultation' (196–202). The Poet is changed, just as the Solitary is changed, and just as Wordsworth of *The Excursion* is changed. He is no longer a Poet in pursuit of Nature's 'secret steps' (81–2), but seeks in vain and vainly for his own exalted reflection, which ends in self-extinction. This parallels the change Shelley saw in Wordsworth, for Shelley praised the early Wordsworth for his struggles with (and between) mind and nature, and despised the later Wordsworth for giving up this struggle. Again, the death of the Poet is Shelley's comment on the limitations and failure of the Solitary, Wordsworth's self-centred vision, and the poem as a whole. This self-pursuit Shelley saw as a poetically narcissistic regression on the part of Wordsworth, and the epigraph to *Alastor* from St Augustine's *Confessions* (III.i) expresses this regression perfectly: 'Not yet was I in love, but I was in love with loving; I sought what I might love, being in love with love'. But Shelley's identification with the Poet is his identification with Wordsworth's problem, and the Poet's failure is Shelley's warning to himself and others who might be tempted to follow. Shelley does, after all, state in the Preface that his poem should act as an 'instruction to actual men', and Mary comments in her Note that the poem 'ought rather to be considered didactic than narrative'.

In *Alastor* the Poet desperately follows the memory of his vision to the point of no return, to a 'solemn pine' (561, 571) where at its base 'Upon an ivied stone [he] / Reclined his languid head' and dies (634–71). This death scene appears to have been lifted out of Wordsworth's *Excursion*, where 'at the root / Of that tall pine', 'beneath / A plain blue stone, a gentle Dalesman lies. . .' (VII. 395–400). Imagery of death, as we have already seen in *To Wordsworth*, and as we shall see in other poems where Wordsworth is the concern, dominates Shelley's portrayals of Wordsworth and his attitude towards him; at the end of *Alastor* the speaker says:

>   when those hues
> Are gone, and those divinest lineaments,
> Worn by the senseless wind, shall live alone
> In the frail pauses of this simple strain,
> Let not high verse, mourning the memory
> Of that which is no more, or painting's woe
> Or sculpture, speak in feeble imagery
> Their own cold powers.
>   (703–10)

The 'high verse', the 'mourning' and 'the memory / Of that which is no more', is the loss expressed in Wordsworth's seminal line in the *Intimations Ode*, 'The things which I have seen I now can see no more'; but this is also the irony of pathos because that 'high verse' is Shelley's very poem on Wordsworth, and 'that which is no more' is also the Wordsworth who once *was*. The 'mourning', then, is over Wordsworth's 'death' as well. Shelley's ambivalence is thus the test of loss against gain, of Shelley figuratively 'killing' his Wordsworthian hero in order to perhaps establish his own poetic identity and destiny. Appropriately, it is as if Wordsworth and Wordsworth's poetry are being buried in the final passages of *Alastor*.

II

A little-discussed poem written by Shelley in July 1816 while he was in Switzerland living near Byron is also about Wordsworth. It was during this month that Shelley mentioned in a letter to Peacock: 'I have a study here in a tower something like Scythrop's – where I am just beginning to recover the faculties of reading and writing'

(*Letters*, II, p. 100). Indeed, besides *The Sunset* (written in the spring), Shelley had hardly written a line so far in 1816; but in July he produced *Mont Blanc* and probably the *Hymn to Intellectual Beauty*, the latter conceived in the last weeks of June while sailing around Lake Geneva with Byron. Also, as mentioned in the previous chapter, it was at this time that Byron records that Shelley was 'dosing' him with Wordsworth's influence. The poem overshadowed by *Mont Blanc* and the *Hymn* is *Verses Written on Receiving a Celandine in a Letter from England* (hereafter cited as *Verses Written on a Celandine*). The poem is central to Shelley's problematical response to Wordsworth.

Why *Verses Written on a Celandine* remains a relatively obscure poem is not altogether clear. It may simply be because of its lack of audience. It is printed neither in the 'corrected' 1970 Oxford Standard Authors edition, nor in today's most popular collection, the Norton Critical Edition edited by Donald H. Reiman and Sharon B. Powers (1977). The poem therefore remains out of the view of most students and casual readers.

Walter Peck discovered *Verses Written on a Celandine* at Harvard in 1925, and subsequently published the poem in the *Boston Herald* (21 December 1925), the Julian Edition (1926–1930, edited with Roger Ingpen), and his *Shelley: His Life and Work* (2 vols, Boston, Mass., 1927). Peck found the poem in a notebook willed to Harvard library in 1902 by Edward A. Silsbee of Boston who apparently acquired the notebook from Claire Clairmont after he met her in Florence. He wrote in pencil on the MS – which is a fair copy in Mary Shelley's hand (Harvard University: Houghton Library, MS. Eng.258.3) – the following note: 'Celandine sent from Marlowe to Shelley by Peacock.'[16] Beneath Mary's fair copy Silsbee made a further note: 'Shelley came in from his study to hand them this – They were delighted – C remembers it.' The 'C' must refer to Claire, but what Shelley actually handed to those present, giving them such delight, is a mystery. It may have been Peacock's letter containing the celandine, or it may have been the actual flower itself; but it seems more likely that what Shelley emerged with from his study was his new poem on the celandine.

We have no direct evidence of such a letter sent by Peacock, although there is no reason to doubt Claire's account as recorded by Silsbee. While composing the poem in July 1816 Shelley was in close correspondence with Peacock, having sent extended daily accounts of his sightseeing throughout that month. There is, however, in one of the letters from Shelley to Peacock, written at the end of July 1816, a passing hint that Shelley and Peacock shared an interest in celandines.

The poet wrote that at Mont Blanc he purchased some seeds of Alpine plants which he intended to take back to England:

> They are companions which the celandine, the classic celandine, need not despise; – They are as wild & more daring than he, & will tell him tales of things even as touching & as sublime as the gaze of a vernal poet. (*Letters*, I, p. 501)

This gazing 'vernal poet', of course, can be none other than the Wordsworth who himself 'gazed – and gazed' on flowers (*I Wandered Lonely as a Cloud*, 1807).

The first five stanzas of this poem's nine stanzas seem clear enough. The speaker begins by addressing a Celandine and then comparing it with what he thought of the flower (while it grew naturally) with 'a poet's' portrayal of the same type of flower:

> I thought of thee, fair Celandine,
>   As of a flower aery blue
> Yet small – thy leaves me thought were wet
>   With the light of morning dew.
> In the same glen thy star did shine
> As the primrose and the violet,
> And the wild briar bent over thee
> And the woodland brook danced under thee.
>
> Lovely thou wert in thine own glen
>   Ere thou didst dwell in song or story;
> Ere the moonlight of a Poet's mind
>   Had arrayed thee with the glory
> Whose fountains are the hearts of men –
> Many a thing of vital kind
> Had fed and sheltered under thee,
> Had nourished their thoughts near to thee.
>
> Yes, gentle flower in thy recess,
>   None might a sweeter aspect wear,
> Thy young bud drooped so gracefully,
>   Thou wert so very fair, –
> Among the fairest, ere the stress

> Of exile, death and injury,
> Thus withering and deforming thee,
> Had made a mournful type of thee,
>
> A type of that when I and thou
>   Are thus familiar, Celandine –
> A deathless Poet whose young prime
>   Was as serene as thine!
> But he is changed and withered now,
> Fallen on a cold and evil time;
> His heart is gone – his fame is dim,
> And Infamy sits mocking him.
>
> Celandine! Thou art pale and dead,
>   Changed from thy fresh and woodland state;
> Oh! that thy bard were cold, but he
>   Has lived too long and late.
> Would he were in an honoured grave!
> But that, men say, now must not be,
> Since he for impious gold could sell
> The love of those who loved him well.
>
>   (1–40)[17]

But the scene in the first stanza is somewhat ominous. It is how the speaker *imagined* the Celandine to be in its natural surroundings. We may expect, then, that this is not how we will in fact find the Celandine. The implication is that the flower idealised by the speaker's imagination will not be the flower he plans to tell us about. He only tells us (in rather conventional terms) how he thought the Celandine *was* in order to make a point about how it *is*. But before he gets to that Celandine he has before him, he refers to another, one that exists in 'song or story', a celandine that has been imaginatively endowed with 'glory' by 'a Poet's mind'. The Celandine celebrated by this Poet seems to have drawn many 'vital' things under its nurturing influence.

By the third stanza, after the speaker nostalgically sighs over how the Celandine once was, the speaker at last directly addresses the flower he has before him: a withered, deformed, and 'mournful' type that seems to have been sent to him in a letter. And into the fourth stanza the speaker compares this desiccated flower to a 'deathless Poet' whose youth likewise represents some form of tranquillity. Like the Celandine before him, this Poet is also now 'changed and withered'; moreover, this Poet has lately become heartless and infamous. The speaker expresses his deep concern by expressing the wish that this Poet would have died before his negative transformation, before he had a chance to disappoint those who, like the speaker, 'love him well'.

The relationship between the Poet of the second stanza and the 'deathless Poet' of the fourth is somewhat problematical. They seem to be the same Poet, and so we are encouraged to make parallels with the two versions of the Celandine: the 'gentle flower' the speaker idealises as opposed to the 'mournful type' he has before him. We had a partial resolution to this when we found out that the 'deathless Poet' too had a 'young prime . . . as serene' as that of the flower, but like the Celandine he is 'changed and withered now'. What constitutes the tension in the poem up to this point, then, is the now possible association of not only the two versions of the poet, but of the relationship between the two versions of the poet and two states of the Celandine, the withered and the idealised versions. Further, this is made more difficult when we add the speaker to the matrix of associations and relationships: What is the speaker's attitude towards the Poet and the Celandine? The speaker is talking to a dead flower before him about a living poet who is represented by that flower, a poet who, no less, himself represents that flower. The Celandine in its changed state is an inferior, pathetic representation of the flower in its past, organic prime; and the same can be said of the Poet: the later Poet is, in the view of the speaker, an inferior and corrupted version of the earlier Poet.

What began as a poem about a flower now becomes more strongly a poem about this Poet and the speaker's feelings toward him:

> That he, with all hope else of good
>   Should be thus transitory,
> I marvel not; but that his lays
>   Have spared not their own glory –
> That blood, even the foul god of blood
> With most inexpiable praise,
> Freedom and truth left desolate,
> He has been bought to celebrate!
>
> They were his hopes which he doth scorn;
>   They were his foes the fight that won;

> That sanction and that condemnation
>   Are now forever gone.
> They need them not! Truth may not mourn
> That with a liar's inspiration
> Her majesty he did disown
> Ere he could overlive his own.
>
> They need them not, for Liberty,
>   Justice and philosophic truth
> From his divine and simple song
>   Shall draw immortal youth,
> When he and thou shall cease to be
> Or be some other thing, – so long
> As men may breathe or flowers may blossom
> O'er the wide earth's maternal bosom.
>
> The stem whence thou wert disunited
>   Since thy poor self was banished hither,
> Now, by that priest of Nature's care
>   Who sent thee forth to wither,
> His window with its blooms has lighted,
> And I shall see thy brethren there.
> And each, like thee, will aye betoken
> Love sold, hope dead, and honour broken.
>   (41–72)

This Poet and his poetry apparently once did represent and celebrate the righteous values of Liberty, Justice and Truth, but now he has turned from them and has become not only a traitor to himself and those causes, but also to those who once believed in him – those we gather, like the speaker. The only compensation is that long after the Poet is dead his early poetry will continue to inspire.

The Celandine has had a connected, vital past, but now has a withered, disconnected present (in that, as a dried flower, it is in a preserved state). This reminds the speaker of a Poet who in the past was a poet of vitality and honourable motives, but who is now, like the flower representing him, changed for the worse. And ironically, it was this very Poet who apparently once represented the revitalising quality of flowers, yet he has now, in effect, plucked them. He is, so to speak, both plucker and plucked. Just as the Celandine in 'exile' is disconnected from its roots and stem, so too is the Poet disconnected from his past self, as is now the speaker from one aspect of the Poet. The poem is about loss, separation and a form of death, but it is also about an attempted preservation – the Poet's preservation of the flower through his poetry, and the speaker's attempted preservation of a Poet who he once held in high esteem.

Behind the shifting allegorical structure which depends on making cross-identifications, there is a more dramatic structure which suggests a further irony. It appears as if a reconstruction or redemption might be taking place in the poem, but after the frustrated outburst of the middle stanza the calmness is broken. Compensation is sought in the immutable aspects of the Poet's work, but a total recovery never takes place, and the poem which began on a feeling of prospect ends on a note of dissipation. The irony which evolves is this: the speaker's regret over the loss is paradoxically bound to his condemnation. His is compelled to write about a poet he has written off. In this way the poem becomes an act of preservation, for the poem itself becomes an everlasting sign of and witness to a poet's success and failure. The speaker doesn't stop much short of making the Poet a tragic figure.

Verses Written on a Celandine turns on the ambiguous notion of deathlessness and the status of preservation as applied to the Poet and his work. Preservation within the context of the poem means withered, live suspended, but it also suggests a form of permanence, life extended. As an extension to this, poetry itself as an object of permanence must come under suspicion: If a poem is of lasting value, is it necessarily doomed to desiccation? Are poems merely the 'dried' remains of some intensely experienced moment? Certainly Shelley's fading-coal theory of creativity as described in the *Defence of Poetry* would support this view. There Shelley notes that even 'the most glorious poetry' is but a 'feeble shadow of the original conception of the poet'. Striking too is that in this very same passage from the *Defence* Shelley says the power of creativity is like a 'flower which fades and changes as it is developed'. This is the fading and changing of the Celandine as a symbol for a poet and his poetic creativity on the decline.

The Poet – more precisely, that is, the two aspects of this one Poet – is, of course, Wordsworth. And we see here in the speaker's reaction to the Poet an ambivalence similar to Shelley's reaction in *To Wordsworth* and *Alastor*. We recognise too the elegiac tone – in rejected lines from the draft Shelley in fact calls his poem a 'lament' (University of Oxford: Bodleian Library, MS. Shelley adds. e. 16).

Praise and reproach, celebration and castigation, creatively feed off each other in a form of poetic equivocation. The early Wordsworth, the Wordsworth Shelley has sympathy and praise for, evoked a picture of youthful vitality and honesty plus revolutionary zeal, but like the Celandine he is changed now, leaving Shelley as his disappointed witness. Yet at the same time Shelley feels that Wordsworth's poetry will continue to prove inspirational, and in this sense he is the witness and heir to the older poet's past glory.

Wordsworth's own poetry is the origin of Shelley's central idea. As Wordsworth himself lamented in his *Intimations Ode*, 'nothing can bring back the hour / . . . of glory in the flower' (181–2) – precisely Shelley's expressed point transformed symbolically in *Verses Written on a Celandine*. Shelley notes that it was Wordsworth who in the first place 'arrayed' the Celandine with 'glory' (12). Also in Wordsworth's poem it is suggested that we must find

> Strength . . .
> In the faith that looks through death,
> In years that bring the philosophic mind.
> (183–90)

Shelley in his poem believes Wordsworth in his 'Poet's mind' (11) has lost 'faith' – 'His heart is gone', writes Shelley (31), the 'heart' that before leaped up when beholding those glories around him (*My Heart Leaps Up*, 1807). In that poem Wordsworth himself sternly states that if his 'heart' doesn't respond, that is, if it fails to leap up, he should be allowed to 'die':

> My heart leaps up when I behold
>   A rainbow in the sky:
> So was it when my life began;
> So is it now I am a man;
> So be it when I shall grow old,
>   Or let me die!

In *Verses Written on a Celadine* Shelley symbolically effects this drastic wish: Shelley allows one aspect of Wordsworth to die. In doing so, Shelley is able to hold on to early Wordsworth, punish Wordsworth for later failings, and, as a psychological ploy, clear the way for himself to become Wordsworth's successor. As in the case of Shelley's response to Keats's actual death, the retentive aspects of this strategy in letting Wordsworth 'die' permits the older poet to be saved 'From the contagion of the world's slow stain' – salvation and cleansing by death (*Adonais*, 356). Ironically, but appropriately, this is the same strategy Wordsworth himself employs in his 'Lucy poems', where death renders mutability powerless.

We might also note that the association Shelley makes between Wordsworth and the withered Celandine may derive from Wordsworth's own poetry. For example, the wandering poet of Wordsworth's *Stanzas Written in My Pocket-copy of Thomson's 'Castle of Indolence'* (1815), a figure who in some ways is an idealised portrait of Wordsworth himself, and with whom Shelley must have identified, is described both in terms of colourlessness and as a dried flower:

> Ah! piteous sight it was to see this Man
> When he came back to us, a withered flower, –
> Or like a sinful creature, pale and wan.
>
> (19–21)

Peacock in fact records how 'particularly pleased' Shelley was with this poem.[18]

But of Wordsworth's poems it is obvious that three poems in Wordsworth's 1807 volumes that are actually on Celandines demand to be brought into the discussion: *To the Small Celandine, To the Same Flower* and *The Small Celandine*. In fact, I could have introduced *Verses Written on a Celandine* with these poems, which are essentially in praise of the flower's unassuming beauty. Like the opening stanza of Shelley's poem, the opening of *To the Small Celandine* also refers to both a primrose and a violet, and Wordsworth identifies himself with the flower by making it his own possession:

> Long as there's a sun that sets,
> Primroses will have their glory;
> Long as there are violets,
> They will have a place in story:
> There's a flower that shall be mine,
> 'Tis the little Celandine.
>
> (3–8)

Shelley, of course, identifies the Celandine with Wordsworth because Wordsworth identifies himself with the flower, 'a flower that shall be mine'. Further, in *The Small Celandine* the speaker comes across an old Celandine in 'altered form' (10) unable to 'help itself in its decay' (18). And like the 'pale', 'withered' and 'changed' Celandine of Shelley's poem, Wordsworth's is 'Stiff in its members, withered, changed of hue' (19). Again, this is Shelley usurping Wordsworth's own imagery to disclaim yet credit the older poet: he turns the language of the younger Wordsworth against the older Wordsworth. Imitation is a form of flattery, but it is also here for Shelley a poetic expression of despair through absence and change, for an aspect of the Celandine to which Shelley addresses himself (that is, the Celandine in the past) is no longer present. Like Wordsworth in some of his strongest poetry, Shelley is struggling to reconstruct a memory in order to revive what it represented. Shelley, however, fails: mutability supersedes permanence, yet what is held as a symbol – the dried flower – represents both change and continuity. We recall the opening lines of Shelley's 1821 *Mutability*:

> The flower that smiles to-day
> To-morrow dies;
> All that we wish to stay
> Tempts and then flies.

Nothing remains constant; and especially those things which attract us, those things that we emulate and hold in high esteem, inevitably flee from or fail us. Wordsworth, I would say, falls into this category for Shelley.

III

So far we have a picture of Shelley as a young poet attempting to establish his own identity by contending with an important influence that is both celebrated and castigated. Shelley's reaction to Wordsworth is easy to keep on a purely rhetorical level, relegating his emotional responses to metaphorical or contextual status, but while analysing his poetic responses we must also try to imagine Shelley's feelings working behind his words – ultimately, of course, this is where all outward expression must originate, in terms of both motivation (why he would write on Wordsworth) and formulation (what he would write on Wordsworth). It must be admitted, even so early, that in his poetry on Wordsworth Shelley reveals himself troubled by the older poet's absent vitality and 'deathless' presence. In *Peter Bell the Third*, even though the mode of expression is satire, Shelley's ambivalence continues to be expressed in a way that displays a serious concern with the older poet and his poetry.

Notice that Wordsworth's *Peter Bell* would be published some time near the end of April 1918 caused quite a stir among his detractors. First off the mark was John Hamilton Reynolds, who in the middle of that month brought out a satire entitled *Peter Bell: A Lyrical Ballad*. Reynolds then asked Keats to draw attention to his skit by putting a notice in Leigh Hunt's *Examiner*, which Keats did (anonymously) in the 25 April issue. A week later, in the 2 May edition of the *Examiner*, Hunt himself quite ruthlessly attacked Wordsworth's *Peter Bell*; and in the next issue, 9 May, he continued his attack, this time comparing *Peter Bell* with Shelley's *Rosalind and Helen* (1819), and Shelley with Wordsworth. Hunt's views are obviously biased, but he nonetheless makes some interesting points. Wordsworth, Hunt wrote, 'always carries his egotism and "saving knowledge" about him, and unless he has the settlement of the matter, will go in a pet and plant himself by the side of the oldest tyrannies and slaveries'; but Shelley, Hunt says, is the opposite of selfishness itself, and has no greater desire than to see his fellow men happy. Hunt rejects Wordsworth on two points – essentially the same two Shelley expresses in *To Wordsworth* and *Verses Written on a Celandine*: first, he condemns Wordsworth for his servility to the status quo; second, he dismisses Wordsworth's type of imagination which selfishly binds itself to the subject's egotism. Unlike Shelley, however, Hunt finds nothing positive or even partially redeeming in Wordsworth. Hunt also underlines the irony that two poets who are essentially so similar, 'who ought to have agreed', have become so different.

Shelley is really the last to jump upon this pile, writing his response to Wordsworth's poem in Florence in the middle of October 1819.[19] But Shelley's *Peter Bell the Third* in its digressive wit goes beyond mere parody. Unfortunately, although the poem upon completion was immediately sent off to Leigh Hunt on 2 November, to be passed on to a publisher and published anonymously, for unknown reasons it did not see print until Mary's second edition of Shelley's collected poetry in 1839.

Shelley's accompanying letter to Hunt is uneasy in its humility regarding the poem. He says his motives are 'solely not to prejudge myself in the present moment' since he has spent little time on this 'party squib', and that he 'has no objection to the author being known but *not now*'. He does desire, however, 'that it should both go to press & be printed very quickly' (*Letters* II, p. 135). On one hand Shelley wants to dismiss *Peter Bell the Third* as trite, while on the other he wants to have it published immediately. In subsequent letters he continued to inquire about the fate of his poem, still apologising for its slightness and reminding his potential publisher (Charles Ollier) of his wish for the poem's anonymity (*Letters*, II, pp. 164, 181, 189, 196). We might be led to think that Shelley's insistence regarding these two matters (the non-importance and anonymity) are related: because the poem is so bad why bother putting a name to it? But two further possibilities can be suggested. First, Shelley may not have wanted the attention of the authorities drawn to him again, perhaps because of the possibility of libel. Second, Shelley may have felt that his own identity as a poet was not yet firmly established enough to sound such a challenge. Shelley might have felt that by 'next year' his poetic status would be sufficient to do so – certainly the completion of two of his best works that very month (*Prometheus Unbound* and *Ode to the West Wind*) must have encouraged him.

To assume that *Peter Bell the Third* is mainly a diatribe against Wordsworth or, for that matter, a general criticism of the contemporary socio-political scene, is a mistake. Richard Holmes and Paul Foot have perpetuated and popularised this error: Holmes says that the 'core of *Peter Bell the Third* is a political attack on Wordsworth', and Foot concludes that Shelley's poem is 'political from start to finish'.[20] These are misplaced evaluations of the main issue of the poem, perhaps only the most obvious or sensational. The poem is as much an evaluation of Wordsworth's poetry and poetics as it is of his politics. And what must lie beneath all of this is a genuine concern over Wordsworth's fate, a certain responsibility determined by the conscientiousness of a younger poet who was aware of his debt to an older poet.

Compared to the reactions of the others who decided to take on Wordsworth, there is something more discriminating in Shelley's response, something both more playful yet more serious. It might be called a double ambivalence. The first, we know, is between Wordsworth the man and Wordsworth the poet. There appears to be little sympathy or concern for the former while there is definite reverence for the latter. The further ambivalence, the one most central to this discussion, and one that became apparent in *Verses Written on a Celandine*, is between the two poet-types, again distinguished most clearly by time – an earlier Wordsworth and a later Wordsworth, the turning point being *The Excursion*. For the later Wordsworth Shelley has little affinity; this is the Wordsworth who, in *Verses Written on a Celandine*, is allowed to wither and die in order that the early poet will be preserved (at least in memory) as an ideal type. The early Wordsworth, represented by the 'fair Celandine', is the vision Shelley desires to maintain and, of course, to emulate. Further, what can also be seen in Shelley's taking-on of Wordsworth, beyond the parody which Reynolds offered, is Shelley's sympathetic interest in the effect of the change in Wordsworth.

In *Peter Bell the Third*, which Shelley nevertheless believed might be taken too seriously, this further ambivalence becomes more apparent when we note how Shelley is reacting at different points in the poem. We find that, yes, Shelley is often critical of Wordsworth's poetry, but he also frequently praises it; just as often we find that he is positive and negative at the same time, and at moments he is neutral. Take, for example, these three consecutive stanzas from Part the Fourth:

> But Peter, though now damned, was not
>   What Peter was before damnation.
> Men oftentimes prepare a lot
>   Which ere it finds them, is not what
> Suits with their genuine station.
>
> All things that Peter saw and felt
>   Had a peculiar aspect to him;
> And when they came within the belt
>   Of his own nature, seemed to melt,
> Like cloud to cloud, into him.
>
> And so the outward world uniting
>   To that within him, he became
> Considerably uninviting
>   To those who, meditation slighting,
> Were moulded in a different frame.
>   (268–82)

Shelley in the first stanza distinguishes between a Peter – that is, Wordsworth – before and after damnation, with some suggestion of blameless regret for the latter. In the next stanza, with ironic reference to Wordsworth's *I Wandered Lonely as a Cloud* (1807), Shelley describes Wordsworth's manner of internalising all that is outside of him, the result being, in Shelley's opinion, a cloudy (con)fusion in Wordsworth's poetry. The third stanza makes the point that this Wordsworthian perception of 'uniting' the object with the subject is merely a different way of perceiving and imagining, 'uninviting / To those' who are a different nature of 'frame' of mind – 'those' like Shelley, that is. Although these three stanzas are about Peter after 'damnation', it would certainly be misleading to say that Shelley here is negative towards Wordsworth; at the most he expresses a slight pessimism and regret, but more precisely it is an objective but teasing assessment of Wordsworth's mode of perceptual imagination.

In those places in *Peter Bell the Third* where Shelley comments upon Wordsworth's poetry this same mixed attitude continues, although the positive and the negative become more pronounced:

> He had a mind which was somehow
>   At once circumference and centre
> Of all he might or feel or know;
> Nothing went ever out, although
>   Something did ever enter.
>
> He had as much imagination
>   As a pint-pot; – he never could
> Fancy another situation,
> From which to dart his contemplation,
>   Than that wherein he stood.
>
> Yet his was individual mind,
>   And new created all he saw
> In a new manner, and refined
> Those new creations, and combined
>   Them, by a master-spirit's law.
>
> Thus – though unimaginative –
>   An apprehension clear, intense,
> Of his mind's work, had made alive
> The things it wrought on; I believe
>   Wakening a sort of thought in sense.
>   (293–312)

Once more, there is a two-mindedness and a dual response to Wordsworth. As F. R. Leavis noted, Shelley here 'is registering his perception of the differences between himself and Wordsworth', differences which show his simultaneous respect for and need to differentiate himself from his subject.[21] Again Shelley describes how Wordsworth's 'mind' works, how it is 'circumference and centre' of his perception and epistemology, how he has no sympathetic imagination, and how his 'contemplation' remained 'wherein he stood'. Wordsworth's mind, Shelley observes, works on 'things', rather than 'things' working on it. But at the same time he acknowledges Wordsworth's creative originality in making new combinations by his 'clear' and 'intense' understanding of those 'things' his mind fixed on. So although Wordsworth never moved out of the realm of his mind, his poetic powers were in making new associations and in bringing to life the subjects of his contemplation. Shelley understands that Wordsworth simultaneously examines his responses as much as those things which solicit those responses.

One excluded passage from *Peter Bell the Third* not published until 1967 makes a further comment on Wordsworth's poetic 'spirit':

> The beam-anatomising prism
>   Of his keen spirit once was clear;
> He of the pantheistic schism,
>   Was, once concealed Don Juanism
> He acted in his seventeenth year.[22]

Besides a slighting reference to a possible early affair of Wordsworth's, Shelley comments here on the clarity of Wordsworth's analysis which broke things down in the same way a prism breaks down light into its components. He calls Wordsworth 'of the pantheistic schism' – that is, one who sees the Creator in everything. The obvious should again be emphasised: namely, that Shelley's admittance of Wordsworth's 'keen spirit' and clarity is early Wordsworth – Wordsworth before 'damnation'.

All of these are fair and accurate criticisms of Wordsworth's poetry. Like Shelley, Geoffrey Hartman observes exactly this process in Wordsworth: what they both see

> is the minute attention he gives to his own most casual responses, a finer attention than is given to the nature he responds to. . . . When Wordsworth depicts an object he is also depicting himself or, rather, a truth about himself, a self-acquired revelation.[23]

On one hand Shelley disclaims this type of imagination – 'He had as much imagination / As a pint-pot'. This is negative. On the other hand, 'though unimaginative', Shelley states that Wordsworth has an 'apprehension clear, intense', making 'alive' what it perceives, 'Wakening a sort of thought in sense'. This obviously is favourable. But Shelley's responses to Wordsworth are, if not totally ambivalent, at least mixed. This indicates Shelley's deep preoccupation with trying to *fix* Wordsworth (in the sense of both holding and correcting), yet it also indicates that Shelley finds it impossible to reach a single judgement. Leavis notes the same point but presents it in a different light: Shelley, who had been 'drawn to read Wordsworth with that devoted intensity', is obviously an admirer, for Wordsworth made it possible for Shelly and his 'younger contemporaries . . . to achieve the means of expressing their own distinctive sensibilities'.[24] But by clearing the ground for individual expression, Wordsworth himself had to become part of that to be cleared. Unless imitation is the calling of the day, and the Romantic credo stressed originality, perhaps every major poet becomes an ambivalent configuration for his followers to contend with. Wordsworth was such a figure, and all of his important contemporaries – Coleridge, Keats, Shelley and even Byron – wrote with one scrutinising eye on Wordsworth's accomplishments.

This ambivalence toward Wordsworth's poetry, the condemnation of his type of imagination yet with some recognition of his achievement, holds for most of the poem. Shelley enlarges his disapproval by calling Wordsworth a kind of 'moral eunuch' and 'Male prude' whose poetry remains impotent because it only touches 'the hem of Nature's shift', and dares not 'uplift' the 'all-concealing tunic'; thus from Nature Wordsworth receives but a 'sister's kiss', his efforts 'stagnant' (Part the Fourth, 313–32). Shelley apparently has little sympathy for those who hold back, those who do not seek beyond or beneath. Some lines later Wordsworth's manner of recollecting and his choice of rather commonplace subject matter is gently mocked (Part the Fifth, 403–32) yet at the same time his 'verse' and 'language' is complimented for its clarity and universality, its life- and light-giving qualities:

> But Peter's verse was clear, and came
>   Announcing from the frozen hearth
> Of a cold age, that none might tame
> The soul of that diviner flame

It augured to the Earth:

> Like gentle rains, on the dry plains,
>   Making that green which late was gray,
> Or like the sudden moon, that stains
> Some gloomy chamber's window panes
>   With a broad light like day.
>
> For language was in Peter's hand
>   Like clay while he was yet a potter;
> And he made songs for all the land,
> Sweet both to feel and understand,
>   As pipkins late to mountain Cotter.
>   (433–47)

Shelley in *Peter Bell the Third* does not totally blame Wordsworth for the 'dullness' in his poetry. In the poem the Devil and the Reviews for the most part bring damnation to Wordsworth: 'Pray abuse', the Devil tells the critics, with a 'five-pound note as compliment'; and so they do, as did the critics in reviewing so harshly Wordsworth's volumes of 1807. The result in *Peter Bell the Third* is Wordsworth going 'half mad' (Part the Sixth, 464–92) and becoming a 'walking paradox':

> For he was neither part nor whole,
> Nor good, nor bad – nor knave nor fool;
> – Among the woods and rocks.
>   (543–7)

This too must have been Shelley's paradoxical description of Wordsworth: for Shelley, Wordsworth was neither one thing nor another – he always solicited two responses at once, making it impossible to censure without at least some praise.

What follows Peter's stunned reaction to the critics is a delusive ride upon a horse, with obvious reference to the ride of the idiot boy in Wordsworth's poem of that name (Part the Sixth, 548–58). From this point on, the Peter or Wordsworth of the past is no more, his 'heart' now being diminished and his 'thoughts' impaired, existing in limbo where 'happiness is wrong' (Part the Sixth, 559–73).[25] Thus Peter 'grew dull, harsh, sly, unrefined' (582), and his verses which were once described as 'clear' become 'verses dark and queer', 'ghosts of what they were' (Part the Sixth, 609–13). And of course now

> the Reviews, who heaped abuse
> On Peter while he wrote for freedom,
> So soon as in his song they spy
> The folly which soothes tyranny,
> Praise him, for those who feed 'em.
>
> (619–23)

Reinforced by this treatment from the Tory critics, poor Peter continues to produce like verses, until, after promotion from the Devil's friend Lord MacMurderchouse, he becomes struck with the contagious disease of dullness and yawning.

IV

With a reading of *Peter Bell the Third* as given above, it would be a misrepresentation of the poem to gloss it as a diatribe against, or total dismissal of, Wordsworth. Even in his dedication 'To Mary' from *The Witch of Atlas* (1820), where Shelley outwardly laughs at Wordsworth's *Peter Bell*, he is in two minds:

> My Witch indeed is not so sweet a creature
>   As Ruth or Lucy, whom his graceful praise
> Clothes for our grandsons – but she matches Peter,
>   Though he took nineteen years, and she three days
> In dressing.
>
> (33–7)

Shelley belittles Wordsworth for the nineteen years of 'blundering toil' (32) he spent dwelling over *Peter Bell*, when it took him only three days to complete *The Witch*. Shelley thus intends his poem to act as a counter-example to Wordsworth's, both in the tone and spirit of poetic creation.[26] None the less, Shelley is humble enough to note that Wordsworth's other early poetry, the poems of Ruth and Lucy (the *Lyrical Ballads*), are 'graceful' portrayals fit for posterity. As in *To Wordsworth* and *Verses Written on a Celandine*, a distinction is made between the earlier and later poetry, between his good and bad poetry. This again is what Shelley states playfully but clearly in the

Dedication to *Peter Bell the Third*: 'He was at first sublime, pathetic, impressive, profound; then dull; then prosy and dull; and now dull – oh so very dull! it is an ultra-legitimate dulness'. Mary too feels she must remind us of Shelley's regard for the older poet: in her 'Note on Peter Bell the Third' she says 'No man ever admired Wordsworth's poetry more; – he read it perpetually . . .'.

In *Peter Bell the Third* we tend to remember, or are given to remember, the poem's most famous stanza as Shelley's last word on Wordsworth:

> Peter was dull – he was at first
> Dull – oh, so dull – so very dull!
> Whether he talked, wrote, or rehearsed –
> Still with this dulness he was cursed –
> Dull – beyond all conception – dull.
> (703–7)

But as we have seen, this is only one part of Shelley's reaction to Wordsworth, and certainly not one that dominates *Peter Bell the Third* or any other of Shelley's poetry on Wordsworth. That critics can so damage a poet, as he partly implies in Wordsworth's case, is confirmed just a few years later in the Preface to *Adonais* (1821). Here Shelley says that the 'savage criticism' of Keats's *Endymion* actually 'produced the most violent effect' on the young poet's mind, and eventually killed him. Shelley must therefore be taken seriously when he suggests external causes for Wordsworth's failure. And when Shelley does make Wordsworth at least partly responsible for his 'dullness' and 'damnation', he implies that it is either a fateful mistake in preparation which people often unknowingly bring upon themselves –

> Men oftentimes prepare a lot
> Which ere it finds them, is not what
> Suits their genuine station.
> (270–6)

– or just a human flaw we all share;

> His virtue, like our own, was built
> Too much on that indignant fuss
> Hypocrite Pride stirs up in us

> To bully one another's guilt.
> (289–92)

As in the case with the Poet in *Alastor*, Shelley does not make Peter directly or totally responsible for his negative condition – it is more a fatalistic predicament, an outcome that is, paradoxically, just as predictable and unavoidable as it is inexplicable.

In a fragment of 1819 Shelley similarly appears to excuse Wordsworth for making an erroneous remark, but the tone is less apologetic, and certainly more cynical:

> A poet of the finest water
> Says that Carnage is God's daughter
> This poet lieth as I take
> Under an immense mistake
> As many a man before has done
> Who thinks his spouse's child his own.[27]

The remark condemned by Shelley ('Carnage is God's daughter') is from Wordsworth's *Thanksgiving Ode* (1816). (In subsequent editions of the poem Wordsworth excluded the line.) Shelley also refers to it in *Peter Bell the Third* (Part the Sixth, 634–40). Although Wordsworth 'lieth . . . / Under an immense mistake' – 'lieth' punningly used here as meaning both reclining ('under') and untruth ('mistake') – Shelley passes this error back to Wordsworth's predecessors. But what we have is Shelley sarcastically praising Wordsworth as 'A poet of the finest water', perhaps suggesting some clarity and pureness, while at the same time reproaching him for a false judgement.

V

Shelley's poetry owes a great deal to Wordsworth, and even in his later work where he apparently moves further away from the older poet, the Wordsworthian presence at his back is still identifiable. In one of the fragments of Shelley's last poem, the unfinished *Triumph of Life*, there is a fleeting but revealing reference to Wordsworth. In the passage the poet-speaker is uninterested in those of the past who influence, for better or for worse, 'this new tide of time'. Among those are 'others' who 'tell our sons in prose or rhyme / The manhood of the child'.[28] This must be a generalised reference to Wordsworth; specifically, to Wordsworth in the *Intimations Ode* who claims the child is father of the man. Wordsworth's dismissal by the poet-speaker is reprimanded by Rousseau, the other speaker in the passage. That Shelley until the end was still ready to censure Wordsworth while at the same time acknowledge his debt to the older poet takes Shelley's ambivalence one step further. It can only indicate that Wordsworth was still a significant part of the image of a poet Shelley kept as his lost leader.

Regardless of whether Wordsworth's contemporaries parodied or imitated him, reacted against or dismissed him, he dominated the poetry of the time – the era has been called, after all, 'the Age of Wordsworth'. Shelley's poetry perhaps best marks this ambivalence of the age, the simultaneous imitation and rejection of Wordsworth. Even at the level of verbal influence, we can note how, for example, Shelley might use a Wordsworthian lexicon to construct his own particular syntax, or conversely, how he might take Wordsworthian syntax and substitute his own vocabulary, or how he might create a Wordsworthian scene only to transcend it. Take this fragment written in 1818:

> My head is wild with weeping for a grief
>   Which is the shadow of a gentle mind.
> I walk into the air (but no relief
>   To seek, – or haply, if I sought, to find;
> It came unsought); – to wonder that a chief
>   Among men's spirits should be so cold and blind.

The opening words, 'My head', echo Wordsworth's manner of centring a poem on a part of the speaker's physical self, as in 'My heart leaps up . . .' or in

> My heart is at your festival,
> My head hath its coronal . . .
>   (*Intimations Ode*, 39–40)

The phrase 'a gentle mind' likewise recalls Wordsworth's profuse use of 'mind', especially in combination with delicate modifiers such as 'tranquil mind' (*An Evening Walk* (1793), 384), 'patient mind' (*Michael* (1800), 156), or 'mind serene' (*Is There a Power* . . . (1815), 11, and *Peele Castle* (1807), 40).[29] Yet even though *walking* is one of

Wordsworth's most popular conventions for poetic discovery, he could never write 'I walk into the air', nor would we expect Wordsworth to emotively describe (especially in the present tense) his head as 'wild with weeping'.

Given Shelley's ambivalent attitude towards Wordsworth in *Peter Bell the Third*, Edward Dowden's passing suggestion that this very fragment of 1818 'may refer to Wordsworth' is worth considering.[30] Since Wordsworth's own ideas and words are used for and against him by the younger poet, and since Shelley holds a high opinion of the Wordsworth who *was*, he would ascribe to the older poet a 'gentle mind', and he would call Wordsworth 'a chief / Among men's spirits'; and at the same time he would describe him as 'cold' and but a 'shadow' of his former self. This is the same 'cold' and colourless trace of a 'Poet's mind' that can be seen in *Verses Written on a Celandine*, and the same lack of colour of the failed lizard-poets in *An Exhortation* (1820), which Shelley in a letter to Maria Gisborne said was an 'excuse' for Wordsworth (*Letters*, II, p. 195):

>   Chameleons feed on light and air:
>   Poets' food is love and fame:
>   If in this wide world of care
>   Poets could but find the same
>   With as little toil as they,
>   Would they ever change their hue
>   As the light chameleons do,
>   Suiting it to every ray
>   Twenty times a day?
>
>   Poets are on this cold earth,
>   As chameleons might be,
>   Hidden from their early birth
>   In a cave beneath the sea;
>   Where light is, chameleons change:
>   Where love is not, poets do:
>   Fame is love disguised: if few
>   Find either, never think it strange
>   That poets range.
>
>   Yet dare not stain with wealth or power
>   A poet's free and heavenly mind:
>   If bright chameleons should devour

> Any food but beams and wind,
> They would grow as earthly soon
> As their brother lizards are.
> Children of a sunnier star,
> Spirits from beyond the moon
> Oh, refuse the boon![31]

When potential for light and colour is forfeited, when poets are bought by 'wealth and power', this is a poetic failure. Wordsworth is, as the poem suggests, a chameleon turned lizard – a turncoat. He has lost the power of positive mutability and has become earthbound, uninspired and uninspiring. And this too is the colourlessness and coldness in the death scene at the end of *Alastor* (703 ff), the light of hope once represented by some 'surpassing Spirit' now becoming for 'Those who remain behind' a scene of 'pale despair and cold tranquillity' where things 'are not as they were'. This is the scene that Shelley believes Wordsworth left behind. This is the scene that Shelley inherited from his precursor. When Shelley in a fragment poem wrote 'Proteus Wordsworth who shall bind thee,'[32] he is expressing his personal frustration about the changing Wordsworth and wondering who it might be that can master the master. Shelley, of course, had himself in mind.

What is pervasive in Shelley's poems about Wordsworth is the imagery of death: *To Wordsworth* is essentially elegiac; the Poet of *Alastor* cannot avoid death; *Verses Written on a Celandine* draws a comparison between Wordsworth and a dead flower and wishes that Wordsworth were dead; *Peter Bell the Third* takes place after death and damnation; and *My Head is Wild*, like *To Wordsworth*, uses the language of death and loss. The reason why Shelley would use death as the dominant metaphor to approach the problem of Wordsworth is on one level straightforward, that for Shelley Wordsworth changed, and his previous self no longer existed. This breaks down into three further answers: first, Wordsworth was figuratively 'killed' for his failure, as a punitive reaction on Shelley's part; second, the symbolic death of Wordsworth would clear a space for Shelley to fill; and third, Wordsworth, allowed to die, permits Shelley to hold on to the inspiration of Wordsworth's early poetry. And behind Shelley's poetic laments on Wordsworth was another strategy. He believed his words on Wordsworth would survive because he knew that Wordsworth would, in terms of posterity, survive. Wordsworth, in effect, represented Shelley's ticket to join the greats, those whose words endure time. For Shelley, the act of writing about Wordsworth amounts to an intimation of immortality.

Freud would say that this type of relationship that Shelley constructed would obviously place Wordsworth as a father figure to the younger poet, in that a father 'becomes a model not only to imitate but also to get rid of, in order to take his place'.[33] Appropriately, Freud describes this as an ambivalent attitude. Since Shelley never met Wordsworth, he could only contend with him in his poetry, as a substitute relationship. And according to the Oedipal complex theory, the son has fantasies about killing the father. Poetry is, of course, always a form of fantasy.

It is an indication both of Shelley's genius and deep worry about Wordsworth that his responses to the older poet were expressed in so many modes, all the way from the dedication and despair in *To Wordsworth* and *Verses Written on a Celandine* to the praise and playfulness in *Peter Bell the Third* and the Preface to *The Witch of Atlas*. But the obvious point must be emphasised, although it is one that is easy to forget in studying the influence of one poet on another: that behind the rhetoric of parody and lamentation there exists a young poet deeply concerned with a great predecessor and contemporary, compelled to cope with his troublesome identification. The figure of Wordsworth must in some ways have been a burden for Shelley, and although each attempt to overcome the problem (if we believe in a cathartic effect) was an attempt to lighten the load, he could never totally unburden himself.

We gain from Shelley's writing on Wordsworth the sense that the older poet could not totally achieve the sublime status of Lucan, Henry Kirke White, Chatterton and Keats, the elevation through early death that many protagonists of Shelley's poems also achieve. There is also the fictional author of *Epipsychidion* whom Shelley claims to have died. Shelley too was tragically (and ironically) to fulfil his own design. His misuse of Wordsworth's own words in the Preface to *Alastor* now take on a new significance of disappointment and wish-fulfilment:

> The good die first,
> And those whose hearts are dry as summer dust,
> Burn to the socket!

At least one aspect of Wordsworth's figurative death made him the 'good' hero Shelley desired. For Shelley, the only way to union and completion is through separation. When Shelley in *Verses Written on a Celandine* chose to describe Wordsworth's state as 'deathless', when he could have used 'living' to say what might be the same thing, Shelley's irony is intentional. As in *Adonais*, he could 'No more let Life divide what Death can join together' (477).

Part II
Speculations

Introduction

Shelley's poet figures are often viewed as rather pathetic and indulgent self-portrayals, over-done and over-personal. But this is an old-fashioned interpretation, attributing to them qualities stemming from what is believed to be some kind of emotional or personal flaw in Shelley's make-up. I too read these figures as personal, but in the way of exemplifying (allegorising) Shelley's deep concern with his idea of himself as a poet. He is not so much exhibiting flaws in his own character, but expressing the very real problems of becoming a poet, which in Shelley's scene of influence is always the problem of becoming a poet relative to other poets. Judith Cherniak says 'the figure of the Poet is significant not only because it dominates several of Shelley's major works, but because it exemplifies that complex relationship between the personal and traditional which is at the heart of his poetry, the recasting of subjective experience in terms suggested by the greatest of poetic and philosophical traditions'.[1] This is one premise from which a consideration of Shelley and influence can begin – that Shelley was writing with other poets and other works of literature in mind, and with a firm acknowledgement of literary history. Shelley, more than anything else, was a student of literature, and his work must always be seen as an engagement with literature, and especially with the literature closest to him.

Wordsworth's presence in Shelley's poetry is manifest in three ways. The first is in the manner of his poetry, especially where Shelley uses Wordsworth's figurative language. The second is in matter, where Shelley takes up the same problems or topics as Wordsworth (for example, the states of permanence and mutability, outlooks of idealism and scepticism). And the third is via the figure of the poet, both as a subject of poetry and as a figure of poetic authority. This study is for the most part concerned with those moments when the three are problematically intertwined: Shelley writing about Wordsworth or Wordsworthian subject matter in a Wordsworthian way.

One is tempted to note those passages where Shelley's obvious design is to disintegrate Wordsworth's most sustained images:

> When the lamp is shattered
> The light in the dust lies dead –
> When the cloud is scattered
> The rainbow's glory is shed.
> (*When the Lamp is Shattered* (1822), 1–4)

Wordsworth's tropes of self-preservation that we know so well become in Shelley's hand intimations of dissemination and death. But more interesting are those cases when it appears that Shelley revised his poetry in order to erase something he felt may have been too Wordsworthian. In *Revaluation* Leavis notes an instance of this when he claims that an 'obvious touch of Wordsworth' has been cancelled out of the final version of one of Shelley's poems.[2] The passage is the third part of *To Jane: The Recollection* (1822). I put in brackets the significant revisions Shelley made (the text is the one printed in *Revaluation*):

> How calm it was – the silence there
>   By such a chain was bound,
> That even the busy woodpecker
>   Made stiller by her sound
>
> The inviolable quietness;
>   The breath of peace we drew
> With its soft motion made not less
>   The calm that round us grew.
>
> It seemed that [there seemed] from the remotest seat
>   Of the white mountain ['s] waste
> To the bright [soft] flower beneath our feet,
>   A magic circle traced; –
>
> A spirit interfused around,
>   A thinking [thrilling], silent life;
> To momentary peace it bound
>   Our mortal nature's strife; –
>
> And still, it seemed [I felt], the centre of
>   The magic circle there
> Was one whose being   filled with love
> [Was one fair form that]
>   The breathless [lifeless] atmosphere.
>   (33–55)

The only revision Leavis draws our attention to is the substitution of 'thrilling' for 'thinking'. Leavis says this 'serves to call attention to the complete and radical contrast'. He continues:

> The calm is the reverse of Wordsworthian; the peace is indeed momentary. What is bound is not the silence, but the impending violation – the chain will break; for 'inviolable' suggests the opposite of what it says, and the characteristic leaning movement conveys the opposite of security. A Wordsworthian atmosphere is never filled with love, and love here is at the same time a sultry menace.

Leavis is correct – correct, that is, in what he does say. Even with a rather pesty woodpecker chipping away at things, the 'atmosphere' of silence, stillness, quietness, peacefulness, softness, calmness and breathlessness that Shelley describes does seem to invoke the 'spirit' of Wordsworthian 'thinking, silent life'. But to call this 'thrilling' certainly turns the calmly cognitive experience into an emotional or sensational one. Leavis is also correct in pointing out that Wordsworth would not fill an 'atmosphere' with 'love'; rather, he would create within it intimations or remembrances of the past in order to relocate his own presence. Leavis doesn't mention it, but the change from 'breathless' to 'lifeless' also intensifies the experience by altering an auditory suspension to a suspension of vitality. But the significance of another revision that Leavis passes by must also be questioned: what about the change Shelley made in altering a generalised and uncertain qualification ('it seemed . . .') to one of a specific and specified response ('I felt . . .')? Certainly the speaker's strength in affectively centring himself within this type of recollected experience is drawn from Wordsworth. Recall what was for Shelley one of the most engaging passages in Wordsworth's poetry: 'And I have felt / A presence that disturbs me with the joy / Of elevated thoughts . . .' (*Tintern Abbey*, 94–103).

So what conclusions can be drawn? It can only be said that Shelley's attempt to erase Wordsworth's presence in his poetry is selective. Shelley is just as willing to use Wordsworth's techniques (ideas or diction) as he is to drop them. Likewise, he is willing to purposefully misuse or revise them. Consider too the opening part of Shelley's poem I have just been discussing:

> Now the last day of many days,
>   All beautiful and bright as thou,
>   The lovliest and the last, is dead.
>   Rise, Memory, and write its praise!
>   Up, – to thy wonted work! come, trace
>   The epitaph of glory fled, –
>   For now the Earth has changed its face,
>   A frown is on the Heaven's brow.

Shelley's hurrying invocation to 'Memory' and the 'epitaph of glory fled' appears to derive from Wordsworth's questioning in the *Intimations Ode*:

> Whither is fled the visionary gleam?
> Where is it now, the glory and the dream?
>   (56–7)

But what has to be decided is whether or not these two poems drawn together tell us something about how one influenced the other, how they are similar and different, how they share a problem. For the moment I would suggest this: here and elsewhere Shelley, following Wordsworth, is attempting to formulate stability and permanence through poetical discourse. He has seen Wordsworth go to the landscape; he has seen him find images which transcend mutability and impermanence, giving him a style of poetry that communicates what appears to be an emotional and lasting balance. The older poet has created a 'faith that looks through death' (*Intimations Ode*, 189). Shelley's poem too seems headed towards such an achievement by settling on an image of stability. Close to the end of *To Jane: The Recollection* he believes he has found boundless depth, purity and clarity in pools which reflect the sky and the forest (53ff.). It is a picture in which he sees himself as part of the lasting scene. But by the end of the poem Shelley acknowledges that this image can never be; the feeling cannot be sustained. The picture reflected on the pool only remains permanent

> Unlike an envious wind crept by,
>   Like an unwelcome thought,
> Which from the mind's too faithful eye
>   Blots one dear image out.
> Though thou art ever fair and kind,

The forests ever green,
       Less oft is peace in Shelley's mind,
          Than calm in waters, seen.
                                         (81–8)

The broken surface of the water erases the scene and its continuity, its holding power; moreover, it erases the tranquil picture of 'peace in Shelley's mind'. He cannot even have the lasting fate of Narcissus gazing at his own image in a pool.

Because Shelley troubles over following Wordsworth's picture of calm perdurability – a picture in which Shelley questions his own status as a figure of stability – the younger poet must develop other strategies to deal with Wordsworth's presence and poetic accomplishment. In other words, Shelley finds imitation of Wordsworth not just implausible but impossible. Shelley must develop other ways of being influenced by the poet he knows he must be influenced by, even when it means defying the influence. Shelley must in a sense 'deconstruct' his poetic experience of Wordsworth in order to discover the antithetical terms and positive limitations of his own relationship with the older poet.

4
Poets, Princes and Fallen Figures

Between *Queen Mab* and *Alastor* a significant change takes place in Shelley's poetry – not necessarily a change for better or worse, but a change in the fundamental character of his work. This can be phrased more subtly: *Queen Mab* is Shelley's first major poem, but *Alastor* is Shelley's first major *Shelleyan* poem. Two questions come quickly: What took place between the writing of *Queen Mab* in June 1812 and the composing of the poems making up the *Alastor* volume of 1816? What is a 'Shelleyan' poem?

To the first of these it could be answered 'a great deal' or 'very little'. On one hand, Shelley separated from Harriet Westbrook and eloped to Europe with Mary Godwin, and between he fathered a daughter and son by Harriet and a son by Mary (Mary also lost a daughter); on the other hand, Shelley wrote very little poetry, and so minimal development might be expected in his artistic interests or creative skills. One could, of course, speculate and suggest that the former caused the latter, that his rather unstable personal life pulled him away from any sustained artistic endeavours. However, central to my discussion, and as one answer to what also took place over those three years, is that Shelley discovered Wordsworth in a new way and attempted to come to terms with him. That is, roughly between 1812 and 1815, beginning with his renewed interest in Wordsworth which began during his stay at Keswick (1811–12) and compounded with his disappointment over *The Excursion*, Shelley read Wordsworth, thought about Wordsworth and, as I have shown, towards the end of those years began writing about Wordsworth in a Wordsworthian way.[1] Remember that previous to this time Shelley was uninterested in Wordsworth's poetry.

Does this undermine the second question? Could a 'Shelleyan' poem in some ways be a 'Wordsworthian' poem? To a particular degree, and to a particular point, I would answer yes, to the extent that an anti-Wordsworthian poem is also a Wordsworthian poem, and to the extent that what I mean by a 'Wordsworthian' poem is one which deals with both Wordsworth and Wordsworth's (good and bad) poetry, often simultaneously, often indistinguishably, in a

Wordsworthian way. Here I acknowledge Harold Bloom when he says that the meaning of a poem can *only* be another poem:[2] because Wordsworth stands as Shelley's most influential predecessor, the meaning of a Shelleyan poem can be a Wordsworthian poem. The problem throughout this study has been and continues to be the way in which Shelley's poems are in fact Wordsworthian.

In attempting to establish his own individuality as a poet, in order to grow as a poet, it was necessary for Shelley to create a protagonist who, also as a poet, would be successful and exhibit qualities of originality and poetic self-determination. Because Wordsworth was singularly important for the young poet, these poet figures are often entangled with Shelley's ideas of Wordsworth. That is, Shelley's idea of a poet is in some ways tied to his idea of Wordsworth. It seems to have become imperative for Shelley to test the failure or negative side of Wordsworth's poetic stance (especially as embodied by the Solitary of *The Excursion*). Could he take the Wordsworthian figure any further than Wordsworth? But this set a kind of trap for Shelley: once having modelled his figures on the Wordsworthian type, could he ever escape this influence on his own figures? Could he, in other words, make a successful poet out of a figure he both condemned and emulated? And one important step further: could he, using this figure, become a successful poet himself? Could he ever write as if he were Wordsworth's own precursor?

I

Queen Mab lacks typical Shelleyan characteristics: it lacks a dominating 'I' (or a significant 'Other') who is involved in either dramatic or rhetorical action. (By rhetorical action I mean a poem like *Adonais*, where Shelley is not telling a tale of events *per se*, but trying strongly to make or illustrate an exigent point, one that obviously displays an emotional – rather than logical, doctrinal or philosophical – commitment.) In other words, *Queen Mab* is heroless and without any particular tension associated with its central figure. In his later poetry, Shelley often insists on a solitary figure or speaker who is the integral part of the particular poem's problem, a figure often struggling with the production of successful poetry. *Queen Mab* remains, nonetheless, as a vehicle expressing Shelley's early views, an interesting poem, but it lingers over another tradition and calls forth didacticism, something which six years later in the Preface to

Prometheus Unbound Shelley says he abhors. Into *Queen Mab* Shelley enthusiastically threw the sum of his youthful knowledge and the various dimensions of his beliefs, as his copious 'Notes', which are perhaps a sign of his lack of confidence in his actual poetry, cover everything from vegetarianism to astronomy.

One can summarise *Queen Mab* as negatively as Carlos Baker when he says 'it is a distempered and unoriginal vision, mediocre as verse, and less than mediocre as history';[3] but one can also be fairer to the poem's genre and workmanship, as Gerald McNiece is: '*Queen Mab* is largely poetry of statement. The organisation is logical and chronological rather than narrative or dramatic. . . . [T]here is no really vital mythic structure to the poem'.[4] McNiece's remarks implicitly suggest what happens in Shelley's *other* poetry when a central figure *is* at work: rather than 'statement' there is narrative and drama. And I would also add that when there is a creative conflict revolving around that figure, one that often puts the production of successful poetry at stake, Shelley's poetry is most engaging. Ahasuerus, the archetypal solitary wanderer, does make an appearance in *Queen Mab* (VII. 66ff.), but he seems to be neither on a quest nor intimately tied to the narrator; instead, he tends to weakly echo Milton's Satan.

At this point in Shelley's poetry the potential in such a figure as Ahasuerus is not fully attractive in a poetically innovative sense. The point is this: many of Shelley's poems revolve around a central 'I' or significant 'Other'; and what requires examination (in this and the next two chapters) is the extent to which these protagonists are prefigured by the idea of Wordsworth and/or the Wordsworthian figure.

II

Like Shelley's portrayals of Wordsworth in *Alastor*, *Peter Bell the Third*, *To Wordsworth* and *Verses Written on a Celandine*, the Solitary of *The Excursion* is a fallen figure, yet paradoxically he is in part redeemed by the poetic elegance of his reasoning and expression, as well as by his stubborn individuality. He is as his name, and this too engages our attention, if not also our 'romantic' sympathy. We are always interested in the plight of outcasts and underdogs. Because of all of this the Solitary can be placed beside Goethe's Faust and Werther, or beside the fictionalised 'I' of Rousseau (for example, in the *Confessions* and *Rêveries d'un promeneur solitaire*); but he stands closer to Milton's Satan in that it is not so much his quest that makes him remarkable, but that which he stands against: not only the Pastor, as well as the Wanderer and Poet, but also against the 'will' of *The Excursion*. So too does the Solitary stand against himself, against human nature (or at least the kind of human nature presented by the Wanderer and Pastor). And so too must the Solitary stand against Wordsworth, yet he is part of a troubled Wordsworth – perhaps, it might be suggested, a part of himself that Wordsworth feared. There is a feeling that Wordsworth really never quite knew what to do with this figure, with the problems or issues represented by the Solitary. Like Frankenstein's monster, he got rather out of hand, leading his creator to uncharted regions.

Through the tragic circumstances of his life (which in some ways parallel Wordsworth's experience), the Solitary has fallen from a belief in mankind and from God. His hopes in France fell just as did his service in the Ministry. He has had a glorious but foreboding vision of death-in-life (II. 834–81) and has suffered the woes of others. Now he chooses to suffer his own woes. Fortified by his solitude, it paradoxically becomes both his strength and his weakness, and within the context of *The Excursion* we are led to feel that his 'self-indulging spleen' (II. 311) functions contrary to any natural life-force. The Wanderer tells us what was behind the Solitary's inward discomposure:

> The glory of the times fading away –
> The splendour, which had given a festal air
> To self-importance, hallowed it, and veiled
> From his own sight – this gone, he forfeited
> All joy in human nature.
>
> (II. 293–7)

Wordsworth too feels this 'splendour' and 'glory' vacate him in the *Intimations Ode*, but in the *Ode* he manages to reformulate his losses and find strength in a discourse of poetic introspection. The Solitary cannot, or at least he chooses not to; rather, in the words of the Wanderer, he 'wastes the sad remainder of his hours' in moroseness, settled on the decision 'that he will live and die / Forgotten' (II. 310–15.

Shelley, though he too like the Solitary challenges the sentiment of the *Intimations Ode*, would also rebuke the Solitary for not at least attempting an alternative solution to total resignation. As the Solitary says of himself, he is 'Stripped . . . of all the golden fruit / Of self-esteem'(III. 488–9). For Shelley, this is to be scorned: despair must always be paired with hope, even if it entails a painful and continual dilemma for the individual. If they are not maintained life itself must be given up, for life is just this very dilemma. Think of the Poet's death scene in *Alastor*: at the moment when the Poet lays himself down, and the 'hovering powers of life' are about to dissipate, 'Hope and despair, / The torturers, slept' (639–40) – the Poet dies. The dilemma must exist for life to continue. For Shelley there is always uncertainty and irreconcilability, but it must be endured. Even the 'self-esteem' that the Solitary claims to have lost must, according to Shelley, be understood as a loss that comes and goes. Using one of Wordsworth's strongest images in his *Hymn to Intellectual Beauty* Shelley points this out:

> Love, Hope, and Self-esteem, like clouds depart
> And come, for some uncertain moments lent.
>   (37–8)

There is no way round this paradox: uncertainty is man's lot, yet it must be fought against and not be submitted to. Part of the Solitary's failing is this sort of resignation.

At the end of *The Excursion*, in spite of its reconciliatory tendencies, the Solitary survives in his negative singularity. It is difficult to say whether this is meant to be a victory for apathy or an unintended irony. The others move towards the vicar's door, but the Solitary declines and takes the path towards that 'one cottage in the lonely dell' (IX. 773–4), moving, yet unmoved. The poet of *The Excursion* ends by saying his 'future labours' will tell us whether or not the Solitary has been or will be healed in his ways, renovated and reformed (IX. 783–96). But Wordsworth never does come back to reformulate the possibility of outcomes for the Solitary, or any figure like him, perhaps because he was uncertain about the outcome, perhaps because he could not bring himself to write about a recovery he himself no longer believed in. (That is, Wordsworth never gave us the third and final part of *The Recluse*.) Shelley, beginning where Wordsworth left off, does come back. The figure who for Wordsworth was an antagonist becomes for Shelley more of a protagonist. By taking up this Wordsworthian figure, Shelley attempts to take his own poetry up.

III

Besides those poems discussed in the third chapter, two other poems written between 1815 and 1816 address themselves to the problematic central figure inherited from Wordsworth: *The Sunset* and *Prince Athanase*. This figure in these poems is always pure, idealised and idealistic in his origins (nurturement), yet, paradoxically, he meets with spiritual disaster, a hermetic melancholy feeding off either itself or an unknown or unknowable grief. All fail inasmuch as they meet with death. And the poems themselves exhibit some aspects of failure inasmuch as they remain unresolved, inexplicable, fragmented. Within the poems the protagonists appear as failed poet figures; outside the poems Shelley figures as a poet bordering on the failure of a vision.

The Sunset and *Prince Athanase* in less sustained and fragmentary ways attempt to bring *Alastor*'s poet figure back to life again. Both poems are deliberately narrative, beginning with and revolving around a central figure: just as the story proper of *Alastor* begins 'There was a poet' (50), the openings of *The Sunset* and *Prince Athanase* are, respectively, 'There late was One' and 'There was a youth'. *The Sunset* and *Prince Athanase* do not pursue solitude as doggedly as *Alastor*, although the central figures in these poems are just as mysteriously possessed or enigmatically defeated by unknown quantities. In *Prince Athanase* this unknown is no more explicitly expressed than as a disquieting 'grief' (65–85); in *The Sunset* 'None may know' what killed the One (4–6).

Like the Poet of *Alastor*, the One and the Prince have idealised backgrounds. When speaking of the One's 'subtle being' (1) we could just as well be referring to the 'gentle yet aspiring mind' of the Prince (22) or the delicacy of the *Alastor* Poet's disposition (55, 58, 67–75). *Prince Athanase* remains, however, more closely tied to *Alastor*. Mary Shelley points this out in her Note to the poem when she says that the 'idea Shelley had formed of Prince Athanase was a good deal modelled on *Alastor*'. But we do not really know the story of Athanase's enigmatic despair, or why his disappointment should lead to death. Shelley only left us with this ending to the problem: 'And so his grief remained – let it remain – untold' (124). He also left us with a footnote to the poem saying that he 'was pursuing a fuller development of the ideal character of Athanase, when it struck him that in an attempt at extreme refinement and analysis, his conceptions might be betrayed into the assuming a morbid character'. Shelley seems to be saying that any more work on this particular character would be futile; it would lead to a yet more desperate or hopeless portrayal of him. In other words, Shelley, at this point, in this poem, could not take this figure any further. The subject of the poem was creatively stifling him.

If the fragments of *Prince Athanase* are pieced together it appears that indeed the poem was going to follow a similar pattern as *Alastor*. We discover that, like the Poet, Athanase's feelings of 'grief' may be relieved if he can find the object of his love (Fragment, III. 232–5). But this rather vague object cannot be found in the exterior world. Instead, again as in *Alastor*, it appears that Athanase in solitude turns inward for the object of his love (251–3).

Standing between *Prince Athanase* and *The Sunset* is the influence of the elements in Wordsworth's narrative pattern, with *The Sunset* especially deriving from Wordsworth. As mentioned, the youthful One of *The Sunset* dies enigmatically, leaving his lover Isabel to live on with the burden of loss. Besides the 'Tale of Margaret' from Book I of *The Excursion*, this is immediately identifiable with many of Wordsworth's tales in the *Lyrical Ballads* where loss and separation through death originate in and are bounded by humble decorum. In *The Sunset* there is, in fact, a reference to Wordsworth's many tales of forlorn women. In the morning, after Isabel and the youth 'lay / In love and sleep' (24–5), she discovers the youth is dead. Isabel lives on, tending her old father. This suffering in silence leads us back to many of the tales in the *Lyrical Ballads* (especially to *The Female Vagrant*, *The Mad Mother*, *The Complaint of a Forsaken Indian Woman*, *Ruth*, *Michael* and *The Thorn*) in which women are left behind to endure in the absence of a loved one. The favourable reference to these tales by Wordsworth in Shelley's poem is given when we are told that to 'see' Isabel 'were to read the tale / Woven by some subtlest bard' (34–5). To look at Shelley's heroine is to be reminded of Wordsworth and his figures; to read Shelley's poem, then, is to re-read some of Wordsworth's work. Wordsworth's early poetry is still influencing Shelley.

What Shelley took from the total effect of these narratives of Wordsworth, which can be seen in *Alastor*, *The Sunset* and *Prince Athanase*, is death fading into the narrative, not ending it, and not really a part of it, but built mainly within the structure of the imagery. ('Athanase' actually means *deathless*.) Wordsworth's *The Thorn* is perhaps the best example of this, where death, although being central to the poem, is in fact anterior to it, suggested only by imagery hinting strongly at an infant's grave. This parallels the case in *Alastor*, where the actual death within the narrative becomes secondary to the imagery bounding it. The similarity between the graves in *The Thorn* and *Alastor* is striking: the Poet's grave on the 'edge of that vast mountain' (573) is but a pile of 'mouldering leaves in the waste wilderness' (54), marked by 'the rugged trunk / Of [an] old pine' (633–4); the grave in *The Thorn* is 'on a mountain's highest ridge' (23) is a 'heap of earth o'ergrown of moss' (49), and is marked by a 'knotted', 'aged thorn' (6–9). Likewise, the death of the Poet, like the death in *The Thorn*, is actually prior to the action, since in the very first line of the Poet's story we are presented with his grave: 'There was a Poet whose untimely tomb' (50). The poem fills in how and why he got there. Of course, death functions differently within the two poems. In *Alastor* it signifies a poetic failure; in *The Thorn* it is the exploration of a loss that can be formulated poetically. Shelley may have taken the descriptive dimensions of Wordsworth's grave into his own poem, and he may have, so to speak, temporarily raised the dead; but the burial place of both figures, the unborn child and the prematurely dead Poet, marks a spot of promise unfulfilled.

I want to return now to the originating central figures of Wordsworth to examine in what ways they 'precurse' Shelley's figures. Although many central figures in the *Lyrical Ballads* can to greater and lesser degrees be brought to Shelley's three poems, *Lines Left upon a Seat in a Yew-Tree* clearly opens up problems of poetical solipsism and solitude in a single figure, a figure much like the Solitary of *The Excursion*:

> He was one who owned
> No common soul. In youth by science nursed,
> And led by nature into a wild scene
> Of lofty hopes, he to the world went forth
> A favoured being, knowing no desire
> Which genius did not hallow: 'gainst the taint
> Of dissolute tongues, and jealousy, and hate
> And scorn, against all enemies prepared,
> All but neglect. The world, for so it thought,
> Owed him no service; wherefore he at once
> With indignation turned himself away,
> And with the food of pride sustained his soul
> In solitude.
> (1800, 1805 version; 12–24)

So too the Poet in *Alastor* was

> Gentle, and brave, and generous, – no lorn bard
> Breathed o'er his dark fate and melodious sigh:
> He lived, he died, he sung, in solitude.
>
> . . .
>
> By solemn vision, and bright silver dream,
> His infancy was nurtured. Every sight
> And sound from the vast earth and ambient air,
> Sent to his heart its choicest impulses.
> The fountains of divine philosophy
> Fled not his thirsting lips, and all of great,
> Or good, or lovely, which the sacred past
> In truth or fable consecrates, he felt
> And knew. When early youth had passed, he left
> His cold fireside and alienated home
> To seek strange truths in undiscovered lands.
> Many a wide waste and tangled wilderness
> Has lured his fearless steps; and he has bought
> With his sweet voice and eyes, from savage men,
> His rest and food. Nature's most secret steps
> He like her shadow has pursued.
>
> (58–60, 67–82)

And now he reappears in *terza rima* as Prince Athanase:

> For none than he a purer heart could have,
> Or that loved good more for itself alone;
> Of nought in heaven or earth was he the slave.
>
> What sorrow, strange, and shadowy, and unknown,
> Sent him, a hopeless wanderer, through mankind? –
> If with a human sadness he did groan,
>
> He had a gentle yet aspiring mind;
> Just, innocent, with varied learning fed
>
> . . .
>
> His soul had wedded Wisdom, and her dower
> Is love and justice, clothed in which he sate

Apart from men, as in a lonely tower,

Pitying the tumult of their dark estate. –
. . .

Fearless he was, and scorning all disguise,
What he dared do or think, though men might start,
He spoke with mild yet unaverted eyes.
(16–23, 31–4, 43–5)

The proximity of Wordsworth's yew-tree figure and Shelley's young men demands little explication other than citation of these passages. The positive qualities of these figures have their origins in the Preface to the *Lyrical Ballads*. Wordsworth says that a poet is 'a man endued with more lively sensibility, more enthusiasm and tenderness, who has a greater knowledge of human Nature, and a more comprehensive soul, than are supposed to be common among mankind'. But still, why this figure? We must conclude the obvious and say that Shelley's idea of a protagonist to a great extent derives from Wordsworth. That is, Wordsworth's idea of himself (or his poetic figures) becomes in part Shelley's idea of himself and his own poetic ideals. But why this particular 'character'? More precisely, what does this portrayal offer in terms of potentiality for both Wordsworth and Shelley?

Let me first of all summarise Wordsworth's yew-tree figure. He has 'No common soul'; he is nursed by 'genius' and led by Nature with 'lofty hopes', which is *exactly* the Poet's projected ideals (in the 'veiled maid') in *Alastor* (159); and he has a pure heart which fights hypocrisy. But the most important aspect of this figure is that the external world does not offer him a vision of what he seeks, and so he turns to a solipsistic and uncreative solitude in which he attempts to create this vision. This is the common flaw which is inherited and worked through by Shelley's protagonists. Shelley is offering a poetical exploration of a particular figure in order to test if this Wordsworthian 'character' has potential for the production of poetry. Shelley finds that it does and does not. It challenges him to create poetry on the subject, but this poetry ends in a poetic vision of despair and grief; more significant, it ends in silence, which is the death or negation of poetry. The strength of this poet figure is thus also its weakness. Wordsworth's poet-figure acts as the anti-inspiration for Shelley.

The problem this figure represents is also in some ways reducible to a psycho-social conflict: What does an honest soul do in a dishonest society? Or, What happens to an uncorrupted person surrounded by corrupt persons? Or it could be given a more philosophical emphasis: What is the end result of following idealism? Is there anything knowable beyond the self? And perhaps most important: Is this particular pose suitable for the production of poetry? The irony, of course, as I have shown in discussing *The Excursion*, is that solitude in itself is not always a resolution or an answer to any of these questions. Although the Solitary returns to his cottage in the lonely dell, no better or worse than when he began, his despondency hardly corrected, the figure in *Lines Left upon a Seat* . . . dies in his deep vale, as does the Boy in *There was a Boy* who, in solitude, communed with the 'solemn imagery' (23) of nature. So too do Shelley's figures die. It might be suggested, however, that the deaths of the yew-tree figure ('The man, whose eye / Is ever on himself', 51–2) and of the Boy to some degree might have satisfied Shelley – this is the fitting end to their vision. The Solitary's living-on is not. Thus Shelley might have agreed with the sentiment in Wordsworth's early poems, and disagreed with it in *The Excursion*. The Solitary may have gone unpunished in Wordsworth's poem, but he does not in Shelley's poems.

Prince Athanase finally leaves behind one other insight into Shelley's attitude towards a teacher-precursor figure. In fragments of the poem (Part II, fragments I and II) Zonoras is introduced, an old man of 'wise words' (125–8) and 'soul-sustaining songs' (137, 171) who travelled afar after the rise of tyranny. The wisdom feeding his 'lonely being' is based on the dictum, 'The mind becomes that which it contemplates' (138–9). Zonoras appears to be modelled on Dr Charles Lind, that strong paternal influence on Shelley during his days at Eton. But I think this might be extended: even if Zonoras is based on Lind, certainly aspects of the Wordsworthian precursor-figure are also present in the older man – specifically, that Zonoras appears to be a poet of mind and solitude who left aspects of his poetic knowledge to his progeny. Whereas Lind taught Shelley much about matters ranging from pamphleteering to Plato, Zonoras's influence goes beyond this. He is also a figure who goes with Athanase out into nature (182ff.), and he is a figure of poetic authority who fills Athanase with poetry (137). Yet Athanase and Zonoras are not alike: They 'mark the extremes of life's discordant span' (181).

Shelley's attitude towards a teacher–precursor figure is important to note here. Zonoras filled Athanase

> With soul-sustaining songs of ancient lore
> And philosophic wisdom, clear and mild,
>
> And sweet and subtle talk they evermore,
> The pupil and the master, shared; until,
> Sharing that undiminishable store,
>
> The youth, as shadows on a grassy hill
> Outrun the winds that chase them, soon outran
> His teacher.
> (168–78)

Shelley, as Athanase, as 'pupil', thus sees his precursor, his 'master', as a figure to *overcome*, to consume and go beyond, just as Shelley took in Wordsworth's 'tales' and 'songs' in order to formulate his own.

The image of Athanase being 'filled / From fountains pure' (168–9) with the overflowings of Zonoras is appropriate in terms of the associative image we have of influence as a kind of overflowing. Think too of Shelley's portrayal of a 'great Poem' in the *Defence* as 'a fountain for ever overflowing', where its 'divine effluence' continually creates 'new relations'. Thus the relationship Zonoras has to Athanase is as a 'great Poem' passed on to the next poet of the next age. In short, he is a source of *poetic* inspiration for the young Athanase.

The imagery of this last passage from *Prince Athanase* (168–78) suggests that Shelley, as the shadow of clouds, must over a 'grassy hill' outrun those clouds overhead, just as he must outrun his poetic predecessor. Just as Wordsworth in his solitude so named himself as a wandering cloud above the hills, here we have Shelley taking up the same figurative relationship and expanding it to create or describe a relationship between himself and an older figure. These Wordsworthian figurations seem at moments like this to become Shelley's figurations, but they do so with the irony that they are being used to both support and subvert Wordsworth's master tropes. This is the sometimes hazy but dynamic mode of relationship involved with poetic influence working at an inter-textual level, complete with a power structure (master/pupil) which, after its implementation, reverses itself: Athanase ends by teaching Zonoras 'truths'. Shelley is just beginning to hint that he believes that as a poet he may yet master a figure of poetic authority.

IV

Alastor, as I have discussed already in the third chapter, is of course most obviously linked to Wordsworth. And it is *Alastor* that deserves most attention. As A. C. Bradley said in his 1909 lectures: 'The *Excursion* is concerned in part with the danger of inactive and unsympathetic solitude; and this, treated of course in Shelley's own way, is the subject of *Alastor*.'[5] Bradley is clearly referring here to the Solitary of *The Excursion* as the subject of *Alastor*, and so he is making the parallel between the Poet of *Alastor* and Wordsworth's Solitary. Unfortunately, Bradley says no more about this deserving subject.

Alastor is modelled on Shelley's idea of Wordsworth's idea of himself as a poet, the protagonist being a solitary poet apparently in pursuit of nature (81–2), yet who is ultimately chasing his own self-created yet deceptive image (149–61). In some ways this protagonist seems to have followed in the footsteps of another of Wordsworth's solitary poets, the one who 'wandered lonely as a cloud' and who 'gazed – and gazed' on a 'never-ending' scene of daffodils, but could not immediately realise the inspirational value of what he saw. Significantly, this action is exactly repeated by the Poet of *Alastor*, who in his 'wandering' 'gazed / And gazed' upon the 'thrilling secrets of the birth of time' (106–28). But ultimately this knowledge fails him, unlike the speaker of *I Wandered Lonely as a Cloud* who can, in his 'bliss of solitude', fill his 'heart with pleasure'. However, the Poet's solitude is anything but bliss: it only fills him with a vision of death.

Just as Shelley felt Wordsworth's perception in *The Excursion* to be solipsistically inclined, he makes the Poet a prisoner of his own perception, his own created vision. In the same way the Solitary is associated with the 'lonely dell' (IX. 774), which marks the enclosure of his activity and outlook, the Poet's pursuit in *Alastor* is determined by the vision he has in the 'loneliest dell' (146). Further, as is well known, *Alastor* is framed, from beginning to end, by unabashed references to Wordsworth's poetry. Shelley prefaces *Alastor* with a foreboding quotation from *The Excursion* (I. 500–2):

> The good die first,
> And those whose hearts are dry as summer dust,
> Burn to the socket!

And within the invocation (1–49) he directly quotes 'natural piety' and 'obstinate questionings' from the *Intimations Ode*. And at the end of *Alastor* Shelley refers to Wordsworth's 'high verse' (707) and quotes 'too deep for tears' (713), the last line from the *Intimations Ode*.[6]

Most important, however, are those starting points that can be found in *The Excursion* which initiate *Alastor*'s subject. These lines from Book IV are central: the Wanderer, holding the Solitary's hand and telling him not to read Voltaire, warns him that

> He, who by wilful disesteem of life
> And proud insensibility to hope,
> Affronts the eye of Solitude, shall learn
> That her mild nature can be terrible;
> That neither she nor Silence lack the power
> To avenge their own insulted majesty.
>
> (IV. 1029–34)

The Wanderer, in his Wordly Wiseman way, discriminates between the two sides of 'Solitude' – one that is 'mild', and one that is 'terrible' and capable of 'the power / To *avenge*'. This darker side of poetic solitude is what *Alastor* is all about, and what the word 'alastor' means (*Alastor*'s second title is, after all, *The Spirit of Solitude*). Peacock tells us that he suggested the title to Shelley, meaning it as an 'evil genius'.[7] But more precisely, 'alastor' in Greek means an *avenging* spirit, or the victim of an *avenging* spirit. Both of these meanings of 'alastor' make a direct connection with the Wanderer's warning of Solitude's 'power / To avenge': in *Alastor* solitude is an avenging spirit by being the controlling agent of the Poet's condition ('He lived, he died, he sung, in solitude' – 60); and the Poet is, as the Preface states, the victim of a 'self-centred seclusion'.

The Wanderer's warning ends up being taken one step further by Shelley than by Wordsworth. The avenging spirit of Solitude makes little impression on the Solitary's outcome – or at least Wordsworth takes it no further. The Wanderer holds that the *milder* type of Solitude in the form of 'seclusion' is to be fostered (IV. 1035ff), and is not subject to retribution; that is, the type of solitude that esteems life and is sensitive to hope (IV. 1029–30) will not be avenged. Wordsworth's demarcation between good and bad Solitude thus makes Solitude a *conditional* state. What Shelley challenges in *Alastor* is this conditionality by addressing himself to the *unconditional* notion of solitude; for the Poet of *Alastor* plainly *does* esteem life and *is* sensitive to hope, yet he is nevertheless avenged by the spirit of solitude. *Alastor* explores the question of whether a solitudinal pose is a suitable state for the production of poetry. Indeed, what Shelley gives to the Poet, who is now like Wordsworth working between potentially successful and failing outcomes, is a quest for 'a dream of hopes' (150). But again, despite this, the Poet is avenged and meets with death on barren heights, an empty (or vacated) sublime.

For Shelley, both sides or aspects of Wordsworth's Solitude are unconditionally disastrous. At this point in his poetry, solitude does not have a good and a bad side: it is an evil. Shelley felt this way about it when he wrote *Alastor*, but he felt this way at least as far back as 1811. In that year he wrote to Hogg that 'I cannot endure the horror of the evil which comes to *self* in solitude' (*Letters*, I, p. 77). Not until 1818 is Shelley able to formulate a more positive version of solitude. In his short essay he entitled *On Love* he puts it this way:

> Hence in solitude, or in that deserted state when we are surrounded by human beings and yet they sympathise not with us, we love the flowers, the grass and the waters and the sky. In the motion of the very leaves of spring in the blue air there is then found a secret correspondence with our heart. There is eloquence in the tongueless wind and a melody in the flowing of brooks and the rustling of the reeds beside them which by their inconceivable relation to something within the soul, awaken the spirits to a dance of breathless rapture, and bring tears of mysterious tenderness to the eyes like the enthusiasm of patriotic success or the voice of one beloved singing to you alone. Sterne says that if he were in a desert he would love some cypress. . . . So soon as this want or power is dead, man becomes the living sepulchre of himself, and what yet survives is the mere husk of what once he was.

This whole scene of natural supernaturalism, with its 'motion' and 'secret correspondence with our heart', its eloquent 'tongueless wind' and melodious brooks, evolved out of aspects of the landscape and all substitutes for unsympathetic human company, openly recalls the means of restoration that Wordsworth developed in his poetry up until and especially in *Tintern Abbey*. Shelley's implicit comment here must be that 'this want or power' is dead in Wordsworth. We have already seen that Shelley considered the older poet as changed from his former self and as the desiccated form of what he once was; and here in this passage we have the man who has fallen out of sympathy with nature described as but 'the living sepulchre of himself, . . . the mere husk of what once he was'. The idea and the imagery is the same. Once more Shelley has condemned Wordsworth in Wordsworth's own terms.

The irony in *Alastor* is not just that a young poet dies for searching after aspects of himself, after a mode of solitudinal creativity, after something that was potentially within him all the time – this reading limits *Alastor*'s scope. The delimiting irony is that Shelley found this Wordsworthian poetic stance attractive, yet possibly destructive – in short, an irresistible risk that he too, following Wordsworth, was prepared to follow through as a creative mode. This once more is Shelley demanding of himself that he continue what Wordsworth discontinued or could continue no further, regardless of the result. It is this dilemma of following or competing which is at the centre of *Alastor* moving outwards to become a test of limitations, the limitations of both Shelley and Wordsworth. How far, and how high, could Wordsworth's influence take Shelley, and Shelley (using the influence) take Wordsworth? And here is where influence becomes a power struggle. *Alastor*, usurped from Wordsworth, extends Shelley's own poetic boundaries as it examines and attempts to surpass the limitations of Wordsworth. *Alastor* is Shelley's test of Wordsworth's poetic vision and capabilities as much as it is a test of his own.

Within *Alastor* it might be suggested that these two competing but allied poets looking at each other becomes apparent in the most prevalent imagery in the poem, the imagery of reflecting light, mirroring and gazing.[8] For example, the last thing the Poet sees while he lives are the tips of the horned moon, but they are as eyes staring back: 'two lessening points of light' (654). The Poet is obsessed with those anti-inspirational 'two eyes, / Two starry eyes, [that] hung in the gloom of thought' (489–90). Indeed, the various presences of 'eyes' and other points of light are so interwoven with each other in the imagery of the poem that these reflective modes are at once and indistinguishably the Poet's eyes (63, 80, 188, 200, 254, 280, 416, 469–70, 535), the veiled maid's eyes (179, 332, 489–90), the fading stars overlooking his search at night (340, 354, 463, 554,* 576[†]), and the eyes of day watching his daytime quest (339). In the end, eyes too are the agents fusing death with sleep (700–1). Shelley works these association by accumulating cross-identifications throughout the poem, but he also condenses them in metaphor. This is a description of the Poet after the visionary encounter:

> His wan eyes
> Gaze on the empty scene as vacantly
> As ocean's moon looks on the moon in heaven.
> (200–2)

The Poet looking at the scene around him is described as the reflection of the moon (the moon's double) looking at its original – in effect, a mirror's reflection having priority over what it reflects. We would have expected the pairings in this case to be the Poet with the moon and the scene with the reflection; but our expectancy is reversed, and the Poet instead becomes associated with the moon's reflection, not the moon. Here in this scopic-reversal is where the solipsistic theme overlaps with the narcissistic theme.[9] And here too, in these presences of eyes, operating both beyond and within the poem, is a shifting synecdoche for Wordsworth's *overseeing* presence. One poet reflects (on) another poet, with the dual sense of meditation and mirroring represented by the idea of reflection.

Shelley is, I think, purposefully playing with the notion of seeing in *Alastor*. The veiled maid is a 'vision' (149), but she is not a vision in the sense that she merely comes into view. She is something that becomes a form of in-seeing, of poetic introspection, so that the Poet's quest is inwards, not outwards. But the Poet is blinded by his in-sight, to the extent that he follows it to his extinction.

The imagery of light and the metaphor of self-seeing also comes into play (as the reflected presence of Wordsworth) once again when the Poet reaches a mirroring well (457ff). The Poet gazes at his image:

> His eyes beheld
> Their own wan light through the reflected lines

---

* Just as the stars are described as 'wan', so too are the Poet's eyes in lines 200 and 470.
  [†] Just as the vision has 'bending' eyes (179), so too are the Poet's eyes bent (416) and the stars are bending (576).

> Of his thin hair, distinct in the dark depth
> Of that still fountain; as the human heart,
> Gazing in dreams over the gloomy grave,
> Sees its own treacherous likeness there.
> (469–74)

Again the particular language and workings of this complicated metaphor must be noted, as well as the significance of the broader associations. The Poet, seeing the reflection of his eyes in the well, is metaphored as the 'human heart' seeing itself in dreams over the grave. Besides foreshadowing the Poet's death, by bringing the metaphored to the metaphor (noting that metaphor itself functions as a kind of rhetorical mirroring), the following is one possible cross-equivalence: the Poet is seeing his own 'human heart' in the grave. This is indeed a drastic vision, made even more so by the further association that can be brought to the 'human heart'. Could this 'human heart' hovering over the grave have been transplanted from the final lines of *Intimations Ode*?

> Thanks to the human heart by which we live,
> Thanks to its tenderness, its joys, and fears,
> To me the meanest flower that blows can give
> Thoughts that do often lie too deep for tears.
> (204–7)

Could it be that the function of this 'human heart' of Wordsworth, which is the organ of tranquil restoration, is condemned by Shelley? It was, after all, 'too deep for tears' from the *Intimations Ode* that Shelley also lifted into the final passage of *Alastor*.

'Neither the eye nor the mind can see itself, unless reflected upon that which it resembles' – so says Shelley in the *Defence*. Shelley, then, may be using this reflective imagery in *Alastor* as presentations of resemblance (between the thing seen and the thing seeing) in order for self-reflection. Shelley's strategy in taking on Wordsworth as a resembling poet is to 'see' himself as poet. Wordsworth is the poet Shelley identifies with and measures himself by. *Alastor* is a poetic mirror into which Shelley gazes, only to see Wordsworth's reflection fused with his own.

This struggle and affinity between these two poets makes the Poet of *Alastor* a protean configuration. It makes the Poet an equivocal configuration of both Shelley and Wordsworth, one looking at the other, one reflecting the other: seeing the self as another through the self and the other. But this makes the Poet neither a multi-headed monster nor a schizoid creation. It is Shelley in the creative process of accommodation and assimilation, becoming another by being as another. The anxiety behind this empathy (or showdown) by gaze precariously manifests itself in that Shelley's idea of Wordsworth is determined by ambivalence, not simply by either veneration or disgust. Pushed further, the dynamics of this extraordinary poetic situation in *Alastor* gives us this consideration, although it almost seems obvious now: when the Poet has the vision of the veiled maid, it is not only Shelley's portrayal of Wordsworth (as the Poet) being seduced by his own idealistic imagination, but it is also Shelley (as the Poet) trying out a figure representing the poetic inspiration (the Muse) behind Wordsworth's poetry. Just as the Poet is a configuration of both Shelley *and* Wordsworth, so too must we admit in this open interpretation that the female vision the Poet follows represents the vision of inspiration behind both Wordsworth's *and* Shelley's poetry. The female vision represents the ideals, knowledge, truth, virtue and liberty which both Shelley and early Wordsworth sought (158–9). But more important, she 'Herself [is] a poet' (161). In fact, she recites a poem to the Poet, 'an ineffable tale' (163–8) leading to the Poet's orgasmic coalescence with her (172–87). She becomes the poetic experience the Poet wants to repeat, and thus she is the motivating and inspirational force behind any continuing of the Poet's action. This is why she is a muse-like figure. She is, however, only a certain type of poetic inspiration, one that (mis)leads to poetic self-destruction and uncreativity.

One conclusion is this: the Poet of *Alastor* cannot be read as either Shelley or Wordsworth; neither can the poetic vision the Poet creates and chases be read as the representative of either Shelley's poetic goals (at the time of composing the poem) or Shelley's idea of Wordsworth's destructive vision. Shelley's Poet and vision defy any either/or criticism. And it is no good saying that *Alastor* is a confused poem. This is unconstructive criticism, as well as a gross underestimation of Shelley's creative skills. *Alastor* is simply Shelley's first poetic attempt to discuss the role of a poet and the production of a certain type of poetry. And it is therefore natural that Shelley might use the most important living poet as a model to test his own poetic strength. Shelley is trying on Wordsworth's poetic guise. *Alastor* is Shelley's impression of Wordsworth's impression of himself.

In the context of what I've just been saying about the situation in

Alastor, Harold Bloom's final revisionary ratio of *apophrades* does not now seem so untenable (*apophrades* being the condition when it appears 'as though the later poet himself had written the precursor's characteristic work').[10] For we only have to go one step further to say that when the Poet has the vision, it is effectively Wordsworth 'creating' Shelley – that is, it is Shelley seeing himself as the idealised product or creation of Wordsworth. It is Shelley letting Wordsworth write his poem. From this angle Shelley's *Alastor* becomes Wordsworth's vision of Shelley. Shelley is giving poetic form to Wordsworth's influence on him. I might also say a little more about Bloom's ratio of *apophrades* when he describes it thus: 'The strong poet peers in the mirror of his fallen precursor and beholds neither the precursor nor himself but a Gnostic double, the dark otherness or antithesis that both he and the precursor longed to be, yet feared to become'.[11] As I've attempted to show, mirroring is in fact the central image in *Alastor*, the place where the poetic dynamics of identification and exchange take place. If there is any validity in Bloom's description, then Shelley is seeing not just Wordsworth as his reflection, but the idealised and dangerous double that Wordsworth beheld in the mirror as his own precursor. This is an endless falling backwards toward that indeterminate precursor for all precursors, the impossible original figure of poetic authority. But for the moment I want to stop Shelley's falling-back at Wordsworth.

This complicated inter- and extra-textual situation existing in *Alastor* might be put more schematically in order to clarify the possible permutations:

Premises

1. the Poet = Shelley and/or Wordsworth;
2. the Vision = Shelley's and/or Wordsworth's poetic vision;
3. the Poet 'seeks' (Preface) the Vision.

Permutations

1. Shelley seeks Shelley;
2. Shelley seeks Wordsworth;
3. Wordsworth seeks Wordsworth;
4. Wordsworth seeks Shelley.

The first permutation presents *Alastor* as Shelley seeking his own idealised vision, which is a fairly conventional reading of the poem.

Shelley's maturity as a poet and *Alastor* as a form of autobiography are often brought into this argument. The second permutation points to a reading where Shelley is following the influence of Wordsworth as a solitary figure. (This is tied to the interpretations of *Alastor* where Wordsworth is taken to be the 'prototype' of the Poet.) The third would indicate that *Alastor* is Shelley's criticism of Wordsworth's own solipsistic quest. And the fourth suggests that Shelley sees himself as the creation or product of Wordsworth, which puts him in the role of a son or inheritor of Wordsworth: Shelley 'created' by Wordsworth's influence.

These permutations are *not*, however, clear-cut alternative readings of *Alastor*. Rather, the power of *Alastor* as a creative work comes from the shifting effect when the poem is read so openly. I called these conditions 'permutations' because this poem is such a changing discourse with possibilities of meaning.

But these possibilities cannot be closed quite yet. One important premise has been omitted. Earlier, I pointed out that there is another problematic presence behind (yet integrally a part of) the poem: the Narrator of *Alastor*. Most frequently we tend to associate the speaking voice of the poem with the designated author – in this case, 'Shelley'. Certainly the author of *Alastor* writes in the manner of certain other poems by this author, as well as holding similar views as the historical individual called Percy Bysshe Shelley. It is thus quite legitimate to tend to equate the Narrator with Shelley. But the Narrator of *Alastor* is Wordsworthian, especially noticeable in the attitude and tone in the invocation (1–49).[12] This of course confounds the situation in the poem and gives us a further premise:

4. the Narrator = Shelley and/or Wordsworth.

There is no need to re-catalogue the resulting new permutations – the reader can be left to work through these almost absurd revisions himself. But what I would like to emphasise by enunciating this further metaperspective of 'voice' is the impossibility of establishing anything like an allegorical/autobiographical reading of the poem. I could, however, say this about *Alastor* (and this may be the safest way of posing the most important point about the poem): Wordsworth is behind (and in) the poem, but how far behind (and in) it is impossible to tell. I can only suggest that Wordsworth's influence is strong, perhaps profound, and always problematical.

One final and important point needs to be made about the

Narrator, that he too is an unsuccessful poet, and that he too experiences a failure paralleling that of the Poet. His failure, as a poet, is his inability to create in *Alastor* the scene (poem) he desires to create. In the invocation his strongest hope is that his poem

> May modulate with murmurs of the air,
> And motions of the forests and the sea,
> And voice of living beings.
> (46–8)

But by the end of the poem the Narrator has created nothing like this. In fact, at the Poet's death the perfect counter-scene is constructed:

> But when heaven remained
> Utterly black, the murky shades involved
> An image, silent, cold, and motionless,
> As their own voiceless earth and vacant air.
> (659–62)

The motion has become motionless; the voice has become voiceless; and the air has become empty. One way of expressing this situation is to suggest that Shelley consciously set out to show the Narrator's poetic ineffectuality: the Narrator cannot do what he says he can do. It is, then, a breach of poetic promise, and Shelley's poem seems to be a portrayal of that breach.

The potential obliqueness of these arguments demands that other links between *Alastor* and *The Excursion* be considered.

Another starting point for *Alastor* in *The Excursion* comes at the important passage when the Solitary tells about his action after the loss of his daughter and his wife:

> I called on dreams and visions, to disclose
> That which is veiled from waking thought; conjured
> Eternity, as men constrain a ghost
> To appear and answer; to the grave I spake
> Imploringly; – looked up, and asked the Heavens
> If Angels traversed their cerulean floors,
> If fixed or wandering star could tidings yield
> Of the departed spirit – what abode
> It occupies – what consciousness retains
> Of former loves and interests. Then my soul

> Turned inward, – to examine of what stuff
> Time's fetters are composed; and life was put
> To inquisition, long and profitless!
>
> (III. 686–98)

This is an appeal for answers which may lurk beyond consciousness and life, for things that are lost or 'veiled from the waking thought'. In this case what is lost are the significant females in the Solitary's life. This parallels the loss of the Poet of *Alastor* after his vision and the loss of the 'veiled maid' (151) where Shelley's protagonist calls on a renewal of sights and sounds (196–202). And like the Solitary who looks to the sliding process of death into sleep, the Poet calls on and questions sleep and death (211–13, 290–5, 304–5). Both figures are wanting the return of that 'departed spirit'. The Solitary turns further inwards for examination, calling on his 'soul', just as the Poet later turns to his to hold 'conference' (222–4). Both of these moments of shock and loss temporarily hold back the Solitary and the Poet, taking them away from normal consciousness and activity; but both return with similar abruptness: the Solitary 'From that abstraction . . . was roused' (III. 706), and the Poet, 'Roused by the shock he started from his trance' (192). Following, both are compelled to travel, the Solitary to France and America, and the Poet, more exotically, to the ends of the earth.

In both poems the pattern is the same. The loss of a significant female figure is followed by a loss of contact with life; following, perhaps as suicidal tendencies, sleep and death are conflated; then intense introspection is taken up; finally, both are 'roused' from their inactivity to a search for the 'spirit' of what is lost.

The Solitary ends by drawing a comparison between his life and the way the reflecting waters of a 'mountain brook' move almost imperceptibly, the movement given away only by the 'onward lapse' of 'conglobated bubbles' as 'Numerous as stars':

> Meanwhile, is heard
> Perchance, a roar or murmur; and the sound
> Though soothing, and the little floating isles
> Though beautiful, are both by Nature charged
> With the same pensive office; and make known
> Through what perplexing labyrinths, abrupt
> Precipitations, and untoward straits,
> The earth-born wanderer hath passed; and quickly,

> That respite o'er, like traverses and toils
> Must be again encountered – Such a stream
> Is human Life; and so the Spirit fares
> In the best quiet to her course allowed:
> And such is mine, – save only for a hope
> That my particular current soon will reach
> The unfathomable gulf, where all is still!
> (III. 967–91)

The Solitary's nihilistic hope is that the course of his life, which has had, like a stream, its shallows and depths, its rapids and calm spots, will end in an 'unfathomable gulf'. This too is the synoptic origin of the Poet's treacherous course as he is compelled over various waters (311ff.) along to an 'unfathomable stream'(373). Shelley, following Wordsworth, also takes up the dynamics of this stream as an allusion to life. As a catharsis the Poet cries out:

> O stream!
> Whose source is inaccessibly profound,
> Whither do thy mysterious waters tend?
> Thou imagest my life. Thy darksome stillness,
> Thy dazzling waves, thy loud and hollow gulfs,
> Thy searchless fountain, and invisible course
> Have each their type in me: and the wide sky,
> And measureless ocean may declare as soon
> What oozy cavern or what wandering cloud
> Contains thy waters, as the universe
> Tell where these living thoughts reside, when stretched
> Upon thy flowers my bloodless limbs shall waste
> I' the passing wind!
> (502–14)

What 'imagest' the changing course of the Poet's life, and what is 'inaccessibly profound', is equivalent to the Solitary's 'stream / (of) . . . Human Life' (III. 986–7). Moreover, just as in the opening section of *Mont Blanc*, there is an implicit questioning of the source of Wordsworth's poetic powers, the source of his poetry. Accordingly, this image of in-flowing, of influence, dictates this: all manifestations of Wordsworth's imagery (*Alastor*, 505ff.) have 'their type' in Shelley, including the 'wandering cloud' (510), which is Wordsworth's most memorable and concise description of his own solitudinal seeking: 'I wandered lonely as a cloud'.

In *Alastor* it is impossible to distinguish between Wordsworth making a prize of his own creation (or wanting to regain his past inspiration) and Shelley wanting to initiate himself to Wordsworth's inspiration:

> Where the embowering trees recede, and leave
> A little space of green expanse, the cove
> Is closed by meeting banks, whose yellow flowers
> For ever gaze on their own drooping eyes,
> Reflected in the crystal calm.
>
> . . .
>
>   The Poet longed
> To deck with their bright hues his withered hair,
> But on his heart its solitude returned,
> And he forebore. Not the strong impulse hid
> In those flushed cheeks, bent eyes, and shadowy frame
> Had yet performed its ministry: it hung
> Upon his life, as lightning in a cloud
> Gleams, hovering ere it vanish, ere the floods
> Of night close over it.
>
>   (404–8, 412–20)

These seem to be Wordsworth's flowers, daffodils and celandines. Indeed, they are, like aspects of Wordsworth's solipsistic entrapment, self-reflexive flowers narcissistically gazing on their own 'drooping eyes'. They also appear later in *Alastor*, now transposed as the 'drooping eyes' of the Poet (601). The flowers are obviously intended to symbolically foreshadow the Poet's fate, as well as to make a possible extra-textual identification of the Poet. We recall here the difficulty in *Verses Written on a Celandine* of distinguishing between the Poet (Wordsworth) and the flower. Once more in *Alastor* this conflation in eye imagery forces us to make pairings, in this case, the flowers with the Poet, thus bringing the self-reflexive qualities of the former to the latter. The Poet's longing is to make a garland of Wordsworth's flowers, perhaps as a form of redemption or protection, or perhaps (if we read the Poet as Shelley seeking Wordsworth) even to crown himself as the heir apparent to Wordsworth. Appropriately, or at least consistent with our reading so far, the Poet is held back at this point by the unconditionality of 'solitude' hanging upon his life.

Poets, Princes and Fallen Figures

Just as the Poet moves back and forth between being Shelley and Wordsworth, *Alastor* itself moves back and forth between discovering and questioning Wordsworth's influence, between taking him on and shaking him off. Hope and fear, sleep and death, also play their part in this relapsing identification. It is as if the poem is like the movement it describes, with its own alternating calms and storms, mountains and dells, dreaming and waking. As the Poet pursues the stream to find its source, to re-chart the course of Wordsworth's poetic failure from beginning to end, the pursuit of life is tragically re-affirmed as one of death, of the failure of poetry. So perhaps within the scope of *Alastor* Shelley has Wordsworth 'change' and age, the life-light of his eyes grown lifeless, his 'flowers' deceased. Here, then, is Shelley's description of Wordsworth's condition, of his tragic yet almost heroic pursuit:

> A gradual change was here,
> Yet ghastly. For, as fast years flow away,
> The smooth brow gathers, and the hair grows thin
> And white, and where irradiate dewy eyes
> Had shone, gleam stony orbs: – so from his steps
> Bright flowers departed, and the beautiful shade
> Of the green groves, with all their odorous winds
> And musical motions. Calm, he still pursued
> The stream.
>
> (532–40)

Of course this is some distance from Wordsworth's own self-projection in old age in the Leech-gatherer of *Resolution and Independence* where 'the sable orbs of his yet-vivid eyes' still had life in them (90–1). *Alastor* re-writes Wordsworth's vision of what he might become.

Yet Wordsworth's accomplishment, though in *Alastor* it ends on a deathly sublime on barren heights, remains for Shelley the courage behind that 'one voice' in solitude, 'one voice' inspiring others to echo that original and originating voice:

> One step,
> One human step alone, has ever broken
> The stillness of its solitude: – one voice
> Alone inspired its echoes; – even that voice
> Which hither came, floating among the winds,

> And led the loveliest among human forms
> To make their wild haunts the depository
> Of all the grace and beauty that endued
> Its motions, render up its majesty,
> Scatter its music on the unfeeling storm,
> And to the damp leaves and blue cavern mould,
> Nurses of rainbow flowers and branching moss,
> Commit the colours of that varying cheek,
> That snowy breast, those dark and drooping eyes.
> (588–601)

We are irresistibly drawn to speculate: Is this Shelley – referring to himself as 'the loveliest among human forms' – saying that he has been 'led' by the influence of Wordsworth to repeat or follow Wordsworth's pattern of poetic seeking? Recall Shelley's more famous solipsistic self-portrayal in *Adonais* as that beautiful 'one frail Form' who is 'Pursued' by 'his own thoughts' (271–306). In this earlier poem it may be Shelley who is pursuing the thoughts of another while thinking of this other. Here in *Alastor* Shelley's identification with Wordsworth and the Wordsworthian poet-figure has once more led him to praise yet reproach, to a scene once more where death can be reformulated as salvation.

Shelley's task remains to continue struggling with this problematic sublime and his identification with Wordsworth, at least until he creates his own sublime and the conflict is resolved, at least until his 'voice' is his own, and not merely an inspired echo.

5
The Maniac Poet

> I send you a little Poem to give to Ollier for publication but *without my Name*. . . . It was composed last year at Este; two of the characters you will recognise; the third is also in some degree a painting from nature, but, with respect to time and place, ideal.

So writes Shelley to Leigh Hunt from Livorno, Italy, 15 August 1819 (*Letters*, II, p. 108). The 'little Poem' is *Julian and Maddalo*, which Shelley later wanted published with *Prince Athanase* (*Letters*, II, p. 196). Curiously, *Julian and Maddalo* was not written at Este the previous year; it was begun early in 1819 and completed later in the summer of that year. And, despite Shelley's repeated desire to have it published, it was not printed until the *Posthumous Poems* of 1824.

Indeed, we do recognise two of the figures in the poem sent to Hunt, Shelley going so far as to write a preface with detailed character sketches of Julian and Maddalo. Maddalo is a rich and intelligent 'nobleman', rather cynical and proud, yet he tells of his exotic adventures with 'inexpressible charm'. Of course this is Byron, as much as it is also the Byronic hero of *Manfred* and *Childe Harold*, IV. Julian is, however, an 'Englishman of good family', and both an idealist and a sceptic; he adds that 'Julian is rather serious'. Just as obviously this is Shelley, with a nice touch of self-mockery.

As far as the third character, the Maniac, is concerned, we are given 'no information' except that in his 'right senses' he was apparently 'cultivated' and 'amiable', and that he has the appearance of having been 'disappointed in love'. We are told, rather mysteriously, that in 'the unconnected exclamations of his agony will perhaps be found a sufficient comment for the text of every heart'.

Because Shelley's idea of a poet is, in important ways, problematically determined by his idea of Wordsworth, once more certain aspects of the older poet's influence are manifest in the poem; and it is to the Maniac we must turn. This identification or association of Wordsworth with the Maniac is important in the general pattern of Shelley's concern with the troubled poet figure it continues. I would like, then, to study the Maniac's circumstances and poetic features in order to continue an examination of Wordsworth's presence as an influence on Shelley's poetry.

I

Julian and Maddalo is an unusual poem for Shelley, especially in its style. The narrative is presented in a straightforward way, and, except for the Maniac's speech, the expression – syntactically and metaphorically – is easy and flowing. Shelley was quite aware of this difference. In his letter to Hunt he says he has

> employed a certain familiar style of language to express the actual way in which people talk with each other whom education and a certain refinement of sentiment have placed above the use of vulgar idioms. (*Letters*, II, p. 108)

A sentence later he adds that this 'familiar style' is not to be permitted 'in the treatment of a subject wholly ideal, or in that part of any subject which relates to *common life* [my emphasis] where the passion exceeding a certain limit touches the boundaries of that which is ideal'. Shelley must have in the back of his mind what Wordsworth in the Preface to the *Lyrical Ballads* writes about the choice of language and subject matter he uses in those poems, how 'language arising out of repeated experience and regular feelings is a more permanent and a far more philosophical language than that which is frequently substituted for it by Poets', and thus how his principal object in the poems was 'to chuse incidents and situations from *common life* [my emphasis], and to relate or describe them . . . in a selection of language really used by men'. Shelley, following Wordsworth, wants to use a style of language resembling speech or conversation; but while Wordsworth holds this is suitable for a depiction of 'common life', Shelley does not – mainly, perhaps, because his subject matter is not at all ordinary.

The narrative of *Julian and Maddalo* begins with Julian's recollection of his ride one evening with Count Maddalo towards Venice. As sunset approaches their talk becomes 'serious' (36), Julian arguing 'against despondency' (48) while Maddalo takes 'the darker side' (49). They substitute a gondola for their horses. Maddalo draws Julian's attention to a ruinous asylum and tower which stands on an island. As the sun sinks, the madhouse fades into the gloomy scene.

But even this early in the poem the asylum's hidden significance is foreshadowed. What does it hold for the two men?

The next morning Julian calls on Maddalo, who is still in bed. While Julian waits he plays with the Count's young daughter. When Maddalo arrives, their conversation from the previous evening is taken up once more, Julian using the example of the child – 'blithe, innocent and free' (167) – to argue how narrow-minded and pessimistic adults can become, and how men have the potential to aspire to a better state. Julian shows that he is a strong idealist. Once more Maddalo responds sceptically to Julian's attitude, and significantly he identifies Julian with someone he once talked to who is now held in the madhouse. Maddalo decides that they should visit this Maniac and listen to his 'wild talk' in order to show that Julian's 'aspiring theories' are 'vain' (195–201). They take a gondola to the island they saw the night before in order to see the 'dejected man' (233). In a chamber in the tower they find him by a window, 'sitting mournfully / Near a piano' with the wind and the sea-spray rushing through his knotted hair (273ff.). His head rests on a music book and his lips are 'pressed against a folded leaf' (278–80).

Julian and Maddalo remain unseen by the Maniac and listen to his words, which in their emotive and almost incoherent quality contrast completely with Julian's controlled and conversational narration. He speaks of how life drags on, of an unspoken despair, and of how he wishes he were dead. He wonders too how much he is responsible for his present state. He only knows that in the past he 'met pale Pain', and it has not left him (324–5). He addresses a figure whom we associate with the cause of his present state:

> O Thou, my spirit's mate
> Who, for thou art compassionate and wise,
> Wouldst pity me from thy most gentle eyes
> If this sad writing thou shouldst ever see –
> My secret groans must be unheard by thee,
> Thou wouldst weep tears bitter as blood to know
> Thy lost friend's incommunicable woe.
>
> (337–43)

What is this reference to 'sad writing'? Is the Maniac a poet of sorts? At the point of climax in the Maniac's monologue he has a vision of coupling with his soul mate in a scene with overtones of necrophilia (382–92). After this fragmented outburst he calms down somewhat, but he is still unable to forget his aspirations of the past, what idealised love has done to him, and what creative powers have left him: his life, he says, is exemplary (459–60). Finally, he realises that his words are ineffective, and he hopes that death will end his despair. He is left sleeping.

Julian and Maddalo are deeply moved by the Maniac's words, and they decide that the poor man must have been abandoned by some 'dear friend' (527). Julian tells us that if he didn't have commitments elsewhere he would have stayed in Venice. He believes that if he studied the Maniac he might learn from him and be able to bring him out of his despair.

Julian finally records how many years later he returned to Venice, and how, through the Count's daughter, he learned that the Maniac's lover came back, only to leave again. Julian seeks further details of the Maniac's story, and after much persistence he learns 'how / All happened' (616–7). The daughter's final gesture is to point out 'yon mute marble where their corpses lie' (615); and Julian's is to withhold the complete story from us.

II

More so than even *Alastor* (to which I will return in a few moments), biographical criticism has been brought to the figures and circumstances of *Julian and Maddalo*, and especially to the significance of the Maniac. The Maniac's soliloquy has been viewed as an outpouring of Shelley's feelings about Hogg's amorous pursuits of Mary Shelley,[1] as well as Shelley's feelings about the short separation from Mary after the death of their son.[2] The Maniac's story has also been read as the growing emotional and intellectual gap between Shelley and Mary.[3] Other interpreters have seen the Maniac's words as Shelley's reflection on his disastrous relationship with Harriet Westbrook;[4] and still others say the monologue has to do with Shelley's feelings for Claire Clairmont.[5] Further, it has been suggested that it has something to do with Shelley's response to the death of his daughter Clara.[6] The Maniac has also been seen as an extension of Byron, or a Byronic hero.[7]

Of course, like the Poet in *Alastor*, he is often seen as Shelley or Shelley's *alter ego*.[8] The most convincing identification to be made with the Maniac is with the Italian poet Tasso (1544–95), who was declared mad and incarcerated; just before composing *Julian and*

Maddalo Shelley was contemplating a poem on Tasso, and we also know that he was greatly impressed by Byron's *The Lament of Tasso* (1817).[9] But Shelley would have had models for the mad poet much closer to his time: William Collins, Christopher Smart and William Cowper all had fits of insanity. Julian's horse and gondola ride with Count Maddalo in Venice is also made parallel with Shelley's actual visit to Byron and his illegitimate daughter Allegra in Venice, August 1818. Yet although there is a very good chance that Byron and Shelley may have seen an asylum on their outing, there is no evidence to suggest they visited a madman in the fourteen hours of continuous company they kept through that night of 23–4 August. In Shelley's letters to Mary written after this meeting with Byron there is only mention of going on a gondola 'across the laguna to a long sandy island which defends Venice from the Adriatic'. Their talk did include, Shelley adds, 'literary matters' (*Letters*, II, pp. 36–7). We can only deduce that the Maniac represents some shared issue or problem between the two poets, or perhaps a problematic figure Shelley and Byron debated over, perhaps something to do with literature.

Where this matching and paralleling of Shelley's work with 'real-life' events and characters gets us with the poem, and especially with the significance of the Maniac, it is hard to tell. We may, nevertheless, derive some assurance from factual and fractional observations like the one Carlos Baker makes: 'one-third of the poem is approximately true to autobiographical fact, another third is true to what Shelley thought to be historical fact, and the final third is demonstratably a piece of fiction'.[10]

There are important issues to be questioned and discussed: Why are Julian and Maddalo drawn to this apparently enigmatic figure? And we cannot escape the biographical question: Is this figure representative of anything or anyone between Byron and Shelley? But these questions, and especially the second one, lead our reading of the poem back into that rather precarious area where fact and fiction often overlap. The usefulness of this practice is to be determined by the credibility of the problematic identification of the Maniac, and whether it adds to our critical understanding of the poem; for the structure of the poem challenges us to interpret the Maniac along with Julian and Maddalo. And then there is Shelley's teasing gloss in the Preface to the poem: 'the unconnected exclamations of his agony will perhaps be found a sufficient comment for the text of every heart'.

But before beginning to work towards this end a clue might be thrown out. It might be suggested that Shelley was encouraged to write about a friendship between two dissimilar characters by Wordsworth's *Stanzas Written in My Pocket-copy of Thomson's 'Castle of Indolence'* (1807). One of the characters in the poem (the 'One') is a transient sort, somewhat mysterious in his action, but an observer of nature and lover of poetry. The other character ('A noticeable Man') is rather more down to earth, or at least less mysterious; he too is a lover of song-making. But what they share, what brings them together, is their love of nature. Peacock says that Shelley was 'particularly pleased' with this poem by Wordsworth, and he recorded in his 'Memoirs of Shelley' what Shelley actually said about the poem, although he doesn't say when the comments were made:

> It was a remarkable instance of Wordsworth's insight into nature, that he should have made intimate friends of two imaginary characters so essentially dissimilar, and yet severally so true to the actual characters of two friends, in a poem written long before they were known to each other, and while they were both boys, and totally unknown to him.[11]

I would suggest, then, that Shelley's attraction to Wordsworth's creative 'insight' led him to write about a similar situation. Shelley, looking at himself and Byron, must have seen the poetic potential in the circumstances of their relationship.

The Maniac remains, in spite of the title of the poem, at the centre of *Julian and Maddalo*. Appropriately, the dramatic and narrative structure of the poem draws us, through the words of Julian and along with the two characters, towards an encounter with the Maniac. They believe their differing opinions will be proved or disproved by his example. But (and this is a noteworthy twist in the poem's unfolding) the Maniac's soliloquy does nothing to resolve the conflicting views of Julian and Maddalo. Rather, after his disjointed but impressive words, Julian says 'our argument was quite forgot'(520). His words create a vacuum, a silence. Moreover, as mentioned, the details of the Maniac's story are withheld from us, as if they offered no solution either; or (and this is a more interesting proposition) perhaps Shelley could not bring himself to formulate a completed story. But why?

More sense must be made out of the Maniac's significance as something standing *between* Julian and Maddalo, Shelley and Byron, yet joining the parallel pairs. Here we can go further into the history of the relationship between Shelley and Byron, and here is where the significance of Wordsworth may prove to be helpful. Before October 1815 Byron found Wordsworth disappointing and incomprehensible. Everything written after the *Lyrical Ballads* he considered second rate. He writes to Leigh Hunt on 30 October:

> I take leave to differ from you on Wordsworth as freely as I once agreed with you – at that time I gave him credit for promise which is unfulfilled – I still think his capacity warrants all you say of *it* only – but that his performance since 'Lyrical Ballads' – are miserably inadequate to the ability which lurks within him: – there is undoubtedly much natural talent spilt over 'the Excursion' but it is rain upon rocks where it stands & stagnates – or rain upon sands where it falls without fertilising – who can understand him? – let those who do make him intelligible.[12]

In the rest of the letter he specifies his charges. Yet after his very close association with Shelley in the summer of 1816 at Geneva, Byron is able to say that Wordsworth could have 'few greater admirers than myself'.[13] In his own copy of *English Bards, and Scotch Reviewers* Byron drew a line down the margin of the passage dismissing Wordsworth (236–54) and wrote 'Unjust'.[14] Byron must have felt he had been rather too hasty in his judgement of Wordworth. What brought about this revaluation, this self-correction?

What I think accounts for this dramatic change in Byron, who was not especially known for compromising his opionions, is Shelley's sermonising on Wordsworth's poetic powers. We recall from the second chapter what Byron said of that summer in 1816: 'Shelley, when I was in Switzerland, used to dose me with Wordsworth physic even to nausea; and I do remember reading some things of his with pleasure'.[15] Indeed, Shelley and Byron saw each other almost every day from 29 May to 29 August of that year, which included their journey around Lake Geneva from 22 to 30 June.[16] 'Many and long were the conversations between Lord Byron and Shelley' recalls Mary of this time.[17] Byron's physician, Dr John William Polidori, recorded in his diary that Byron's company 'talked till the ladies' brains whizzed with giddiness, about idealism'.[18] (Mary, nevertheless, managed to survive all of this to come up with the idea for *Frankenstein*.) The proof of Wordsworth-via-Shelley's influence in *Childe Harold* III can hardly be missed (see, for example, lxxii or lxxv). And recall what Mary says about Wordsworth's poetry in her 'Note' on *Peter Bell the Third*, that Shelley constantly 'taught others to appreciate its beauties'. Byron, it appears, was not exempt from Shelley's lessons on the merits of Wordsworth's poetry.

Mary specifically notes the significance of Wordsworth-via-Shelley's influence on Byron and the circumstances of two young, strong poets coming together in her 'Note' on *The Revolt of Islam*. She says that in the summer of 1816 Shelley's 'genius was checked by association with another poet whose nature was utterly dissimilar to his own, yet who, in the poem he wrote at that time, gave tokens that he shared for a period the most abstract and etherealised inspiration of Shelley'. As I will show later, the inspiration behind Shelley's poetry written at this time (*Mont Blanc, Hymn to Intellectual Beauty*) surely came from Wordsworth. (Remember too that Shelley wrote *Verses Written on a Celandine* at this time.) So although other autobiographical circumstances behind *Julian and Maddalo* are ostensibly based on what took place when Shelley and Byron re-met in the summer of 1818, when Shelley went to Venice in order to accompany and assist Claire Clairmont in her dealings with Byron over their child, it is clear that Shelley had inspired Byron earlier in a particular way, a way, it might be suggested, that originated from Shelley's own inspiration by Wordsworth. In a sense, then, what was between Shelley and Byron, what was 'shared' by them, from 1816 when Shelley and Byron first met, until 1818 when they met again in Venice, was a poetical concern; and the influence of Wordsworth, the figure and poetry of Wordsworth, seems to have played a significant part in that concern. Two such poets meeting are bound to talk about poetry, and they are bound to debate about the contemporary scene and its most problematical figure.

III

Now, turning to the Maniac in relation to Julian and Maddalo, what we have is an experienced figure between two inexperienced ones, in that the validity of their arguments depends upon the *words* of the Maniac (286–7; 291; 299). That is, what will apparently prove either Julian or Maddalo right in their views is the substance (the persuasiveness and eloquence) of the Maniac's story and language. It must be emphasised that Shelley has the Maniac portray himself as a despairing poet whose words are 'sad writing' (340). This is rather.

odd, considering that words are spoken. Either Shelley meant the Maniac's words to be as a piece of writing, a poem, or that with some irony he is undercutting the real-life pretence of a dramatic monologue, drawing our attention to the fact that he is, after all, giving us a text, a poem in a poem. In either case, Julian himself hints at the priority of the written over the spoken when he says that the Maniac 'spoke – sometimes as one who wrote' (286). This encourages even more a view of the Maniac's story as a poem within the poem – moreover, as the Maniac's obstinate questionings of his poetic powers. There is also the passage in the *Defence* which seems to point strongly to the Maniac as a Poet and to the situation in the poem. Shelley writes: 'A Poet is a nightingale, who sits in darkness and sings to cheer its own solitude with sweet sounds; his auditors are as men entranced by the melody of an unseen musician, who feel that they are moved and softened, yet know not whence or why.' This is the situation in Shelley's poem when Julian and Maddalo are so deeply impressed by the Maniac's words, except this poet is seen by his 'auditor', and his 'sounds' are failing. This, then, is another portrait of a failed poet, a poet who cannot 'cheer [his] own solitude'. The obvious connection is with the Poet of *Alastor*, who likewise is a prisoner of poetic solitude.

The Maniac is frustrated over the stifling emptiness he now sees in his poetry. At one time what he wrote was worthy, but his present utterances only serve to erase the positive values of his past poetical formulations:

> How vain
> Are words! I thought never to speak again,
> Not even in secret, – not to my own heart –
> But from my lips the unwilling accents start,
> And from my pen the words flow as I write,
> Dazzling my eyes with scalding tears . . . my sight
> Is dim to see that charactered in vain
> On this unfeeling leaf which burns the brain
> And eats into it . . . blotting all things fair
> And wise and good which time had written there.
> (472–81)

This problem of speaking (and writing) to the heart is strikingly reminiscent of Wordsworth. Shelley's portrayal of him now is of an unsuccessful poet, a dissipated authority, one unable to retrieve or recollect the 'wise and good' which at one time must have been his subject, and fearing what might happen to him. His vision is now 'dim'. Is this what became of the Wordsworthian figure? To speculate even further: Is this Shelley speaking *for* (giving imaginative voice to) Wordsworth who can no longer revive the inspiration of the past? If it is, this once more exhibits Shelley's mingled concern for and condemnation of Wordsworth the poet. In this crucial passage Shelley does portray the Maniac as a poet whose present ineffective poetry devalues his past work, just as Shelley felt *The Excursion* devalued Wordsworth's early work. The fluency of the Maniac's past poetry only serves to accentuate the deep feeling of inability he presently experiences. Perhaps Shelley is also projecting his fears of what might happen if he follows this model, if his own creativity deserts him: he too must avoid the fate of uncreativity which comes in solitude, and which, once more, is the fate of the Poet in *Alastor*.

With reasonable certainty we can take it that, to begin with, Byron contested Wordsworth's value as estimated by Shelley. Of course this put Shelley on Wordsworth's side, just as Julian is said to be like the Maniac (195). After the Maniac's soliloquy, Julian confesses he was never before so 'impressed' (517), and he goes elsewhere to seek solace:

> I sought relief
> From the deep tenderness that maniac wrought
> Within me – 'twas perhaps an idle thought –
> But I imagined that if day by day
> I watched him, and but seldom went away
> And studied all the beatings of his heart
> With zeal, as men study some stubborn art
> For their own good, and could by patience find
> An entrance to the caverns of his mind,
> I might reclaim him from his dark estate:
> In friendships I had been most fortunate –
> Yet never saw I one whom I would call
> More willingly my friend; and this was all
> Accomplished not; such dreams of baseless good
> Oft come and go in crowds or solitude
> And leave no trace – but what I now designed
> Made for long years impression on my mind.
> The following morning, urged by my affairs,
> I left bright Venice.
>
> (565–83)

Again, is this perhaps the Shelley who wanted to learn from the art of Wordsworth, and at the same time save his older colleague from the 'dark estate' of failure? The example Shelley uses is revealing: the way he believed Julian will study the Maniac is the way 'men study some stubborn art / For their own good'. This anticipates what Shelley writes about influence in the Preface to *Prometheus Unbound*, that 'one great poet is a masterpiece of nature which another not only ought to study but must study'. The implication is that the Maniac is someone whose art is to be examined, someone who is to be learned from. Moreover, the Maniac with his flaws makes him the perfect poetic figure; that is, his imperfections are poetically perfected by Shelley. He is a figure of inspirational equivocation, at once a model and anti-model. And even though this fate of the Maniac is to be avoided, he is portrayed as noble in his pathos. Again, as in *Alastor*, through the failure of a poet figure Shelley produces successful poetry.

Julian calls the Maniac his 'friend', even though he is unacquainted with him except through his words; he can ony experience the account of the other poet's experience. He only has the Maniac's spoken-but-written text. Once more, all of this may suggest that Julian wants to save the Maniac from poetic failure, yet at the same time learn by his example. Julian can still perceive glimmerings of the poetic powers the Maniac once may have possessed:

> The colours of his mind seemed yet unworn;
> For the wild language of his grief was high,
> Such as in measure were called poetry.
> (540–2)

Maddalo, however, points out that poets like the Maniac pay a great price:

> Most wretched men
> Are cradled into poetry by wrong,
> They learn in suffering what they teach in song.
> (544–6)

The warning is, of course, directed to Julian.

Julian is given qualities which lead us back to, on one hand, the figure of Wordsworth and Wordsworthian sentiment which Shelley constantly describes –

> I love all waste
> And solitary places; where we taste
> The pleasure of believing what we see
> Is boundless, as we wish our souls to be
>
> . . .
>
> And, from the waves, sound like delight broke forth
> Harmonising with solitude, and sent
> Into our hearts aëreal merriment.
>   (14–17, 25–7)

– and on the other, to Shelley's displeasure with the Solitary's state of despondence (as named in Books III and IV of *The Excursion*): 'I . . . / Argued,' says Julian, 'against despondency' (46–8). Julian, then, has aspects of his character which recall the early Wordsworth, yet other characteristics which remind us of Shelley's condemnation of the later Wordsworth.

Is this interpretation of the Maniac (that is, the Maniac is to Julian and Maddalo as Wordsworth is to Shelley and Byron) just as reductive and inconsequential as those other readings that have already been slighted? Must I now, somewhat embarrassingly, trump Carlos Baker by saying that *Julian and Maddalo* is maybe two-thirds approximately true to autobiographical fact? Well, not quite, mainly for two reasons: first, Shelley and Byron did not pay an actual visit to Wordsworth, though they certainly appeared to have discussed him a great deal; and second, a reading of the Maniac as Wordsworth leaves *Julian and Maddalo* in part as a poem about Shelley's *idea* of a poet, which in turn will always recall Shelley's *idea* of Wordsworth or a Wordsworthian figure, something which I hold is central to the development of much of Shelley's poetry. But this last point must be qualified with even more tentativeness. The poem cannot be expressed in such a way that 'the Maniac = Wordsworth' and Wordsworth only. It can only be said that the Maniac represents Shelley's continuing concern with the desperate and disconsolate poet figure, and that significant aspects of this figure are in some important ways determined by Shelley's concern with the man who he felt was the most important poet of his time: Wordsworth.

It might be suggested that *Julian and Maddalo* is instigated by Wordsworth's own words. For it is conceivable that Shelley's poet-madman is prefigured by these lines spoken by the Wordsworthian poet-traveller from *Resolution and Independence*:

> We Poets in our youth begin in gladness;
> But thereof come in the end despondency and madness.
> (48–9)

This truly is the thematic situation of the Maniac (as it is of the Poet in *Alastor*). The circumstances and ideas behind *Resolution and Independence* support *Julian and Maddalo*, so that a cross-identification might be made between the Maniac and the Leech-gatherer. Both can perhaps be seen as idealised projections of Wordsworth as a potentially pathetic poet figure, differing, of course, in that one is how Shelley sees Wordsworth (a victim of his own circumstances, yet desperately enduring with at least some eloquence and nobility), and the other is how Wordsworth sees himself (eternally a solitary figure, but firm in mind).

Thus there is, beyond the figures within the poem, but dependent on them, a poetic situation where Shelley approaches Wordsworth as he has seen Wordsworth approaching himself. This is justified in that Shelley's strong yet ambivalent identification with the older poet has already been shown. Shelley is as much interested in the fate of Wordsworth's poet-figures as he is in Wordsworth, and because of this it can be said that Shelley's idea of Wordsworth is entangled with his own portrayals of the Wordsworthian poet figure. Taken back into the poems in question, Julian approaching the Maniac parallels the Traveller approaching the Leech-gatherer. The specifics of the narratives bear this out: both the Traveller and Julian set out in the morning, and in dream-like or unreal circumstances they encounter infirm figures whose poetic words and 'posture' are impressive. The past lives of these men, which only suggestively account for their present conditions, are drawn in mysterious circumstances,

> As if some dire constraint of pain, or rage
> Of sickness felt by him in times long past,
> A more than human weight upon this frame had cast.
> (*Resolution and Independence*, 68–70)

This too is an exact summing-up of the Maniac's condition, but it also sums up aspects of the burden passed on from Wordsworth's figures to Shelley's central figures. These figures appear to be idealists whose idealism has not been accommodated or proved by the real world. The Leech-gatherer does not appear to have totally recovered from failed expectations. In more extreme form, this burden of the past is inherited by the Solitary of *The Excursion*, who never recovers the loss of hope sounded by the French Revolution. And of course many of Shelley's poet figures following the Poet of *Alastor* often seek their ideals in the real world, only to be blasted by disappointment.

Here then is a point where it might be said that Shelley's and Wordsworth's figures come together and pull apart, and where, accordingly, in terms of influence, Shelley and Wordsworth come together and pull apart. Wordsworth's strongest figures are for Shelley vulnerable, but they are not necessarily impotent. That is, Shelley feels there is a flaw in Wordsworth's figures, but it is a flaw that he can creatively utilise (idealise) in his own poetry. Shelley takes up both the vulnerability and the potency of these figures, Wordsworth himself built within these figures as an aspect of Shelley's problematic identification with the older poet. This composite figure is what was meant to be suggested by previously framing Wordsworth in inverted commas: 'Wordsworth'; and the phrase 'these figures' now here becomes '*this* figuration'. Wordsworth is, as I attempted to explain at the beginning of this study, a *figurative* problem for Shelley, both in the sense of Wordsworth being a figure of paternal and poetic authority, and Shelley having to cope with Wordsworth's authority in a figurative mode, in poetry.

What Wordsworth subtly projected in such poems as *Resolution and Independence* and *The Excursion* is partly an attempt (but an unsuccessful attempt) to distance something within himself, making himself the major figurative presence (but a negative presence) in his own poems. (We know what Shelley didn't know, although at times he appears to have intuited it: that the Solitary was an attempt to rewrite or rework *The Prelude*'s account of Wordsworth's own past.) In poetic acts of empathy, and with resulting complexity, Shelley develops both a pro- and anti-Wordsworth sentiment from this projection, made even more difficult in that at times it is impossible to tell the real Wordsworth from the fictive creation, or, for that matter, at more extreme moments, Shelley from Wordsworth. Shelley is not perhaps so much trying to correct 'Wordsworth' as he is trying to *redeem* him, as the latter suggests not only an attempt to save the older poet but to fulfil his promise as well.

IV

Can the workings of *Julian and Maddalo* be seen as a sophisticated development out of *Alastor*? Certainly the action and the imagery in the later poem are less extravagant. But the essential circumstances remain: the Maniac, like *Alastor's* Poet (who is also described as a maniac of sorts after his vision – for example, 244–54), is a poetic visionary whose vision fails him and leads him to desperate ends;[19] or, in more philosophical terms, the Maniac, like the Poet, is an idealist ruined by the failure of the world to match up to his own idealism. And here, if we can move sideways for a moment, is where the function of Maddalo as Byron is important. We must believe that Byron warned Shelley about following too closely Wordsworth's inspiration. This is, of course, the situation in the poem: Maddalo means the Maniac as a warning to Julian as to what he might become. 'I knew one like you,' Maddalo says to Julian, 'and he / Is now gone mad' (195–8). Beneath all of this must be Shelley's real fear that he may become like the Maniac, that he may meet the same fate as Wordsworth. Thus in one sense the poem functions as Shelley's warning to himself. Once more an ambivalence towards the older poet becomes apparent. Shelley's simultaneous wants are to be both like and unlike the Maniac. The Maniac's poetry may have collapsed into fragments, but for Julian his story persists in having a strong and affective quality; the Maniac's 'text' demands study. The same applies to Shelley's relationship with Wordsworth: the older poet may have produced poetry that disappointed Shelley, but the story of Wordsworth's own failure as a poet persists as a sort of myth in Shelley's poetry, a myth that may also hold a prophecy. Whether it becomes a prophecy of success or failure is a cause of Shelley's poetic anxiety. Poetic failure is more of an attractive poetic circumstance than poetic success: the threat of uncreativity incites creative output.

Like the Poet of *Alastor* who wakes from his dream of the 'veiled maid' (151) to find everything changed (192ff), the Maniac wakes 'as one from dreaming' to find that his 'state' is changed and that he is separated from his 'spirit mate', yet remembering her eyes (335–43, 423, 468). He is left confused and distraught in this desertion, just as the Poet is when the 'veiled maid' disappears before him. Like the Poet, the Maniac's thoughts turn to death (*Alastor*, 211–22, 292–5, 368–9; *Julian and Maddalo*, 315–16, 369), of tearing away the 'veil' from his mind in order to transform his inevitable funeral into a wedding. His state is such that thoughts of self-castration become the expression of his frustration and guilt (420–38). After resisting these morbid temptations, his resolve becomes one of exemplification, 'to show / How much men bear and die not' (459–60); so too in the Preface to *Alastor* does Shelley say his story 'is not barren of instruction to actual men'. As his soliloquy reaches a climax, and he sees the grave yawning before him (505–10), like the Poet of *Alastor* lying down at the base of the pine in order to meet death, the Maniac reclines (513), as if to surrender himself. This is where we leave him, only to come back in later years to find him dead and buried with his 'spirit mate' (615). He has died with his vision. He too seems to have failed as a poet.

By virtue of the Maniac's significance as a representational figure, he takes the Poet's circumstances one step further. What makes the Maniac so potent a figure is this: he is both a vision (seen by Julian and Maddalo) *and* a visionary, having had his own vision. As a narrative strategy on Shelley's part, this has the effect of distancing him from his subject, somewhat in the same mode as a tale within a tale. But this distancing reveals two things to us. First, it gives us another connection with *The Excursion*. Besides the similar distancing that Wordsworth attempts between himself and the Solitary (by putting the speaker of the poem, the Wanderer, and the Pastor between himself and his problematical protagonist), there is an important plot parallel: just as the speaker and the Wanderer in *The Excursion* set off to visit the Solitary, in an attempt to draw a moral lesson from his account of his unhappy life, so too do Julian and Maddalo set off to visit and learn from the Maniac's distraught account. The Solitary and the Maniac are both held up as examples of estranged yet poetic figures of hopelessness.

Second, and finally, this distancing reveals something more to us – a possible anxiety regarding Shelley's approach to the subject. Transferred into the poem, to Julian, this works so strongly that after many years he is compelled to return to the scene of his encounter to make further inquiries about the Maniac (583ff.), only to ironically withhold his further findings from the 'cold world', from us. Once more, as in *Alastor*, *The Sunset* and *Prince Athanase*, the story of the poet figure is left open-ended, inexplicable and perhaps unfinishable. What would have been gained by giving us the further history of the Maniac? It could only lead to a regression, an anticlimax to the actual encounter with the Maniac. But Shelley's anxiety is revealed in that he does return to this same central figure who is in some ways like Wordsworth, but now it is a Wordsworth whose moments of finding strength in the past, of invoking immortality and 'splendour in the grass' (*Intimations Ode*, 182), become the burden of an eternal pain: the Maniac exclaims:

> You say that I am proud – that when I speak
> My lip is tortured with the wrongs which break
> The spirit it expresses. . . . Never one
> Humbled himself before, as I have done!
> Even the instinctive worm on which we tread
> Turns, though it wound not – then with prostrate head
> Sinks in the dust and writhes like me – and dies?
> No: wears a living death of agonies!
> As the slow shadows of the pointed grass
> Mark the eternal periods, his pangs pass
> Slow, ever-moving, – making moments be
> As mine seem – each an immortality!
>
> (408–19)

If I were to go all the way with my thesis, this passage might be read as Wordsworth addressing Shelley's charges as a failed poet; more precisely, this may be Shelley imaginatively having Wordsworth acknowledge (apologise for) his failure as a poet. It is important to remember that the Maniac's 'lips [were] once eloquent' (454), but are no longer so – that is, he can no longer compose fluent poetry. The 'immortality' that Wordsworth always worked towards, that 'glory' to be extended eternally as an inscription of memory, is now fragmented into moments of agony. His vision has deserted him, and his death-wish is to be denied. Note too that Shelley preserves Wordsworth by giving him a 'living death'. And how much do the Maniac's early characteristics coincide with early Wordsworth? Appropriately we find that he is one

> Who loved and pitied all things, and could moan
> For woes which others hear not, and could see
> The absent with the glance of phantasy,
> And with the poor and trampled sit and weep,
> Following the captive to his dungeon deep.
>
> (444–8)

This does sound remarkably like the poet of the *Lyrical Ballads*.

The Maniac is the failed solitary poet whose idealism has collapsed under the weight of disappointment and disillusionment. He is a figure of dissipated poetic authority, yet paradoxically this is what ennobles him. Julian approaches to learn from him and, if he can, to save him. Whether or not this exactly corresponds with Wordsworth is not altogether the point, although Shelley's poetry on the failure of the solitary poet always in some important ways derives from Wordsworth. *Julian and Maddalo* is unique (relative to Shelley's other poems which I have discussed) in that it is less impassioned, less breathlessly heading towards solipsistic destruction. Yet Shelley can still not fully capture his subject, nor claim it as fully controlled. He can only frame within his poem the Maniac's fractured verses. But he knows that if he wants to control the Maniac he would have to have him speak no longer, kill him, or say no more about him. Shelley almost manages all three in *Julian and Maddalo*. This does not, however, mean that the problem of the failed poet, the problem of Wordsworth, will go away, any more than the problem of influence will go away. But it may mean that through the experience of the poem Shelley will become a stronger poet, one whose confidence in his poetic powers will take him one step closer to Wordsworth, yet one step further away.

Part of the Maniac's poetry may be read as a drastic rendition of Wordsworth and Wordsworth's words and vision, indicating to this reader that Shelley is at a 'make it or break it' point with Wordsworth. But Shelley's genius, his want, is such that in *Prometheus Unbound* he both makes *and* breaks it. The Maniac's story, 'a sufficient comment for the text of every heart', continues as Shelley's text.

The Maniac's soliloquy is an account of loss, of diminishing poetic and visionary powers. He is a Promethean who fails. His powers are diminished to the extent that his attempts to write are ineffective: he can no longer coherently reflect his feelings. And even his soliloquy has been perceived as but a series of fragments. He suffers from a poetic form of aposiopesis. Whatever he had before – whether creativity or hope – he has no longer. If, as I have been suggesting, some elements of the Maniac are based on Shelley's creative engagement with Wordsworth, then the Maniac is certainly the most pitiful yet pitied representation of the older poet which Shelley makes in the poetry discussed so far. Shelley does, however, make the Maniac more self-conscious; he has him acknowledge aspects of his change,

> as when a boy
> I did devote to justice and to love
> My nature, worthless now!
> (379–81)

but like all of the poems up until this point, the pity is still not impressive enough to have Shelley's ambivalence resolved and a successful outcome for his protagonist take place. How is it, then, that this is achieved in *Prometheus Unbound*?

6

Shelley Unbound

I

To Wordsworth, Alastor, The Sunset, Prince Athanase, Verses Written on a Celandine and *Julian and Maddalo* are in various ways and to various extents Shelley's attempts to resolve his ambivalent identification with Wordsworth and Wordsworth's central figures (as well as his attempt to engage Wordsworth's poetic lexicon). And up until *Julian and Maddalo* this identification has been a source of restrictive anxiety yet poetic productivity. The Maniac, like the protagonists in those other poems, represents a failure or failed vision, a poet whose values and powers of poetic articulation have deserted him.

Shelley does not appear to be able to take these central figures beyond the situations or conflicts into which he leads them. The story left untold at the end of *Julian and Maddalo* is, however, ironically suggestive of a resolution on the brink of expression: Julian says he knows the complete story of the Maniac, 'but the cold world shall not know' (617) – at least not yet, anyway. *Prince Athanase* also contains an uncompleted narrative: 'And so his grief remained – let it remain – untold' (124). Accordingly, a statement made by Arthur Clutton-Brock about *Prince Athanase* – 'One feels that Shelley could not have made Athanase do anything' – can be applied further:[1] it seems that Shelley does not really make the Poet of *Alastor*, the One of *The Sunset* or the Maniac of *Julian and Maddalo* do much either. But Clutton-Brock's additional charge that in *Prometheus Unbound* Shelley was also 'hard put to it to make anything happen at all'[2] is a rather myopic reading of the poem, and I would conclude that he was looking either at the wrong stage or for the wrong mode of action. In *Prometheus Unbound* a great deal takes place, especially in terms of the crucial exchange of power in the poem and the resulting ramifications of Prometheus's recovery of power. All of this suggests a new level of achievement for both Shelley and his protagonist. I would like to propose that the action that takes place in *Prometheus Unbound* can be read as the freeing of poetic creativity from a particular tyranny of influence, and that the stage, the site of the poem where the struggle takes place, is poetic language. In short, *Prometheus Unbound* is another poem about the production of poetry. But now Shelley appears to know what he wants to do, and a successful outcome indicates a conflict resolved. That is, a successful poet-figure within the poem may mean that Shelley, as a poet relative to his great contemporaries, and especially relative to Wordsworth, has achieved poetic self-determination. Anna Balakian points out that to justify the study of influence one must attempt to discover 'the turning point at which the writer frees himself of the influence and finds his originality'.[3] In the context of the present study *Prometheus Unbound* is that 'turning point' for Shelley.

Yet when I say that in *Prometheus Unbound* Shelley frees himself from Wordsworth's influence, I do not mean that he consciously set out to do so. He did not necessarily have Wordsworth in mind when he composed his poem. What I do mean is that in *Prometheus Unbound*, and especially via the figure of Prometheus, Shelley reaches a new level of expression, and that within the form that expression took, even at the level of plot, he purposefully gives notice of his own poetic individuality. Because Wordsworth is Shelley's strongest poetic influence, because Shelley felt so strongly for and against Wordsworth, the older poet was first of all given power by Shelley, then endured for a time, and finally put down. This also happens to be the structure of the plot of *Prometheus Unbound*, and I would suggest that the authority manifest in Jupiter with which Prometheus struggles in some ways intimates Wordsworth's presence as a figure of poetic authority. Here I would look to David Simpson's suggestion that 'it is tempting to regard the movement of *Prometheus Unbound*, involving as it does the education of the hero away from "his self-torturing solitude" (I. 295), as an appeal for a reborn Wordsworth'.[4] If, as I believe there is, any validity to this idea, the situation in the poem is an interesting one: my reading of *Prometheus Unbound* as a poem about the breaking away from a figure of authority is thus also marked by the return of a 'reborn' authority: and at the edge of the text, as a kind of Bloomian revisionary ratio of *apophrades*, the new Shelley invokes the return of the old (dead) Wordsworth by simultaneously putting him down. The 'reborn Wordsworth' is Shelley.

More so than with any of his other productions, Shelley was well aware of his new poem's significance. In his letters and conversations he repeatedly maintained that *Prometheus Unbound* was his most important poem, his best and most unique poem, and the poem costing him his severest effort (*Letters*, II, pp. 94, 127, 164, 174). But more significantly, besides evaluating it relative to his own poetry, he placed it in comparison with the works of others: 'It is a drama, with characters & mechanism of a kind yet unattempted' (*Letters*, II, p. 94).[5] Shelley was determined to stress the poem's unique qualities: 'It [*Prometheus Unbound*] is in my judgement, of a higher character than any thing I have yet attempted; and is perhaps less an imitation of any thing that has gone before it' (*Letters*, II, p. 116). And once more: 'It is original; and cost me severe mental labour. Authors, like mothers, prefer the children who have given them most trouble.'[6] Stated clearly here is Shelley's belief that at last he has achieved separation from his models and found his own originality. He himself realised his poem was a turning point, and that what influenced him had been accommodated and assimilated. Suggested too is that Shelley is rewriting (or completing or correcting) his old poems, those poems in which he could not, to use Clutton-Brock's phrase, 'make anything happen at all'.

It is as if that story of the Maniac left untold at the end of *Julian and Maddalo* is in some ways taken up by the story of Prometheus unbinding himself from the curse of Jupiter, a curse which Prometheus ironically set in motion himself. Indeed, the final words of the Maniac's soliloquy not only clearly anticipate Prometheus's unsaying of his binding curse and the purging of all his spiteful feelings, and so hint at a positive outcome, but also the Maniac even sounds like the redemptive Prometheus:[7]

> Here I cast away
> All human passions, all revenge, all pride;
> I think, speak, act no ill; I do but hide
> Under these words, like embers, every spark
> Of that which has consumed me.
>
> (501–5)

As I have argued earlier, the basis of Shelley's canon is his concern with a central visionary figure struggling with a *self-determined* problem – in the case of Prometheus it is this binding curse. Those thousands of years of chained suffering parallel Shelley's years of enduring Wordsworth's influence, expressed from *Alastor* to *Julian and Maddalo*. And the figure of the suffering Maniac incarcerated in his tower does seem to anticipate the tormented figure of Prometheus chained to a mountain precipice.

But Shelley intuited that at least Prometheus's suffering would have both purposeful and redemptive ends: in order to free one's self, one must first become enslaved; more pragmatically (as in *Prince Athanase*), in order to become a master, one must first serve as an apprentice or pupil. That this theme is at work in *Prometheus Unbound* is evidenced in its Preface, which must, as I shall suggest, be read as an integral part of the poem. I pointed out in the first chapter that more than in any other place, including the *Defence*, Shelley in the Preface to *Prometheus Unbound* describes how strongly a poet is *bound* not just to the influence of his precursors, but even more strongly to contemporary influence. Poets, says Shelley, are both the creators and creations of their time: 'From this subjection even the loftiest do not escape.' Remember that Shelley specifically had Wordsworth in mind in the Preface, the final five paragraphs being a direct response to the charge made by a reviewer in the April 1819 *Quarterly Review* that Shelley was imitating Wordsworth: 'Mr Shelley indeed is an unsparing imitator; and he draws largely on the rich stores of another mountain poet'. Shelley begins his response by saying, 'One word is due in candour to the degree in which the study of contemporary writings may have tinged my composition', and after demonstrating that all great writers necessarily share a common influence and resemblance with those with whom they share the same time, he throws the charge back at his accuser: 'If this similarity be the result of imitation, I am willing to confess that I have imitated.' Yet, in relation to the Preface, which is all about the impossibility of escaping influence, *Prometheus Unbound* has this noteworthy twist: it is about a poet successfully freeing himself, successfully escaping.

To maintain that aspects of *Prometheus Unbound* can be read as Shelley freeing himself from a figure of poetic authority, two readings of the poem must be brought together. The first is that *Prometheus Unbound* takes the form of a father–son conflict to be resolved, resolved in order that the son can be freed from the repressive (and oppressive) influence of the father. Obviously I am taking it that Prometheus is in some ways representative of both Shelley's role and his poetic aspirations, and that Jupiter, whom I take as a father figure to Prometheus, is partly representative of Wordsworth's binding influence as a figure of poetic authority. I will further point out that the background and dramatic structure of the poem is determined by a number of cross-identifications based on father–son conflicts. On all sides the poem is intent with a struggle against paternal authority.

The second reading that must be brought to *Prometheus Unbound* is also suggestive of a form of emancipation. Here I believe *Prometheus Unbound* to be about poetry (language in various re-creative formations) striving to achieve its own unique power. 'Prometheanism', as Harold Bloom defines it, is 'the quest for *poetic strength*'.[8] These two readings, then, are not as exclusive as they might have at first seemed, for bringing them together the suggestion can be repeated that on one level *Prometheus Unbound* is about Shelley freeing himself from an authorial and authoritative influence, and that this is an influence which can only be binding in creative acts of language. The means of achieving freedom, of becoming *unbound*, are thus other creative acts of language, new forms of lyric. The poem, in short, is an account of a struggle against paternal and poetic authority.

II

The reading of *Prometheus Unbound* I am working towards is, admittedly, narrow – perhaps even reductive. I say this because themes taken from (or brought to) Shelley's poem are normally on a grander scale: for example, the destruction of Tyranny and the regeneration of Mankind; the need for Revolution; and the call for Social Reform; or on more abstract levels: Good triumphing over Evil; the power of Necessity; Imagination displacing Reason; Hate overcome by Love. In *Shelley's Mythmaking* Bloom says that 'the poem is so multiform a creation that it can sustain a great many commentaries. No one approach will exhaust it; no approach responsible to the primacy of the poem's text will disfigure it'.[9] The poem allows for philosophical, political, and moral readings of the suffering, struggle and defeat that takes place within what Shelley called a 'Lyrical Drama'. The idea of *defeat* should be emphasised (I could have said victory), for Shelley notes in the Preface that, unlike Aeschylus, he does not want his Prometheus to merely compromise with Jupiter: 'I was averse from a catastrophe so feeble as that of reconciling the Champion with the Oppressor of mankind'. He does not want his hero 'unsaying his high language and quailing before his successful and perfidious adversary'. Shelley apparently wants his Prometheus to celebrate his freedom through the dismissal of Jupiter. He wants his representative's 'high language' not only to stand up to Jupiter's, but to put him down as well. What remains to be shown is how, on a less grandly thematic scale, the struggle and defeat has a more personal and poetical significance for Shelley. It is not just the achievement of composing this particular work that made Shelley regard his poem so highly: it is that the poem itself is in some ways a description of that very achievement, the production of successful poetry.

To come to Shelley's *Prometheus Unbound* as a naïve reader is almost impossible; that is, it is impossible to come as a reader of the poem without some prior knowledge of the Prometheus story. The result, of course, is that we bring some expectations to both the narrative and its meaning, as well as to the relative accomplishment of Shelley. And even if we knew nothing of the Prometheus myth – Prometheus who made mankind out of clay; who stole fire from the gods and gave it, along with the arts, to man; who was punished by Zeus (Jupiter) and chained to a rock and daily had his liver eaten out by an eagle or vulture – even if we knew nothing of this, Shelley in the Preface makes sure that he informs us of particular aspects of Aeschylus's version of the myth. Thus before we come to the actual text of Shelley's poem we are given the literary and historical context of his achievement. Shelley must want us to know this background information. But at the same time he states very emphatically that in his version, his rendition, he is going to use the myth to his own purpose. In Harold Bloom's terms, this is indeed a very conscious effort to 'misread' his precursors. This is the first thing Shelley states in the Preface: he says that like the Greek writers who 'employed . . . a certain arbitrary discretion', using myths to their own purposes, he too wishes to 'employ a similar licence'. What Shelley clearly invites here is a comparison of his 'original' poem with the other, earlier version. Like the Greek writers, Shelley feels that he too is not *'bound'* to 'common interpretation' or imitation of his 'rivals and predecessors'. Here is an important point: before we even enter the text Shelley has set it up as both an original work and a discourse of poetic originality. And so we find we are being directed to the significance of those things which Shelley accented, added or changed in his version of the story. We also become aware that Shelley's desire is to extend, complete and over-turn Aeschylus's *Prometheus Bound*.

In the Preface Shelley also invites us to compare the 'imagery' of his work with that of Dante and Shakespeare. More strongly, he draws attention to similarities his poem has with *Paradise Lost*, and especially to a comparison between Satan and Prometheus. In Shelley's rather immodest 'judgement', he feels his protagonist is 'a more poetical character' than Milton's – Prometheus is free of vices, and 'the type of the highest perfection of moral and intellectual nature, impelled by the purest and the truest motives to the best and noblest ends'. To say the least, Shelley is putting himself not just in good company, but above it. Nowhere else is Shelley quite so publicly confident about one of his own poetic accomplishments, about himself as a poet.

III

Prometheus's curse is repeated; Jupiter is put down; Prometheus is freed and united with Asia. Because the action in *Prometheus Unbound* is minimal, discerning the work's 'meanings' does not seem particularly dependent upon examining this plot. It is, after all, an old story with familiar types: the good guy overcomes the bad guy and then gets the beautiful girl. And because the players are not 'human', not 'characters', we might be drawn to consider the poem as straightforward allegory: for example, Prometheus = value A, Jupiter = value B, and so on.[10] But this doesn't quite sound like Shelley's intentions. 'Didactic poetry is my abhorrence,' he says in the Preface; and didacticism in narrative form often smacks of allegory, inasmuch as instructional lessons are sometimes instilled by exemplary tales. Neither does *Prometheus Unbound* stand well as a simple play or story – again, action and plot are lacking. The general problem is that the play's action is abstract and supernatural. The result of this is troublesome: characterisation can be confused with abstraction, or plot with argument. Is Prometheus a strong character or representative of an admirable principle? I would suggest a compromise that would leave the poem open. Shelley, as a poet of ideas, is too enthusiastic to leave his own concerns out of the poem; but he is also too much a philosopher and politician to omit these interests as well. Thus the poem does not just move between these levels, but carries them simultaneously. This perhaps is *Prometheus Unbound*'s most unique quality as well as its greatest achievement, but it is also one of its sources of difficulty. So much is written about the poem because so much was written into it.

Despite the archetypal nature of all the poem's major *dramatis personae*, interpretations of *Prometheus Unbound* have followed from interpretations of the poem's central figure. I can rely on Earl Wasserman for support here: he says the meaning of *Prometheus Unbound* must ultimately be 'a function of what its protagonist represents'.[11] Lawrence John Zillman, in classifying various interpretations of Prometheus, says that they generally fall into four areas: 'Prometheus as (1) Humanity; (2) the Mind or Soul of Man; (3) a religious manifestation; (4) a political manifestation'.[12] Indeed, few readings of the poem have come outside these areas. But some critics dispute these interpretations. Bloom says that critics are just bringing their own meaning to the text;[13] Wasserman says that other critics fall short because they assume that 'the central subject of the drama is a mankind having autonomous reality and that Prometheus is a fictional abstraction of earthly man or of his faculties or ideals'.[14] In spirit the solutions of Bloom and Wasserman to these failings are similar. Both critics return to Shelley for their interpretations, Bloom to the context of Shelley's personal mode of mythmaking, and Wasserman to Shelley's particular brand of metaphysics. The results of their work (as any reader will testify) is to give readings of *Prometheus Unbound* more complex, more eclectic than other accounts. Whereas to impose a philosophy (for example, Necessity) or a social comment (for example, Reform) on the poem makes it 'easier', more simple, it is also reductive and follows the worst application of the law of parsimony. My intention, as I have stated, is also to return in part to Shelley for the context of *Prometheus Unbound*. I will not lay claim to a reading equalling the scope achieved by Bloom or Wasserman – at any rate, that is not my intention. But I can, by situating Shelley's poetic self in the poem, highlight what surely must be an important aspect of Shelley's poetry and an important moment in his growth as a poet.

If establishing *Prometheus Unbound*'s genre is difficult, then perhaps it encompasses more than one classification. A suggestion evolving in this present chapter is to read Shelley's work as both a mythic narrative and a lyric poem, yet with the latter having priority over the former. This must be explained. *Prometheus Unbound* as mythopoeic is easiest to defend, since Shelley's source is a myth. Accordingly Shelley's characters are supernatural beings engaged in titanic struggles: the fate of the World and Mankind is at stake. When I say *Prometheus Unbound* is a lyric poem, however, a fuller explanation is needed. I do not merely mean that parts of it are lyrical. First of all, I use the term 'lyric poem' in the sense that the poet makes a personal discovery or realisation by dwelling on a subject or thing outside of himself. That is, the poet uses something outside himself to find out or prove something about himself. Thus the lyric poem can be an expression of personal growth or accomplishment. What I am suggesting in this case is that the Prometheus myth itself is the subject outside Shelley that the young poet goes to; and it engages his expression to such a degree that he discovers himself as a poet. *Prometheus Unbound*, the poem, is proof of the accomplishment. Again, the Preface offers a key. A lyric poem normally contains the poet's presence as 'I'. In Shelley's work this personal presence is felt very strongly in the Preface (which is Shelley's strongest statement as a poet), and in the poem is transferred from Shelley to Prometheus. For example, note the tone of the opening sentence of the last paragraph in the Preface: 'The having spoken of myself with unaffected freedom will need little apology with the candid'. That Shelley saw himself as Prometheus (or carried the concerns of the Preface over into the poem) is in some ways obvious. Compare the description of Shelley's own poetic aims outlined in the Preface with a description of Prometheus's character and his action in the poem. Shelley's admission that he himself has a 'passion for reforming the world' is certainly not unlike Prometheus's accomplishment of such an end. Consider too Shelley's desire to acquaint his readers 'with beautiful idealisms of moral excellence'; similarly, as Shelley tells us, Prometheus represents 'the type of the highest perfection of moral and intellectual nature'. Shelley adds that Prometheus has no personal aims, but only the 'truest motives'; so Shelley implies about himself in the last paragraph of the Preface, that he is 'bound' to do his best, and is concerned with neither success nor failure. What differentiates my reading of Shelley's poem from other readings is directly related to this: *Prometheus Unbound* may abound in grand themes, but like *Alastor*, like *Prince Athanase*, *The Sunset* and *Julian and Maddalo*, it is also significant in once more expressing Shelley's problem of becoming a poet.

What makes *Prometheus Unbound* stand out is that unlike the central figures in these other poems, Shelley at last found in the figure of Prometheus a poetic potential that simultaneously challenged his creative powers and paralleled his situation as a poet. In other words, the timing and the subject matter come together. Benjamin Kurtz noted this as well: in Prometheus Shelley 'found a figure so elevated by popular tradition and former poetic treatment, that no splendour of phrase could seem inappropriate; and so peculiarly suited to his own experiences and temperament, that it inevitably called forth his greatest poetic genius'.[15] That is to say, the figure of Prometheus created Shelley as a great poet. William H. Hildebrand observes something quite similar about Prometheus's creative potential: that Shelley now 'found a myth that enabled him to give cosmic dimensions to his own spiritual struggles and aspirations', and he could now fuse 'his own self-myth with the mythic Prometheus'.[16] Of course Shelley's 'self-myth' is intimately tied to his desire to be an original poet. My argument, though overlapping with those of Kurtz and Hildebrand, should be differentiated on one main point: they talk more in terms of self-discovery, while I am centring more on a poetic coming-of-age in a poem in part concerned with that process itself.

What must be developed now is, first, the structure of the father–son relationship in *Prometheus Unbound*, and second, how this structure encourages a reading of the poem as about the production of poetry. The poem is about a poetic success as well as being a poetic success.

IV

My reading of *Prometheus Unbound* as a father–son conflict or power struggle in part coincides with the argument that the relation Prometheus has with Jupiter is that of a son attempting to contend with a tyrannical father.[17] This reading is complemented by the fact that in Shelley's re-working of the myth Demogorgon acts as Prometheus's spiritual double, and Demogorgon is the child of Jupiter (III. i. 54). By association, then, Prometheus is Jupiter's heir. When Demogorgon approaches the throne of Jupiter in order to take him down, to accompany him on his fall, the double of Prometheus says to his sire:

> Descend, and follow me down the abyss.
> I am thy child, as thou wert Saturn's child;
> Mightier than thee: and we must dwell together
> Henceforth in darkness.
> (III. i. 53–6)

This may be said to be one part of Prometheus falling with Jupiter, a part that can never now be disassociated from his procreator. Note the Oedipal succession here, where the child becomes the father only to have his own power usurped by his own child: the latecomer (the son) wishes to be greater or stronger than his predecessor (the father) by assuming his *creative* power. With some irony the Oedipal struggle is unknowingly voiced by Jupiter himself just before Demogorgon appears to take him down:

> even then,
> Two mighty spirits, mingling, made a third
> Mightier than either.
>
> (III. i. 42–4)

The background of the Prometheus myth is based on what might loosely be called father troubles. From Hesiod's *Theogony* Shelley would have read an account of the myth that would have encouraged the Oedipal accent in his own version. Hesiod recounts the story of Earth (mother) marrying Heaven (father). The products of this coupling were the Titans, among whom Kronos (or Saturn) was one. But Earth also gave birth to three other rather bizarre creatures which Heaven disapproved of, resulting in his having them hidden away. Earth was upset by this, and Kronos was asked by his mother to castrate his father. In this way Kronos took over his father's role and became King of the Titans. But Kronos, now fearing the same fate as his father, ate his own children as soon as his wife, Rhea, gave birth to them. However, through a deception on the part of Rhea, one of Kronos's sons, Zeus (or in the Roman adaptation, Jupiter), managed to survive; and he too brought down his father as well as some of the other Titans. From the Titans allowed to live under Zeus's rule, one generation later Prometheus is born. But Prometheus too defied the word of his ruler, and stole fire from heaven and gave it to mankind. And so we find that Prometheus too is a rebel against authority. Shelley's Prometheus thus comes from a lineage determined by father–son conflict, where usurpation and transference of paternal power is always at stake.

Another piece of evidence suggests that a father–son relationship is the basis of the Jupiter–Prometheus conflict. As a number of critics have pointed out, Prometheus is in some ways a Christ figure.[18] 'Nailed' (I. 20) to the precipice he has, like Jesus, a 'crown of pain' (I. 290), and a Fury holds up the example of Jesus to Prometheus as one of 'those who do endure / Deep wrongs for man, . . . but heap / Thousandfold torment on themselves' (I. 594–6; also I. 546–72). In the second act Panthea also recalls for Asia a dream she had of Prometheus: she tells of his 'pale wound-worn limbs' and of lifting her eyes to see 'the overpowering light' of Prometheus's 'immortal shape' and experiencing the 'love' and warm 'power' emanating from him (II. i. 62–78). On its own this is reminiscent of Christ's pose on the cross, but it is even more apparent that Shelley had Christ in mind as a model for Prometheus when it is compared to his description of Correggio's painting of Christ beatified, which he saw in Bologna on 8 November 1818, just when he was beginning to work on *Prometheus Unbound* (*Letters*, II, pp. 49–50).

Also recall Jesus's words on the cross: 'Father, forgive them; for they know not what they do' (Luke, 23: 24). Interestingly, these are the words which end a Fury's final attempt to make Prometheus despair over man's imperfect character:

> Many are strong and rich, and would be just,
> But live among their suffering fellow-men
> As if none felt: they know not what they do.

Prometheus answers:

> Thy words are like a cloud of wingèd snakes;
> And yet I pity those they torture not.
> (I. 629–33)

We would have expected Prometheus to be the one to repeat Jesus's words. But the effect of having an evil Fury say them is an interesting reversal. It is the tormentor, not the tormented, who is speaking. But further, this reversal disclaims Jesus's statement of forgiveness. By making Prometheus respond in terms of pity, not forgiveness, Shelley gives his figure a superiority in response over Jesus. Forgiveness does not always suggest an emotive quality, but can be just a one-sided statement of agreement; on the other hand, Shelley would say pity is a truly empathetic response.

Like Jesus, the hero in Shelley's poem appears as a god in human form, and his effort is to awaken a 'clear knowledge' for man (I. 542); and his suffering is on behalf of the earth and mankind (I. 118–19, 305, 815–17). If this parallel between Prometheus and Jesus is an intentional one, as it appears to be, we would expect some further homology between the double pairings of Prometheus/Jupiter and Jesus/God. But as Stuart Curran points out, 'A Christian mythographer is naturally loath to equate Prometheus with Christ, since the correlative is to cast God as the vindictive Jupiter, torturing his victim on the cross.'[19] Given Shelley's sceptical stance towards

Christian faith, one would have to hold that in his myth the parallel works for just that reason, in order to demonstrate the vindictive and tyrannical nature of God. Simultaneously it suggests Shelley's belief that Jesus was betrayed by his Father (as well as by some of his followers). Jupiter put down is the autocracy of the Church put down, and the resurrection of Prometheus is the renovative hope for mankind creating its own destiny.

All that has been said about the father-son struggle in *Prometheus Unbound* must be considered in the light of Shelley's relationship with other figures of paternal authority. In fact, Shelley sought out a series of father figures in response to the bitter disappointment he had in his relationship with his own parent. He sought out Dr Lind, Captain Pilfold, Southey and Godwin. But with all, except Lind, he felt let down, and one by one discarded their influence and denounced their authority. My thesis has been that Wordsworth too fits within this pattern, and that *Prometheus Unbound* reflects particular aspects of this struggle and disappointment. Shelley, achieving simultaneously poetic individuation and a form to express it, 'creates' himself while putting down the restraining force he clothed as Jupiter. And it is the presence of Wordsworth that most strongly figures as a paternal and poetic father to be dealt with in the poem. Finally, to justify this claim, the degree to which *Prometheus Unbound* is about a poetic struggle must be determined.

V

The resolution to Prometheus's problem appears to be simple: he decides he is going to 'hate no more' (I. 57). But for this to be effective it must be put into words. (I. 69–73). More properly, the self-set curse of Prometheus (I. 262–301) must be unsaid to be undone (I. 58–9). (A curse is, literally, a *mis*use of words – bad words.) Thus the crucial notion in *Prometheus Unbound*, where power resides, is in the performative action of words, whether they take the form of voices, prophecies, curses or echoes. Voices lead; prophecies are made; curses are placed and undone; echoes repeat. The mechanisms for change are put in motion, and all through the power of utterance. Note how frequently speaking is invoked or referred to throughout the play. Appropriately, death is associated with the inarticulate (I. 183), and thus with uncreativity.

The action in *Prometheus Unbound* (remembering that ostensibly it is a 'drama') is not so much determined by the movement of the players, their physical action, but by their speech acts: their speech *acts*. The site of the poem's struggle is always language, speech, invocation.[20] Thus one strategy for authority is repetition – to say again (or even to say together, as in a chant or chorus or refrain) is not just to say once more: it is to add power and direction by referring not only to itself but to its original as well. This aspect of repetition is also a part of the cumulative nature of influence, just as it is part of the father–child/father–child relationship, each new son having not only his father's power, but his father's father's as well: Saturn → Jupiter → Prometheus. Every newcomer contains his precursor; every precursor continues to speak through his followers. This is to say that Prometheus must, as the offspring-poet, recycle the father-poet's poetry in his own verse. The themes of poetic individuation and the father–son conflict overlap considerably. It might even be put that the father–son conflict is the narrative construction through which the theme of poetic individuation is expressed.

Prometheus knows the power of utterance better than anyone else, but not just because he has been bound by his own words; for as his soul-mate Asia tells Demogorgon, it was Prometheus who in the first place

> gave man speech, and speech created thought,
> Which is the measure of the universe.
> (II. iv. 72–3)

And appropriately Prometheus's freedom is celebrated by the Earth's concise expression of the range of language's power:

> Language is a perpetual Orphic song,
> Which rules with Daedal harmony a throng
> Of thoughts and forms, which else senseless and shapeless were.
> (IV. 415–17)

What is important here is that Shelley gives speech and language priority over thought. Power and action are manifest in words; and it is through words that Prometheus is bound and unbound. And how is Asia to know Prometheus? Appropriately, she is to 'read his written soul!' (II. i. 110). Prometheus is a textual symbol for both utterance and writing, for the possibility of signification.

Shelley's emphasis on language doesn't have to be extended to see that he is discussing the re-creative power of poetry and the role of the poet. As Daniel Hughes has put it, what we have in *Prometheus Unbound*, especially in Act I, is 'the development of Prometheus as an increasingly capable poet in his difficult mastery of both word and image', which ends in the 'freeing of word and image'.[21] Hughes summarises Prometheus's stance by imaginatively paraphrasing him in the first person:

> I repent being a poet of merely defiant words; I repent answering Jupiter at his own level of language; I will give up such words so that I may discover a language freed from hate and capable of moving towards my release – : I will not be a bad poet.[22]

Hughes is correct here, and his method of expressing it is appropriate. But using his method of giving imaginative voice to Prometheus I would go in a slightly different direction:

> I have been a poet in Jupiter's shadow for long enough; I have used his words and they have used me; I must now work towards a form of poetic self-determination knowing that Jupiter has preceded me but failed in his poetic vision – : I will be an original poet.

Prometheus expresses Shelley's struggle for a new language of the sublime,[23] but the specific workings of the old sublime, its origins, are not specified. An implication behind this is that the 'curse' is the old poetic language, Jupiter's language, which Prometheus – as an unoriginal poet – merely threw back at him. To go beyond Jupiter he must not only repeat, but, as a new and radical poet, revise.

Prometheus as a poet is struggling against his own words and therefore against a part of himself (I. 302–5). This must be his primary, internal level of concern. His secondary and external level springs from the primary, and is against Jupiter, another part of himself, to whom he has given power (I. 273), challenged ('Friend, I defy thee!' – I. 262), and now must defeat in order to pursue his own goals and to establish his own poetic autonomy. Jupiter is invoked by Prometheus, and in this sense he is the creation of Prometheus; but he is, as Prometheus finally realises, the product of a corrupt imagination. The curse that gave Jupiter power (I. 262–301) is a corrupt poem that must be revised. A *new* language, a *new* poetry, is necessary to undermine that power. When Prometheus hears once more his loveless and hopeless poem recited by Jupiter's spirit, he is astonished that these were his 'words' (I. 302). They show no creative foresight, but only an immature vanity. What they implicitly embody is the line from Wordsworth that Shelley so strongly objected to: 'Carnage is God's daughter'.[24] Carnage can also be God's son; and if Prometheus wishes to avoid that fate he must summon another part of himself that is strong and mature enough to both correct and challenge Jupiter and the stifling uncreativity he represents. This is perhaps one of the reasons why Shelley introduced Demogorgon into his poem. He is a figure of defiant imagination confronting that which Prometheus at one time authorised: Jupiter as reigning influence. Demogorgon represents the re-creative inspiration of the successful poet-to-come, the 'voice unspoken' (II. i.191), and he is the supernatural and prophetic manifestation of Prometheus's new poetic strength. Shelley adding the final act effectively balanced the whole play by countering the corrupt poem. Further, just as Prometheus opened the play as a poet hoping for vision of creativity, the end of the added final act is Prometheus's newly created poetic strength, Demogorgon, reciting the new poetic vision of hope. 'All' wait for Demogorgon's first poem of the new age: 'Speak: thy strong words may never pass away' (IV. 553). Demogorgon becomes a sort of Zeitgeist. The opening vision, the opening poem, is at last answered and revised. In the final act Prometheus does not speak: he no longer has to, for now the poem and poet can speak for it-/him-self. Shelley may have added the final act just to advertise further (show off) his newly discovered poetic prowess and authority. The final act is nothing less than an overflowing of a new-found confidence.

The final act also adds another vision which suggestively conjures up Wordsworth's dismissal. It begins with the funeral procession of Jupiter's Time passing near the cave of Arts where Prometheus and the sister Oceanides dwell. The corpse of Time is being borne to his 'tomb in eternity' (IV. 9–14). But this is an 'eternity' which opposed the notion of immortality. Immortality suggests a positive remembrance or existence for the future; the 'eternity' that Jupiter's Time fades into is that of the dark and dead past (IV. 24–5, 39). Accordingly, the petals of flowers strewn on the corpse are of a particular type with which we are already familiar:

> Be the faded flowers
> Of Death's bare bowers

> Spread on the corpse of the King of Hours!
> (IV. 18–20)

The elegiac dismissal of Wordsworth in *Verses Written on a Celandine*, where the older poet is portrayed as a paled and desiccated flower, comes back to us. Here too Shelley uses this strong image of deterioration and change in an attempt to bury those moments of Jupiter's influence.

Jupiter has another function besides standing against Prometheus. He stands between Prometheus and Asia. *Prometheus Unbound* thus not only starts with the same background which marks the beginning of the end for the Poet of *Alastor*, but also falls within the same narrative pattern as *Alastor*, where the tyranny of solitude and uncreativity stands between the Poet and his 'veiled maid'. Both figures are poets; both want to be reunited with their female visions, which suggest a lost Muse of poetic creativity; both are strong yet gentle in character; yet both are to an extent naïve, just as Prometheus was in giving Jupiter power in the first place, just as the Poet was by thinking that he could, in solitude, successfully pursue his own vision of poetic perfection. But the Poet in *Alastor* is Prometheus still bound to the rocks, to his own curse; Shelley in *Prometheus Unbound* is still working on the same problem of 'freeing' his progagonist. (Even a few of the terms from the Preface to *Alastor*, which is a condemnation of Wordsworth's self-destructive form of idealising, anticipate particular devices used in *Prometheus Unbound*. 'The Poet's self-centred seclusion,' Shelley writes, 'was avenged by the furies of an irresistible passion pursuing him to speedy ruin.' This too is the intention of Prometheus's avenging Furies, only now, unlike the Poet in *Alastor*, Prometheus has the strength to resist. We also recall from *Alastor*'s Preface that an 'apportioned curse' is put on those who are loveless and who do not share human passion. The curse Prometheus unthinkingly puts on himself and mankind might also be said to result from selfishness.) What makes *Prometheus Unound* the first successful outcome for Shelley is that Prometheus and Asia (as symbol of completed imagination) actually *do* come together and *stay* together, unlike the failures of coupling in *Alastor*, *The Sunset*, *Prince Athanase* and *Julian and Maddalo*. He achieves this, literally, by evolving a new context, by reformulating new words from old words, not just by making a new poem from an old one, but by countering an old poem with a new one. These were his own words, echoed back to him by the spirit of his precursor, the

Phantasm of Jupiter. Once more, this is the power of repetition and revision when it encourages positive change. The unseen Spirits of the final act give an account of Prometheus' new poetic power:

> The pine boughs are singing
> Old songs with new gladness,
> The billows and fountains
> Fresh music are flinging,
> Like the notes of a spirit from land and from sea;
> The storms mock the mountains
> With the thunder of gladness.
>
> (IV. 48–54)

This suggests that a new poetic spirit has been introduced into the scene of poetry. What Prometheus as poet is doing is taking the 'Old songs' of his predecessor and giving them 'new gladness'. In this passage is even found the repetition of the image Shelley used in the *Defence* to describe how, in the scene of influence, one poem moves through time:

> A great Poem is a fountain for ever overflowing with the waters of wisdom and delight; and after one person and one age has exhausted all its divine effluence which their peculiar relations enable them to share, another and yet another succeeds, and new relations are ever developed, the source of an unforeseen and an unconceived delight.

Prometheus's poetry is 'Fresh music' which comes from this 'fountain' of poetic continuity.

In Prometheus's opening speech there is a strong image of the nature of the poetic transference taking place between Jupiter and Prometheus. In this case it is a negative transference. Prometheus speaks to Jupiter of how he has suffered in his enslavement, how he has been pierced by the ice of glaciers 'crawling' over him (I. 31–3). But this is not all that has penetrated his being. He also refers to Jupiter's eagle that daily visits him:

> Heaven's wingèd hound, polluting from thy lips
> His beak in poison not his own, tears up
> My heart.
>
> (I. 34–6)

Noteworthy here is that the eagle which shreds Prometheus's heart does something first: it dips its beak into the 'poison' from Jupiter's mouth. This accentuates the nature of the relationship between Prometheus and Jupiter. Specifically – and here this mouth-to-heart transference becomes more significant – this can be interpreted as the mephitic utterances of Jupiter influencing Prometheus's pain. The proverbial 'salt in the wound' becomes the anguishing remembrance of Jupiter's oratorical presence: every time he feels the pain he cannot but help be reminded of his master. Unlike Aeschylus's version of the myth which has Prometheus's liver torn out, Shelley prefers to have the eagle set upon his representative's heart, and of course the heart is Wordsworth's most powerful trope of feeling and emotion. But more striking is the image that parallels the act of writing. The beak dipped into Jupiter's poisoned mouth can only be likened to a pen dipped into a poisoned inkwell. And of course the instrument for writing in Shelley's day also has the appropriate ornithic association: the quill-pen. For the present study the workings of this image offers the fitting translation: some of the writings of Wordsworth sent to the heart of Shelley – a heart with a sensitivity learned from Wordsworth – caused Shelley great suffering which had to be overcome; Wordsworth's inked words deeply influenced (flowed into) Shelley's poetical being.

At the opening of the poem Prometheus is still bound to Jupiter's influence. Prometheus endures, unaware of the potential of his poetic power, not realising that his suffering can be ended by an act of revision. But Prometheus had to give power to Jupiter in order to test his own relative creative power (just as Wordsworth had to be emulated by Shelley for a time). By the end of the poem, after Jupiter has been used, he is set aside, *but not forgotten*. To forget his influence would be a bigger mistake than being enslaved by him. To remember (like to master) is to hold, and thus to have some stability; to forget is to let go, and thus to be vulnerable to the abyss, which can be read as a place symbol for eternal infamy and disremembrance.

By saying that Prometheus is assuming the power of Jupiter, the underlying premise must be that in some ways he is dependent on Jupiter, just as Shelley is dependent on aspects of Wordsworth, even though in both pairs the older figure is to be put down. There is in fact a strong instance of this in the spirit scene of the first act (I. 672–800), where a figure representing Wordsworthian sentimentality expresses a hope for Prometheus. Each of the six Spirits who come before Panthea, Ione and Prometheus – countering the Furies who have just vanished (I. 443–634) – enunciates an example of hope, recalling, none the less, a failure (intimating the failure of the French Revolution). The fourth of these Spirits tells of a poet who looks at nature but does not see it; instead, in his own thought he creates other forms, 'Nurslings of immortality!'. The Spirit tells its tale:

> On a poet's lips I slept
> Dreaming like a love-adept
> In the sound his breathing kept;
> Nor seeks nor finds he mortal blisses,
> But feeds on the aëreal kisses
> Of shapes that haunt thought's wildernesses.
> He will watch from dawn to gloom
> The lake-reflected sun illume
> The yellow bees in the ivy-bloom,
> Nor heed nor see, what things they be;
> But from these create he can
> Forms more real than living man,
> Nurslings of immortality!
> One of these awakened me,
> And I sped to succour thee.
>
> (I. 737–51)

This is part of the hope which will fortify Prometheus. It is also quite obviously strongly suggestive of the scene of Wordsworth's transforming imagination: it is the intro- and retro-spective poet who goes to the landscape or nature not to discover its beauty but to intimate a lasting presence (his own) which will defy the forces of mutability. Shelley's analysis of Wordsworth's mode of poetry is as succinct as it is accurate. Just the phrase 'Nurslings of immortality!' captures Wordsworth fostering a form of lasting poetic self; it also calls attention to Wordsworth's 'child' in the *Intimations Ode* who is both the poet's producer ('The Child is father of the Man') and the product of the poet (Wordsworth as poet revives the child's significance). This poet seeks immortal bliss. But how can such a positive rendering of Wordsworth take part in a poem which I am claiming to be about Shelley's ambivalence toward the older poet? The answer is relatively simple: Wordsworth once *did* represent the hope of the French Revolution and the redeeming power of the creative thought; Shelley *does* respect the imaginative strain in Wordsworth's early poetry. What aids the Spirit in aiding Prometheus is one of those transcendent 'Forms' which originated from Wordsworth's imagination, his 'lips'.[25] Appropriately, what is also outlined in this passage is Shelley's scene of poetic influence: the poet is both active and passive, receiving the outside world and combining his own being within to create new forms. But the point is this: Jupiter creates Prometheus as a revisionary poet, for without Jupiter to stand against, to defy and master, Prometheus remains recumbent and nonresistant. Regardless, then, of how negative Jupiter's force has been, Prometheus owes his new powers to his older adversary.

VI

Prometheus Unbound is about defiance, and it is about the clearing away of an old order and the establishing of a new origin through creative acts. But as much as this is a universal story, it is also a point in an individual history. The most radical conclusion I can come to, then, is that through the dynamics of his poem Shelley frees himself from a type of Wordsworthian prefiguration, a 'freedom long desired / And long delayed' (III. iii. 5–6). *Prometheus Unbound* is about the overthrowing of an older, uncreative figure of poetic authority by a younger, regenerative figure of authority, and this happens to parallel Shelley's problematic identification with Wordsworth. The father-son, precursor-progeny relationships which structure the poem induce us to these conclusions; so does Prometheus as a poet struggling against a language to which he was once bound, now only to revise and surpass it. Harold Bloom's theory of influence brings these two concerns (the father-son relationship and the production of poetry) together: 'To live, the poet must *misinterpret* the father, by the crucial act of misprision, which is the re-writing of the father.'[26] Wordsworth is, in this study, the 'father' who must be misinterpreted, re-written, yet always, ultimately, returned to.

The primary associations of the super-ego with the Oedipus complex also comply with this scenario. The rules or laws laid down by the primal, tyrannical father first of all restrictively govern the actions of the sons, in a sense confining their behaviour to imitation of the father; but inevitably the restrictions lead the sons to go beyond the father, to overthrow or kill him. The sons, of course, later become law-giving fathers themselves, repeating and passing the influence down. It is this continual father–son conflict which forms the psycho-dynamic basis of influence. And it is this conflict operating on a number of levels which is one of the dominating structures of *Prometheus Unbound*.

In reality, however, sons do not normally resolve the repressive aspects of their relationship with their fathers by killing them – that is, unless the restraining mechanism fails to check what would be considered potentially psychopathological tendencies. Neither of course do poets actually kill their predecessors, even if, as in the case of Wordsworth and Shelley, they happen to be contemporaries. There are other, more ingenious ways if the concern over influence is great enough, such as the revisionary ratios Bloom outlines in *The Anxiety of Influence*. Yet as I have pointed out, in Shelley's earlier portrayals of Wordsworth there are strong imagistic suggestions of the older poet's death. Indeed, this must be evidence not only of Shelley's anxiety about Wordsworth, but also of his strong ties to him. To hate the father he must first be loved. The desire for detachment comes only after attachment. Acknowledging authority is the precondition for assaulting authority.

Prometheus is interested in freeing man from common discourse in order to make a new harmony, which is Shelley revising and revitalising Wordsworth's language. This is the central passage in *Prometheus Unbound* where the new poetic project is voiced:

> We will entangle buds and flowers and beams
> Which twinkle on the fountain's brim, and make
> Strange combinations out of common things,
> Like human babes in their brief innocence;
> And we will search, with looks and words of love,
> For hidden thoughts, each lovelier than the last,
> Our unexhausted spirits; and like lutes
> Touched by the skill of the enamoured wind,
> Weave harmonies divine, yet ever new,
> From difference sweet where discord cannot be.
> (III.iii. 30–9)

These words are spoken by Prometheus as he outlines what he and the sister Oceanides are going to do in the cave of Arts. They are going to 'search' for progressively new and original 'combinations' in their work. But why is he retiring with these sisters? What do they represent? And why three? One possible answer may be to look at the other offspring of Jupiter. I am thinking of the Muses, those nine daughters of the King of the gods, three of whom represent poetry (Erata, Calliope, and Euterpe). Of course the idea of incest (Prometheus being a son-like figure to Jupiter) was nothing new to Shelley's idea of poetry: it had been included in the original version of *The Revolt of Islam* (*Laon and Cythna*) and was retained in his play *The Cenci*, which, perhaps significantly, was written in the period between composing the third and fourth acts of *Prometheus Unbound*. Shelley did consider incest 'a very poetical circumstance' (*Letters*, II, p. 154). And perhaps it should be pointed out that *The Cenci* itself is about the murdering of sons by their father and in turn the father's murder by his daughter. The play can be read as a description of debauched paternal love and the struggle for power. But more signifiantly, Count Cenci can be seen as a corrupt poet, and Beatrice as his poem.[27] Thus the two dramas, although different stylistically, share the same theme of the production of poetry in the presence of a dissipated authority.

My reading of *Prometheus Unbound* has depended upon maintaining that two orders of relationships govern the identities within the poem, plus of course the further identifications and circumstances being suggested outside the poem (that is, the difficult relationship Shelley had with his father and the substitute fathers he sought). Of the identities within the poem one has already been emphasised and named: the structure of the father-son relationship which primarily exists between Prometheus and Jupiter, and between Demogorgon and Jupiter as well. This structure complements the struggle over poetic power between Jupiter and Prometheus. The second order, partly described but not named, is the relationship existing between Prometheus and Demogorgon. (This was used to help establish the father-son relationship between Prometheus and Jupiter.) Demogorgon is created as the revisionary voice of Prometheus, the spirit of his summoned poetic strength and deep imagination. But this can be extended. Most obviously the Phantasm of Jupiter is the double of Jupiter. Further, and just as important, the Phantasm of Jupiter is also the double of Prometheus. It is not just that the Phantasm has the similar qualities of calmness and strength as Prometheus (I. 238, 259); more important, the Phantasm by repeating Prometheus's curse mirrors the Titan's own youthful image (I. 262–301) and is the agent of Prometheus's hate, the product of his will. Prometheus, after all, *selects* the ghost of Jupiter as his own representative double (I. 210–14).

What this last association suggests is that an aspect of Jupiter is an aspect of Prometheus. Moreover, Jupiter now seems to have no autonomous being, although earlier it was claimed that Prometheus is also dependent on Jupiter. As Prometheus said in his curse to Jupiter, 'I gave thee power, / And my own will' (I. 273–4). Prometheus willed himself to be put under the influence of Jupiter; he *created* Jupiter's authority, used it to his own ends, and finally achieved the sublime moment of poetic differentiation. And there is one final irony which reverses the father–son role, yet again emphasising the power exchange: Prometheus gave power to Jupiter in order that Jupiter might dethrone his own father, Saturn (II. iv. 43–6), yet Jupiter is given this power only to have it turned against him. So whereas above I said how Jupiter created Prometheus, Prometheus likewise creates Jupiter. In other words, in the poem Shelley wishes to show that the relationship between these two figures is one of radical interdependence. And although in the end Jupiter's authority is dismissed, Prometheus's accomplishment can never be evaluated except in terms of Jupiter.

But there remains one question to be answered by the logic of the poem's plot if it is to be maintained that the poem can be brought to Shelley's situation as a poet influenced by a poetic authority. If the old poem (the 'curse') was Shelley's in the first place, how can it be claimed that in *Prometheus Unbound* Shelley is revising something relating to Wordsworth's authorial presence? The answer is this: Shelley may be saying that his earlier poems are under the binding spell of Wordsworth's influence, to the degree of imitation. But now the time (the 'Spirit of the Hour') has come for him to go beyond these earlier 'words' in order to become free; and freedom is, in this context, equivalent to originality. In effect, he has given the 'words' back in order to give them up. Wordsworth is maintained in power (and Shelley in captivity) so long as Shelley does nothing revisionary about his earlier, admittedly Wordsworthian poetry. To break away from this power he needs a new voice, and this comes in the guise of Demogorgon, a force that can confront Jupiter as his progeny, and so as both his destroyer and his preserver. The logic of causation in *Prometheus Unbound* is thus deeply entwined with the principle of Necessity. It is Necessity's power that aligns Prometheus with the irresistible, immanent and unstoppable spirit of History. And so the paradox which becomes apparent by Prometheus's conspicuous absence in the final act, is that our hero has also experienced a sort of loss of selfhood that gave him power in the first place: he has had to give up his role of sufferer and perserver.

Appropriately this is parallel to Shelley's notion of influence, how aspects of a poet's originality are consumed by the greater forces of influence. *Prometheus Unbound* is about the strength necessary to invoke then overcome influence.

Shelley was now, at the beginning of his *annus mirabilis*, at last certain of his individuality and originality relative to his contemporaries. He could now give his central figure the successful outcome so long awaited and striven for. Recall what Shelley said about his poem, that he believed *Prometheus Unbound* to be original not only in the context of his own poetry, but in all poetry; his new poem is, he said, 'perhaps less an imitation of anything that has gone before it' (*Letters*, II, p. 116). In this light his Preface turns out to be a public apology for his own creative genius and new-found poetic autonomy. As such, it is an important part of the poem, not just in the history of the poem, but in the history the poem itself enacts. Shelley has in effect stolen Wordsworth's fire, and has paid the price of getting away with it: he is now original. But can he maintain his originality? He has in some ways escaped the influence which in the Preface he said it was impossible to escape from, but he has done so only by an incorporation and revision of that influence.

As Jupiter is at last put down, his final metaphor before eternal oblivion shows the drastic exchange in power between poets:

> I sink
> Dizzily down, ever, for ever, down.
> And, like a cloud, mine enemy above
> Darkens my fall with victory!
>
> (III. i. 80–3)

Do we again have to be reminded whose movement was also 'lonely as a cloud', and how Shelley sought unsuccessfully to follow that sublime? We think too of Prometheus's vision of Jupiter's 'self-torturing solitude' (I. 295). Now it is Shelley's turn, and it is Shelley who now attempts to overshadow the figure who once overshadowed him. And so what on one level is discontinuity, on another is repetition.

The subject that Shelley goes to is the Prometheus myth; the discovery is of himself as poet; the accomplishment is his poem. The problem stated clearly in the Preface is Shelley's need to establish himself as an original poet, free from possible charges of imitation. This too is part of Prometheus's problem. Shelley, in effect, wants to be Prometheus unbound. He wants to be free from the oppressive influence to which he was bound. Prometheus as Shelley's poetic self must find the 'words' so that he might be poetically creative. Jupiter figures in this as the binding and authorial influence of Prometheus's time. He holds the words. Thus he must be put down, his poetic power usurped, and Prometheus must reverse the order to take his sublime place above Jupiter. Jupiter is the negative force which urges or calls for a positive outcome; and that positive outcome is the imaginative and creative force of Demogorgon, who is at once the son of Jupiter and the active double of Prometheus.

From *Alastor* through to *Julian and Maddalo* Shelley has been unable to make a success of his protagonists – success, that is, in terms of outcomes for these figures. I have suggested that these central figures are in various ways and in varying degrees based on a problematic identification with Wordsworth and the protagonists in Wordsworth's poetry. Wordsworth might be described as a cathartic representation to Shelley, in that in a creative sense Wordsworth has been an outlet and purgative object for Shelley. I am also thinking of Bloom's revisionary ration of *kenosis*, which is an 'undoing' of the 'precursor's strength *in oneself*'.[28] This 'undoing' is the unbinding of Prometheus from Jupiter's 'strength', just as it is Shelley's attempted 'undoing' of Wordsworth's influence. Shelley is engaged in a father–son (precursor–progeny) conflict with Wordsworth; if Shelley is to become a kindred (as well as competitive) 'spirit of the age', it is natural that he must in some way emulate the age's strongest figure. But most important, he must surpass and attempt to break away from that figure.

The question I posed at the end of the previous chapter is still not fully answered: How is it, then, that a successful outcome for Prometheus is achieved, when those other central figures who represent Shelley's problematic identification with Wordsworth meet with disaster? If one were to ask what is the most curious adaptation in Shelley's revision of the Prometheus myth, it might be in having Prometheus give Jupiter power in the first place, only to take it away. What is the effect of this revision? What does this mean in terms of influence, in terms of Prometheus as a poet and Jupiter as the influencing force? Prometheus giving Jupiter power is Prometheus willing Jupiter to power. This is a severe invocation. In the scene of influence, to be influenced, one must first of all seek an authority to be influenced by. It is this retention of Jupiter by Prometheus that is so important; Prometheus *transfers* power to Jupiter and then *transfers* it back so that Jupiter lives on as part of Prometheus. In fact, there is the rather odd suggestion that the 'abyss' into which Jupiter was put down is the same cave in which Prometheus and Asia plan to live (II. iii. 1–10; III. iii. 10ff. and 124ff.).[29] But if we consider that both are poets, or that Prometheus co-inhabits the same imaginative space as his precursor, it makes sense that they should share that same cave of Arts with Muses of poetry. In this cave Prometheus returns to visit the dead. In Shelley's other poems invoking a Wordsworthian central figure this further positive transference was not effected, perhaps because Shelley was not ready to achieve poetic emancipation, or perhaps he had not discovered a plot strategy allowing for the further transference. Perhaps it is not until *Prometheus Unbound* that Shelley can so positively accommodate Wordsworth's influence. In other words, Shelley cannot totally accomplish his goal of poetic individuation until he has come to terms with Wordsworth, and *Prometheus Unbound*, I would hold, represents this coming-to-terms. In any case, the curious exchange between Jupiter and Prometheus allows Shelley now to express not so much an ambivalence, but an acknowledgement.

I come back once again to the terms Shelley used in a fragment in addressing himself to the problem of Wordsworth: 'Proteus Wordsworth who shall bind thee'. Shelley in effect answers 'I will', and through the reversal in the fates of Prometheus and Jupiter it is the older poet whom Shelley now binds, while he himself is unbound.

7
Righting Wordsworth

In the previous three chapters I examined how Shelley creatively contended with a poet figure which, it was shown, in various ways derived from an identification with Wordsworth and a struggle for poetic individuation. But Shelley's engagement with the older poet goes beyond the scope of these problems to the realm of ideas: to such problems as perception, memory, mutability and, of course, the problem of poetry itself. This chapter examines aspects of these problems in a number of shorter poems by Shelley, and considers the important relationship they have with some of Wordsworth's poetry.

I

Let me begin with a generalisation: Shelley sees how Wordsworth sees, but disagrees with how he sees, or at least with how he re-creates or expresses seeing. If Shelley was influenced by Wordsworth, then we would expect his poetry to be in some ways the 'corrective' to Wordsworth's. The response expected would range from imitation to what in psychoanalysis is called reaction-formation: an antithetical response based on a deep desire for likeness. An aphorism of Lichtenberg touches this: 'To do just the opposite is also a form of imitation.'

Both Wordsworth and Shelley imported aspects of their worldview and metaphysics from German philosophy. This system of thought (and accompanying style of expression) influenced how the English Romantics – but especially Coleridge, Wordsworth and Shelley – thought about things ranging from subject and object to the process of history. Most important, it posed the problem of relationships, in thinking, seeing and expressing. Potential disparity was often invoked in order to overcome the disparity. For Wordsworth, reconciliation of disparate or incongruous elements in his experience was often achieved by deferred acts of mind: Wordsworth retroactively creating conformity. But Shelley questioned aspects of this idealised, delaying mode, and he came to challenge Wordsworth's achievement of a poetic sublime on this point. Whether expressed in metaphors of mutability or inconstancy or the unknowable, Shelley's work often appears as various attempts to address the *on-going* flux, to become (or reflect) the motion, as it were, *between* and *surrounding* what he is attempting to describe. This can be seen when, for example, he gazes on Mont Blanc in an attempt to define not the mountain but its boundaries and the source of its inexplicable power, or when he appeals to a skylark: 'Thou art unseen, but yet I hear thy shrill delight'.

In his poetry Shelley doesn't muse on clouds, birds, mountains or leaves, though ostensibly they are his subject. Contemplation is not always an aim in Shelley's poetry, especially contemplation in an accepting or passive sense. Instead, for example, he summons and questions the source of movement, or the source of sound; and ultimately, and perhaps most importantly, the source and mode of his own creativity – in short, what inspires him. These external objects or presences become only points of references to something not-themselves: they are metaphorical, and as such are guides to (creating) relationships. It is never quite enough for Shelley to say, 'There it is'. He finds he has to question, 'What gives it "there-ness"?', and, most important, 'How is "there-ness" to be poetically expressed?'. Unlike Wordsworth he finds that he cannot always accept that the 'mind' as a trope is capable of bestowing 'there-ness' or certainty on relationships, of bestowing meaning. (Shelley is of course a sceptic in the Pyrronic mould.) It is not the case that Shelley denies meaning, but that he denies the constancy, limitations or immutability of *one* meaning. Shelley approaches a point where the figurative aspects of language have priority over meaning, the former being not a clothing for the latter, but its determinant. Shelley recognised the paradox that language is both banal and powerful, conventional and unstable, essential and arbitrary.

When I suggest that for Shelley metaphors are attempts to create referential relationships, however unstable they may be, I am also stating that Shelley believed language to have a life in-itself, and that poetry is the highest form of that life. It is no wonder that Shelley's poetic language tries so hard to 'break form' – this is Shelley pushing language to its limits in a necessary but ultimately futile effort to go beyond those limits. I would, in fact, maintain that Shelley went further than any of his contemporaries in attempting to do so, and perhaps further than any English poet. Of course there is a risk involved, a risk of pushing too hard or too far. Shelley's poetry has been accused of this from the beginning. The belittling view that Matthew Arnold had of Shelley in the nineteenth century was inherited in the twentieth by Leavis, Eliot and the New Critics: Shelley flew too high and burned those ineffectual wings of his. But at the same time his poetry attracted the positive emotional responses expected of music: this is Shelley's achievement of making the reflexive language of his poetry an experience in its own right – not necessarily an account of experience. The 'object' in Shelley's poetry is often language's own seeking. This is another way of saying that Shelley's poetry is about itself, about itself coming-into-being. Again, this ties in with the themes of uncreativity and poetic individuation running through the poetry I have already discussed.

But to 'break form' in his language Shelley had to be certain of achieving an excellence in architectural form. The highly accomplished structural elements in his poetry are often given only secondary consideration. In what Wordsworth himself once said about Shelley there is an awareness of both the positive and negative results of Shelley's risk, as well as an awareness of Shelley's superior formal craftsmanship: on one hand Wordsworth said, 'Shelley is one of the best *artists* of us all: I mean in workmanship of style', and he thought Shelley had the 'greatest native powers of all the men of this age'; yet on the other hand he felt Shelley's poetry fell by attempting to 'outsoar the humanities'.[1] It is interesting that both Arnold and Wordsworth described Shelley as a sort of high flier, the poet equivalent of Icarus.

When Shelley's poetry addresses itself to the problem of flux, of mutability and inconstancy, it attempts to both mime the flux through its language, and display an evanescence of that which inspires it. The trouble is that inspiration too is subject to these unstable forces. Shelley expresses the frustration in the *Defence*, saying that the creating mind is but a 'fading coal', and the resulting poetry but a 'feeble shadow' of its originating inspiration. Shelley's poetry can only make the most of this inadequacy by making the most of it in figurative language. Unlike Wordsworth, whose language offers a rhetoric of constancy, Shelley can only summon a dynamic or unstable rhetoric of shifting metaphors in order to approximate (in terms of his own analogies) as closely as possible the fully glowing coal, the originating shape of the shadow. When we find in Shelley's poetry the regressive metaphor – that is, one figure of speech falling back upon (an)other figures – this is Shelley searching for, as he calls it in the *Defence*, 'the before unapprehended relations of things'. Shelley is looking for that fleeting juncture when two things come together in an original relationship. For Shelley, this is the instant of inspiration that precedes the moment of creation.

Wordsworth and Shelley shared the same problem: the problem of creating effective poetic relationships, not only on a linquistic level, but on an epistemological level as well. They did not, however, share the same solution. (Shelley had the added difficulty: Wordsworth was part of both the problem and the solution.) Admittedly, to overcome disparity as Wordsworth did was one of the greatest creative achievements of the age, or of any time. But Shelley felt Wordsworth overcame it by a subjectively-produced illusion, a false strength, ending in the failure of *The Excursion*, where self-doubt becomes the poetry of hesitancy, inaction and compromise. The greater achievement, the achievement Shelley attempts in his poetry, is to positively and actively struggle with doubt and mutability – to allow questions the same status as statements, to give uncertainty the same value as truth, and to allow language at least the same right as meaning.

II

There is in a great deal of Wordsworth's best poetry a kind of curious logic, not hitherto unnoticed, but not always seen from the particular angle I wish to draw attention to now. That Wordsworth's poetic experiences are ostensibly based on remembered experience is well enough known. Yet is it not interesting that in *Tintern Abbey* Wordsworth returns to the banks of the Wye to remember what he felt five years before, although he claims that it is in fact recollection of these 'forms of beauty' that is the most sublime experience (23–50)? In other words, Wordsworth returns not to re-experience his experience, but to effect the experience of his memory, to recall remembering: thus, the 'picture of the mind revives again' (62), and not the picture of the Abbey. He apparently wants to establish his absence, not his presence. Accordingly, when we think of this poem we do not see Wordsworth actively in the landscape, even though the poem is (as the title tells us) about 'Revisiting' – moreover, revisiting a particular place on a particular month, day and year: 'July 13, 1798'. Transcendent or retroactive memory so dominates him, that while he is revisiting, he recalls what it was like to recall this spot. *Tintern Abbey* is neither much about Tintern Abbey nor about revisiting it; Wordsworth appears to be obsessed with not being where he is but where he was, *even when he is there*. He is, in one sense, revisiting his memory. Further, and perhaps more curious, Wordsworth goes back into the past only to become concerned with a state of being where he has not been, in 'after years' (138).

In *Tintern Abbey* Wordsworth handles his absence or dislocation through a subtle yet powerful rhetoric, although the logic of his experience borders on tautology. In the *Intimations Ode*, another poem that we know Shelley read closely, the struggle warrants more deliberate reasoning to finally reconcile absence (absence in this case being the sense of having left or 'vacated' something irretrievable: childhood). Just as absence in *Tintern Abbey* is represented by 'Revisiting', in the *Ode* it is by 'Recollection'. Both poems are based on the problems of repetition. Moreover, as Stuart Sperry has expressed the *Ode*'s logic, 'the type of recollection celebrated in the "Intimations Ode" is more the memory of a memory than a memory'.[2] Wordsworth begins by lamenting that he can no longer experience what he used to, and that 'there hath past away a glory from the earth' in the process of growing up (1–18). Yet by the end of the poem he is able to say that the 'years that bring the philosophic mind' (190) and the powers of recollection are superior to those glory-filled childhood years. How does Wordsworth make this jump? And does he make it successfuly, or at least convincingly? Similarly, in *I Wandered Lonely as a Cloud* the significance of the daffodils he gazes on in his original experience does not strike him in an immediate sense:

> I gazed – and gazed – but little thought
> What wealth the show to me had brought.
>   (17–18)

Only when Wordsworth is distanced from his experience, at a later time and different place, when through his poetry he has created absence, do those daffodils 'flash upon that inward eye' and his 'heart with pleasure fills' (19–24).

What becomes apparent by these examples is that Wordsworth gives cognitive experience priority over direct experience. Related to this, he portrays the directness of some of childhood's experience as primitive, unthinking, unconscious, as operating on emotive and instinctual levels. 'Childhood,' he says in the *Ode*, 'is the simple creed' (140–1), and a child is 'a Creature / Moving about in worlds not realised' (148–9). Likewise in *Tintern Abbey* Wordsworth recalls the 'coarser pleasures of my boyish days' and his 'animal movements' (74–5). Aspects of the landscape were to him merely an 'appetite'. But

> That time is past,
> And all its aching joys are now no more,
> And all its dizzy raptures.
>
> (77–86)

Childhood's robustness contrasts with adulthood's 'purer mind' (30), 'sober pleasure' (140), and the 'healing thoughts' (145) of recollection. Remembering that for Wordsworth the Child is also 'father of the Man', childhood comes to represent an ambivalent state: a source of pain and pleasure.

In *Nutting* (1800), which is arguably Wordsworth's most vigorous portrayal of an adolescent experience, Wordsworth hopes that his present feelings are not confounding those of his past. But one gets the feeling that in fact they are, that he is troubling to bridge his past experience with his present condition. His aim, of course, is one of understanding, of attempting to come to terms with his past experience, and by understanding it, hold it, fix it and maintain it. Only in *Nutting* this poetic reconciliation is not as successful as Wordsworth might want, perhaps because this particular experience (and the experience of writing about it) is more enigmatic than those of *Tintern Abbey* and the *Ode*. In fact, the imagery of *Nutting* is that of a (first) sexual experience, of rape even. The young Wordsworth sallies forth one day towards 'distant woods' with a 'nutting crook in hand'. Among the woods and rocks he went until he came to an unspoiled 'nook' where 'the hazels rose / Tall and erect, with milk-white clusters hung, / A virgin scene!' (13–20). Here, with 'suppression of the heart' and 'restraint / Voluptuous', he 'eyed / the Banquet' and fondled the flowers (21–5). He visualises an orgasmic scene with 'sparkling foam' (33). After a slight repose he records his action:

> Then up I rose,
> And dragg'd to earth both branch and bough, with crash
> And merciless ravage; and the shady nook
> Of hazels, and the green and mossy bower

Deform'd and sullied, patiently gave up
Their quiet being.

(42–7)

As Wordsworth thinks back upon this experience he now believes he feels that same 'sense of pain' (51), and is touched in the same way. But whereas in the *Ode* the rift between past and present is reasoned out, and in *Tintern Abbey* the distancing between experience and memory is allegedly shortened by actually being there, in *Nutting* the split remains, the crisis situation remains open as a result of the inexplicable nature of the experience as it is recollected. We are not nearly so convinced, first of all, that he feels the same way, and second, that he comprehends his past experience. It is only by comprehension that experience can be held – that is, held in check. Wordsworth does not really know what to make of his excitement in his 'merciless' ravaging of this 'virgin scene'.

Of course the danger of the enigmatic experience for Wordsworth is that the present may become displaced or disoriented in terms of continuity and significance, a fear of the possibility that no stylistic strategy or amount of poetic meditation can conjoin past with present, or even make sense of the past. A generalisation might be inserted at this moment about Wordsworth's poetry: it is most engaging when attempting to conciliate the inexplicable nature of past experience. The 1805 *Prelude* remains the best example of this. Unfortunately, *The Excursion* was the only long poem that Shelley and his contemporaries knew Wordsworth by. One can only speculate on the impact *The Prelude* might have had on Shelley, Keats and Byron.

A fitting image of Wordsworth striving to achieve poetic accordance between past and present evolves in his *Influence of Natural Objects* (1809). Once more Wordsworth speaks of an 'everlasting motion' which begins in childhood to 'build up our human soul . . . until we recognise / A grandeur in the beatings of the heart'(1–14). Because the poem spends more time describing past action than present contemplation of that action, it is more like *Nutting* than either *Tintern Abbey* or the *Ode*. In the end of the poem Wordsworth describes skating on a winter's evening until dizzy, 'as if the earth had rolled / With visible motion her diurnal round!'(59–60). Then the dizziness would subside, 'Till all was tranquil as a summer sea' (63). Like the 'dizzy raptures' of his boyhood in *Tintern Abbey* (86), this dizziness too is part of his past experience, a blurred or decentred vision of the world around him, while the tranquillity to follow is not just the regathering of his balance, but of his senses, of clarity of vision and the possibility of clear expression (yet there is an ironic hint that this dizziness presents an enhanced vision, since there is a perception of the usually imperceptible motion of the earth). No longer is he out of control. But the image of Wordsworth skating is an important one. He describes pursuing the reflection of a star upon the ice, 'flying still before me' (50–2). Of course no matter how fast or far he skates, the reflection 'still' (always) remains just out of his reach, yet it is 'still' (not moving). What is important is that he is chasing not a star, but its reflection. In effect, Wordworth finds that no matter how fast or far he skates, he can never recapture the star's reflection; but he can, through poetry, at least recapture the experience by reflecting on it. When he feels his past dizziness subside, his vision becomes 'tranquil'. The star of his memory is before him, to be captured in his recollection of trying to capture it. Again, the logic is as curious as the expression is ingenious.

In all of these poems, and in *Nutting* most enigmatically, Wordsworth strives to establish some kind of continuity between a number of related but normally antagonistic dimensions: direct experience and recollection of the experience; absence and presence; past (youth) and present (adulthood); dizziness and balance; experience and memory; action and cognition. To balance and make a smooth transition between these is one of the major logical problems in Wordsworth's poetry, to overcome dialectics to make continuities, to establish (create) permanence out of potential flux and mutability. On the surface, through the sheer effectiveness of his language, he appears successful in this struggle, or at least convincing. Thus poems such as *Tintern Abbey* and the *Intimations Ode* are his greatest triumphs, or at least his most convincing attempts. In fact, the success of Wordsworth's poetry depends on that problem existing – that is, the problem of creating and then reconciling antagonistic, perplexing or discordant dimensions. In Wordsworth's later poetry this problem *per se* disappears altogether, and I think the engaging quality of his poetry suffers accordingly. (This corresponds with the so-called 'decline' theory.) There is no longer any triumph because disparity is no longer his subject. Without a problem there is no tension, no struggle, no possibility of triumph. There are solutions without problems, answers without questions. This, we feel, will never do. Likewise Shelley.

III

As much as Wordsworth's rhetorical powers lie in his ability to reconcile disparities, given that it is one of the central projects of his poetry, Shelley's is in his recognition of the irreconcilability of disparities. Although working at the same problem, Shelley must have found Wordsworth's solution lacking, or perhaps superficially formulated. Inasmuch as Shelley felt there was a dynamic and necessary interchange between antagonistic properties, Wordsworth felt that one could always consume the other. This consumption is the function of Wordsworth's 'mind' and poetry as Shelley saw it.

The differentiation of childhood and adulthood is not as much a central issue for Shelley as it is for Wordsworth. Shelley is, however, just as interested in poetically exploring the various conflicting natures of experience. He is perhaps a little more difficult to come to terms with than Wordsworth in his pursuit of the subject, mainly because he 'fictionalises' more than Wordsworth and his language is more reflexive. It isn't easy to gauge whether Shelley is writing about actual 'experience', or whether the experience he appears to be writing about is creative experience. Evidence suggesting that some of Shelley's major poetry challenges Wordsworth's mode of reconciliation must be examined.

'Mutability', as Wordsworth wrote in *The Excursion*, 'is Nature's bane' (III. 458). Taken on its own, this appears to be one of Wordsworth's more radical pronouncements. That it is given to the Solitary to say makes it less so, since the Pastor and the Wanderer attempt to show by reason and example that, on the contrary, change is a harmonious process of constancy – moreover, it can (like Nature) teach moral lessons and offer a form of faith. In Shelley, however, change is reckoned to be a more inconstant thing, and loaded with doubt. Whereas 'power' in Wordsworth is often associated with the retentive nature of creativity – in the sense that the mind makes, then maintains, relationships – in Shelley 'power' lacks that idealising tendency, and 'power' is that which 'un-makes' relationships, differentiates, holds things apart, or at least lends scepticism to knowledge and experience. For Shelley 'power' is confounding; for Wordsworth it is discerning.

Of Shelley's poetry, his *Hymn to Intellectual Beauty* (written 1816) is perhaps his closest attempt at replication of Wordsworth's coming to terms with experience, especially the sort of experience expressed in the *Intimations Ode*.[3] Like Wordsworth, Shelley gestures to effect a continuity between his boyhood pursuits and his present state (between parts v and vi), but the problem of reconciling the power of the experience is inevitably a recognition of flux and doubt, rather than of process and faith.

The *Hymn* does not disguise its view of mutable 'Power':

> The awful shadow of some unseen Power
>   Floats though unseen among us, – visiting
>   This various world with as inconstant wing
> As summer winds that creep from flower to flower, –
> Like moonbeams that behind some piny mountain shower,
>   It visits with inconstant glance
>   Each human heart and countenance;
> Like hues and harmonies of evening, –
>   Like clouds in starlight widely spread, –
>   Like memory of music fled, –
>   Like aught that for its grace may be
> Dear, and yet dearer for its mystery.
>
> (1–12)

This 'power' is an omnipotent yet 'unseen' thing, coming to the world not in the Wordsworthian deeply felt sense of harmony and connection, but as a shadowy 'inconstant wing' and 'inconstant glance'. What it is, or what it appears to be, it is not – it is only '*Like*' other things, and mysterious things at that. In other words, it is only knowable (expressible) as a metaphorical construction, as a relationship between things that it is not, not the things themselves. It is the space between objects in relationship – between, moreover, the antipodes which enclose life itself: 'fear and dream', 'death and birth', 'love and hate', 'despondency and hope' (21–4). It is also the space between ways of knowing, between mystery and certainty. We might be able to differentiate subject from object, but we cannot really know what goes on between them to make them relative. Shelley, forming a question from Wordsworth's statement that 'The rainbow comes and goes' (*Intimations Ode*, 10), wants to know 'why the sunlight not for ever weaves rainbows', why things inevitably 'fail and fade' (18–20). In the same way

> Love, Hope, and Self-esteem, like clouds depart
> And come, for some uncertain moment lent.
>
> (37–8)

Shelley reluctantly notes that true answers to these questions (true reconciliation of these antipodes) have been given neither to philosopher nor poet; superstition has thus invented answers (25–9). All we are left with is 'Doubt, chance, and mutability' (31). A great number of Shelley's poems are discourses on this uneasiness yet celebrations of this mystery.

Uncertainty is the only certainty Shelley acknowledges in the *Hymn*. Those important human ideals ('Love, Hope, and Self-esteem') which we live by are uncertain. But Shelley is strong (or ingenious) enough to formulate something positive out of what potentially might lead to despair. The *Hymn* acknowledges the inevitability of inconstancy, and in this way Shelley develops a counter-strategy to work towards the 'immortality' Wordsworth intimates; he develops a strategy that *uses* the forces of mutability and inconstancy instead of attempting to pacify or sooth them.

In the *Ode* and *Tintern Abbey* Wordsworth differentiates the actions of his youth and those of his later years – specifically, that his youth was unthinking, and hence different in nature and purpose. Yet all is apparently reconciled by 'healing thoughts' (*Tintern Abbey*, 145). But Shelley in the *Hymn* deliberately seeks the same answers 'While yet a boy' (49) and 'even now' (63). Shelley, then, unlike Wordsworth, does not differentiate the project or action of his past from that of his present. Although there is in the *Hymn* a fleeting indication that Shelley, like Wordsworth, finds a form of continuity between the ages, it remains one of enigma (of common questions) rather than one of reconciliation (of past questions *with* present answers). For Shelley, both ages pose questions and seek answers; for Wordsworth, past experience poses a question that the present answers, or that the future will answer. Because for Shelley his past is non-differentiated from his present, his past in effect erases the temporal space it occupies; it does not, as in the Wordsworthian mode, create that space to be filled by retrospective memory or contemplation. So, although time outside of Shelley (external time) can be differentiated – morning from afternoon, autumn from summer – Shelley's poetic experience of time (internal time) is 'As if it could not be, as if it had not been!' (73–7). Time for Shelley is an emptying process; for Wordsworth it is a filling process. And 'Harmony' for Shelley is not something which, as in *Tintern Abbey*, in the moment of perception *connects* 'The Landscape with the quiet of the sky' (7–8). Neither is Shelley's 'harmony' one which, as in the *Ode*, gives

> Strength in what remains behind;
> In the primal sympathy
> Which having been must ever be.
> (184–6)

nor the 'harmony' which is the continuity between seasons.

The synchronisation of external time with internal time perhaps remains the achievement of 'harmony' which Shelley's poetry strives towards. To harness Time is to master Knowledge and Life. Shelley hopes, as it were, to make his own 'uncertain', 'inconstant' time to correspond with time outside of himself. He implicitly wants constancy and certainty. And the agent summoned for this task, to whom the *Hymn* appeals, is called 'Intellectual Beauty'. A great deal of time could be (and has been) spent speculating on the source and meaning of this phrase, but for the moment I will suggest that it corresponds with the production of poetry. In Wordsworth is the hope that poetry can create time; in Shelley is the fear that poetry can erase time. Both poets address the same problem, but whereas the older poet arrives at 'immortality', the younger poet falls on 'mutability' that intimates the silence of death.

Directly countering Wordsworth's notion of permanence that something 'Which having been must ever be', Shelley maintains that something which has been is 'As if it could not be, as if it had not been!' Again, the *Hymn to Intellectual Beauty* is Shelley's rendering of the problem of Wordsworth's *Intimations Ode*, but the repetition of the problem leads to opposite conclusions, opposite sentiments – a challenge over the functioning power of poetry. Perhaps the question in the back of the two poets' minds is this: Will Time (in the form of posterity) maintain the 'life' of my poetry, or will it be passed over, forgotten? The only future they might have, as poets, is their poetry. We know that Wordsworth was concerned that his poetry be as lasting monuments, and we also know how anxious Shelley was to join the greats. All poets seem to share the fear of being forgotten.

Besides the interpretation of the *Hymn* as a reworking of the *Intimations Ode*, the aspect of Shelley's poem I have been edging towards is one that brings together Intellectual Beauty and poetry. Poetry is, strictly speaking, the manifestation of Intellectual Beauty; and Shelley's *Hymn* to it is in hopeful praise of the production of successful poetry, for the ideal combination of imaginative perception ('intellectual') and aesthetics ('beauty'). Moreover, that 'unseen Power' that 'visits' in such an 'inconstant' way anticipates what

Shelley later says about the characteristics of poetic influence in the prefaces to *Prometheus Unbound* and *The Revolt of Islam*, and in the *Defence*. But it is also apparent that Shelley has not yet come to settle on a scene of poetic instruction. In the *Hymn* inspiration is but an idealised and enigmatic moment, something that only peripherally has a debt to the influences of tradition, society and the works of other writers. At this point it is a mysterious and voiceless (unvoiced) force, one that Shelley can only associate with pursuits of speaking to the dead. When Shelley gives the history of his pursuit of this 'high talk' (52), the significant change in Shelley's life is to suddenly have the 'shadow' of Intellectual Beauty inexplicably 'fall' on him (59–60). I read the resulting 'ecstasy' (60) as Shelley's recording of the moment of his first genuine poetic inspiration. The resulting vow that he takes is that he will henceforth continue (61ff.) to employ and liberate this inspiring power. In short, he says he will dedicate his life to Poetry. Shelley wants his new words to proliferate, to always go beyond what his present 'words cannot express' (72). He does not want the inspiration to stop: he wants the 'power . . . to my onward life supply / Its calm' (78–81).

This calmness that Shelley invokes for his 'onward life' follows in the wake of that same tranquillity that Wordsworth moves towards in the *Ode* and *Tintern Abbey*. Shelley wants, if he can, to share in this peace of mind and piece of posterity. He does not want his poetry to stop. Again, this is both his hope and his fear. To regress would be to move towards voicelessness and silence. To spread the word, to scatter or disseminate the inspiration of poetry to all, would be an act of universal reformation. It would acknowledge him, the poet, as a legislator. Shelley's *Hymn* is an interesting poem because, while undermining Wordsworthian permanence, it invokes Wordsworthian tranquillity.

IV

Wordsworth's *Intimations Ode* and Shelley's *Hymn to Intellectual Beauty* set out respective theories of poetic experience. In the same way, and as a balance to this, Wordsworth's *Tintern Abbey* and Shelley's *Mont Blanc* can be seen to represent the practice of those theories, since both are ostensibly based on actual encounters. That is, in these poems both speakers make on-the-spot claims of presence. (Note the similar claims of presence made in the titles: Wordsworth's poem is *Lines Composed a Few Miles Above Tintern Abbey*, and Shelley's poem is *Lines Written in the Vale of Chamouni*.) Both poems, however, in their most crucial passages, appear to think through thinking-through, although Shelley reverses or undermines Wordsworth's order by beginning his poem with the mind rather than with the landscape.

Important too is the development in Shelley's poetry in those seven or eight months between *Alastor* and the achievements of *Mont Blanc* and the *Hymn*. The change is not so great as that between *Queen Mab* and *Alastor*, but rather there can be seen a more specific and controlled application of the ideas and imagery sounded in *Alastor*. What I am concerned with now is how Shelley's grasp of Wordsworth in the *Hymn* and *Mont Blanc* aids him in his quest for poetic maturity.[4] Critics have noted that *Mont Blanc* is Shelley's version of the Wordsworthian poem of Nature, and specifically that *Tintern Abbey* acted as a model for Shelley's poem. They mean, of course, that *Tintern Abbey* acts as both model and and anti-model.[5] Jean Hall in particular has outlined the differences between the poems: how the movement in *Tintern Abbey* is gentle, gradated and smooth, while *Mont Blanc* is abrupt and uncontrolled; how *Tintern Abbey* proceeds by empirical and natural logic, while the logic of *Mont Blanc* is abstract; how Wordsworth's poem outlines a harmony with Nature, while in Shelley's poem there is a discontinuity with natural forms. In short, while Wordsworth's steadfastness allows him to make transitional manoeuvres, Shelley's questionings bring him to radical and 'transformational' moments.[6] But before some of these conclusions are considered in more detail, I will turn to a closer examination of Shelley's text and its probable origins.

First of all, Part I of *Mont Blanc*:

> The everlasting universe of things
> Flows through the mind, and rolls its rapid waves,
> Now dark – now glittering – now reflecting gloom –
> Now lending splendour, where from secret springs
> The source of human thought its tribute brings
> Of waters, – with a sound but half its own,
> Such as a feeble brook will oft assume
> In the wild woods, among the mountains lone,
> Where waterfalls around it leap for ever,
> Where woods and winds contend, and a vast river
> Over its rocks ceaselessly bursts and raves.

This passage has become famous, or infamous, ever since Leavis used it in a comparison with Wordsworth to demonstrate the 'bewildered confusion' characteristic of Shelley's poetry. More specifically, Leavis says that in this passage 'The metaphorical and the actual, the real and the imagined, the inner and the outer, could hardly be more unsortable and indistinguishably confused'.[7] Confusing, yes; but confused, no. Yeats more fairly pointed out the problem when he wrote that the poem is 'so overladen with descriptions in parenthesis that one loses sight of its logic'.[8] The logic is there, only it is imagistic rather than syllogistic logic. But Shelley would have agreed with Leavis. This is just the point he wants to make: it *is* difficult to sort out the real from the imagined, the inner from the outer.

Although the image in this opening section appears to be one extended metaphor, the 'waves' and 'waters' and 'river' are *not* part of one body of water, or any water for that matter. In fact, there are three different waters. More exactly, there are three over-lapping but discontinuous metaphors referring to water within the framework of the continuous water imagery. David Simpson correctly points out that what is generally difficult about Shelley's poetry is that the 'succession of metaphors is . . . organized so that, more often than not, they "interfere" with one another'.[9] And as Harold Bloom has said about the opening of *Mont Blanc*, 'Shelley is not content to describe the second term of his metaphor in its own particulars, but rather alternates its presentation by extensively looting the components of the suppressed first term.'[10] It is Simpson's 'interference' and Bloom's 'looting' that must be recognised and delineated in the opening section of *Mont Blanc*. I believe there are three distinguishable but interdependent metaphors at work.

In the first metaphor Shelley expresses how the 'everlasting universe of things' going 'through the mind' (1) moves like the dynamic nature of waves, as if the universe were a sea or vast body of water; (2) how these waves (as indicators of the universe of things) can enter the mind and withdraw from it (roll up/in/out); and (3) how these waves are 'dark' or 'glittering', 'reflecting gloom' or 'lending splendour'. What Shelley has said in this first metaphor (call it the wave metaphor) is that the universe of things going through the mind is a continuous and variable action, yet it is a dynamic *inter*action of mind and universe.

The second metaphor (beginning 'where from' and ending 'half its own') can be called the spring metaphor. Here is where the confusion can begin, for are the 'secret springs' the 'source' of the waters of which those waves in the first metaphor are composed? Is it the same water? The answer is made difficult because of the prepositional link 'where from', which can be read as either a literal or abstract joining. But it remains helpful to temporarily separate the two metaphors, for the wave metaphor is descriptive of the universe/mind relationship, and the spring metaphor centres on the mind's contribution to perception. What can be said, however, without maintaining a strict demarcation between these two metaphors, is that the spring metaphor is an aspect (even category) of the wave metaphor, determined by the words 'where from'. Shelley here is saying that the mind is both a receiver and sender, end and origin: a spring is both an outlet *and* a beginning. The 'sound' a mind hears is created half by itself (inside/subject) and half by (or from) the 'universe of things' (outside/object). Shelley's concern is with that grey area where overlapping and interaction takes place.

The third metaphor, beginning 'Such as', is a fuller explanation of the spring metaphor by being a part of the spring metaphor, so that in effect it acts as a metaphor for a metaphor. Again, this is confusing in that we might mistakenly take the brook as coming from the spring, instead of being only *illustrative* of the spring metaphor. This final brook metaphor presents the idea of two different but related 'sounds' or forces contending with each other – one sound originating from the brook (the 'mind') and the other from the waterfalls, etc. surrounding it (forces of the 'universe'). All of the 'things' in this metaphor (the brook, woods, mountains, waterfalls, winds, river, rocks) are part of one connected picture, but within the matrix of the picture, within the imagined process taking place, to make it *work* or *flow*, the 'forces' work for and against each other with various strength and varying contribution: the woods with the winds, the river with the rocks, and the brook with the waterfalls. Each is in effect 'half' of the other, but more important, each is dependent on the other. Without the woods moving the winds would be invisible, and without the winds the woods could not move; without the rocks the river could not burst or rave, and without the river the rocks could not cause bursting or raving. And so the sounds the brook creates, like the sound 'human thought' brings to perception, *appears to be* only 'half of its own' – the other half *appears to be* dependent on the outside world: without the mind the universe could not exist, and without the universe the mind could not exist. Shelley repeats this idea in the form of a question in the last lines of the poem.

In short, the 'waves' originate from the universe of things outside the mind; the 'springs' originate in the mind; and the 'brook' is to the rest of the overpowering landscape as the mind is to the overpowering 'universe of things'.

There is one important implication here to be taken up regarding Wordsworth's process of perception as Shelley interpreted it. Wordsworth, as Shelley reads him, makes the mind's workings the most powerful agent in perception, more powerful than what it actually perceives. That is, the Wordsworthian 'mind' would dominate what Shelley's calls the 'universe of things'. Conversely, in *Mont Blanc* there is the suggestion that the mind is dominated by the 'universe of things'. In this way the opening section of *Mont Blanc* is a sort of parody of Wordsworth's model of the Man–Nature relationship.[11] The 'brook', which is the symbol for what human thought brings into the landscape, is 'feeble' relative to the leaping 'waterfalls' and bursting 'vast river'. Shelley, then, questions his model and rejects Wordsworth's form of idealism; he says that his mind influences less than it is influenced. This is consistent with the idea Shelley later develops of the scene of influence in the prefaces to *The Revolt of Islam* and *Prometheus Unbound* as well as in the *Defence*. As we saw in the first chapter of this present study, Shelley holds that the individual's contribution is important to the flow of the greater influence, but at the same time it is consumed or overwhelmed by the greater accumulative (and accumulating) power of influence. The 'universe of things' holds the same power relationship to the mind as the 'spirit of the age' holds to the individual poet: the 'universe of things / Flows through the mind' just as the 'spirit of the age' flows through the poet.

Like Bloom's revisionary ratio of *clinamen*, in the opening passage to *Mont Blanc* Shelley swerves towards and away from Wordsworth, attempting to delineate how in fact *he* sees, what part of his perception originates from the subject, and what part from the manifold objects, the universe. What partly causes confusion is that Shelley employs what we would expect him to see (rivers, woods, etc.) as a series of tropes for what he actually does go on to 'see' in the rest of the poem. The point he makes is a valid one, one of limitations and origins: we really cannot tell where the outside world ends and where the inside world begins. Shelley at this point in the poem only knows that this interaction as a process is continual ('everlasting', 'forever', 'ceaselessly') and continuous (flowing and rolling), and that man (and man's expression of this experience) is subject to this fluctuating movement. That is, man is not only subordinate to Nature, but also at the mercy of his perceiving and creating mind. It is at this last point that an engagement with Wordsworth takes place, the implicit comment being that the older poet is too often a slave to his own mind.

The opening section of *Mont Blanc* has an origin in *The Excursion* which directly takes up this problem of perception:

> Faint, and diminished to the gazing eye,
> Forest and field, and hill and dale appear,
> With all the shapes upon their surface spread.
> But, while the gross and visible frame of things
> Relinquishes its hold upon the sense,
> Yea almost on the mind itself, and seems
> All unsubstantialised, – how loud the voice
> Of waters, with invigorated peal
> From the full River in the vale below,
> Ascending!
>
> (IX. 60–9)

Shelley re-engages some of Wordsworth's phrasing:

The Excursion	*Mont Blanc*
'the gross and visible frame of things'	'The everlasting universe of things'
'the voice / Of waters, with'	'Of waters, – with a sound'
'full River'	'vast river'

In situation too there are similarities. At this point in *The Excursion* the Wanderer is discussing growing older, how direct perception diminishes and 'Relinquishes its hold upon the sense', and how usually we say that 'Man descends into the VALE of years'; but the Wanderer argues that we could also describe ageing in other terms, of ascending to 'a final EMINENCE' where one can look 'Down from a mountain-top' (49–59) and be 'disencumbered from the press / Of near obstructions' (69–80).

In *Mont Blanc* Shelley follows Wordsworth by looking to the summit of a mountain also to imagine his presence there where the winds silently 'contend' (134–5) – beside, as it were, Wordsworth's elevated place (sublime). But Wordsworth's motives, to regain 'Fresh power to commune with the invisible world' (IX. 86), are taken either one step forwards or one step backwards by Shelley: Shelley's aspirations too are for 'power', but he doubts that such 'power' is accessible at all (96–7). What exactly this 'power' is can only be speculated on: it is only 'there' (48, 127, 132). Shelley is concerned that he might, somehow, learn from addressing this 'power' by having his own poet's mind's witness and partake of its influence. 'Power', in fact, as Shelley uses it in *A Refutation of Deism* (?1812–3), is related to the imagination's creative potential: 'The word *power*,' Shelley says, 'expresses the capability of anything to be or act.' What is at the centre of *Mont Blanc* is Shelley's attempt to understand how the 'mind's imaginings' (143) work in this 'awful scene' (15) of influence. We know that for Shelley influence works both ways (that is, the poet is both influenced and influencing). Thus we know better what Shelley means when he says that 'Thou hast a voice, great Mountain' (80): the poet and the mountain bring each other into being by utterance. The relationship of vitality passing between them is what Shelley calls 'fast influencings' (38). We also know that in Shelley's scene of influence the force of influence is more powerful than the individual's own contributions. It is a pervasive force, and not at all unlike the inescapable force of the glacier which flows down from the heights of Mont Blanc, levelling all in its path. In short, the mountain is a symbol for the enigmatic source and power of influence.

The poet brings the mountain into being through his utterance, while the mountain brings the poet's utterance into being by its presence. There is no explicit privileging in this relationship, only an instantaneous exchange of influence, although the mountain is the more powerful. A biological metaphor might be appropriate: the poet and the mountain have a symbiotic relationship: they 'live' off each other. In *Mont Blanc* Shelley is asking a deceptively simply question: How can I differentiate myself from what I see? This question is, in fact, the problematical centre of Shelley's ontology. The mountain makes Shelley exist as much as Shelley makes the mountain exist. And the poem is also an expression of a poetical concern: What is my status as a poet overwhelmed before the force of influence?

Although the opening passage from *Mont Blanc* has origins in *The Excursion*, there is in *Tintern Abbey* a further model which establishes both the language and the idea of Shelley's poem (this is, arguably, the poem's most important passage):

> And I have felt
> A presence that disturbs me with the joy
> Of elevated thoughts; a sense sublime
> Of something far more deeply interfused,
> Whose dwelling is the light of setting suns,
> And the round ocean, and the living air,
> And the blue sky, and in the mind of man,
> A motion and a spirit, that impels
> All thinking things, all objects of all thought,
> And rolls through all things. Therefore am I still
> A lover of the meadows and the woods,
> And mountains; and of all that we behold
> From this green earth; of all the mighty world
> Of eye and ear, both what they half-create,
> And what perceive; well pleased to recognise
> In nature and the language of the sense,
> The anchor of my purest thoughts, the nurse,
> The guide, the guardian of my heart, and soul
> Of all my moral being.
>   (94–112)

Shelley derives from Wordsworth the description of 'things' as *rolling* in or through the mind. Shelley also follows Wordsworth by using the same objects ('woods', 'mountains', etc.), and by noting that these exist not only as things in themselves, but also as created 'half' by 'human thought'. Shelley is attempting to see, or at least think about seeing, in the same mode as Wordsworth. But when these passages are placed within their respective poems, Wordsworth is found to believe that the poetic memory of perception has a reconciling, even moral effect (103–12), whereas Shelley cannot take himself so far from the immediacy and inconstant power that his perception brings to the moment. Hence Wordsworth implores that 'wild ecstasies' mature into 'sober pleasure' (139–40), while for Shelley his 'wild thoughts' (41) remain to the very end of the poem precariously posed as questions of absence and dependency:

> And what wert thou, and earth, and stars, and sea,
> If to the human mind's imaginings

> Silence and solitude were vacancy?
> (142–4)

Both Shelley and Wordsworth open up the possibility of a discursive space by their obstinate questionings, but whereas Wordsworth can fill that space and re-construct what he has pulled down, Shelley cannot, leaving what he has pulled down in an eternal state (but not stasis), of deconstruction, of other questions on the periphery.

Three interrelated notions dominate *Mont Blanc*: mutability, the unknowable and impermanence. These end up being formulated against *Tintern Abbey*, where stability, knowledge (or faith) and immortality form the basis of Wordsworth's experience. Wordsworth says that in his darkest and most doubtful moments he can address his memory of the 'sylvan Wye' (50–8), and formulate a 'tranquil restoration' (31) and 'Abundant recompense' (89). What will last, what can be poetically created and held for the remainder of his years (and beyond), is a lasting inscription of 'sober pleasure'. Shelley finds in the mountain an awesome but ultimately untouchable form of permanence, but for man mutability is its ever-present anti-companion. As he addresses Mont Blanc, all moments become moments of doubt, of eternal impermanence and change. These qualities determine and limit not only mankind's efforts but animated nature's as well: 'All things . . . / Are born and die; revolve, subside, and swell' (92–5). Before the force of the mountain's glacier 'man flies far in dread; his work and dwelling / Vanish' (117–20). What can be learned from this? Only that we are instructed in a paradox of inconstancy:

> The wilderness has a mysterious tongue
> Which teaches awful doubt, or faith so mild
> (76–7)

Shelley controverts the kind of knowledge Wordsworth says Nature teachers. For Wordsworth, Nature

> can so inform
> The mind that is within us, so impress
> With quietness and beauty, and so feed
> With lofty thoughts.
> (*Tintern Abbey*, 123–9)

It is both consoling and consolidating. For Shelley, looking at the inaccessible power of Mont Blanc, even Nature itself is overwhelmed. The powerful presence of the mountain, the unstoppable force of the glacier, overpowers both Man and Nature. Before the mountain the poet stands, and his efforts to know the source and nature of this power emanating from the mountain only lead him to question his own place in the 'awful Scene'.

As mentioned earlier, in *Tintern Abbey* Wordsworth begins in the landscape and works towards the mind, while in *Mont Blanc* Shelley begins with the mind and works towards the landscape. This can be put in a more interesting way: Wordsworth begins his poem with an affirmation of his presence; Shelley ends his poem by questioning his presence. Shelley begins where Wordsworth left off, in the space Wordsworth cleared but illegitimately filled, and negatively ends where Wordsworth positively began; and in the process Shelley alters and questions the poetic sublime. Through this metalepsis he completes Wordsworth by going beyond Wordsworth to the older poet's own beginnings. So although the poem is 'corrective' of Wordsworth, suggesting the first of Bloom's revisionary ratio of *clinamen*, *Mont Blanc*'s relationship to its precursor poem *Tintern Abbey* also seems to correspond with Bloom's second revisionary ratio of *tessera*, where completion and antithesis are the dominating characteristics.[12]

It is interesting to compare Shelley's account of how he composed *Mont Blanc* with Wordsworth's more famous description of how he composes. In the Preface to *History of a Six Weeks' Tour*, Shelley said that *Mont Blanc* was

> composed under the immediate impression of the deep and powerful feelings excited by the objects which it attempts to describe; and as an undisciplined overflowing of the soul, rests its claim to approbation on an attempt to imitate the untamable wildness and inaccessible solemnity from which those feelings sprang.

Wordsworth explains his mode of producing poetry in the Preface to the *Lyrical Ballads*:

> I have said that Poetry is the spontaneous overflow of powerful feelings: it takes its origin from emotion recollected in tranquillity: the emotion is contemplated till by a species of reaction the

tranquillity gradually disappears, and an emotion, similar to that which was before the subject of contemplation, is gradually produced, and does itself actually exist in the mind. In this mood successful composition generally begins.

Shelley obviously had Wordsworth's description in mind in relating how *Mont Blanc* was written. Not only does this further confirm Wordsworth's influence on *Mont Blanc*, but it shows again how Shelley's thinking and writing uses but confronts that of his precursor. Once more Shelley challenges the tactics of deferral and control that Wordsworth employs in the production of poetry. Shelley, following Wordsworth, is interested in the recreation of the original experience; but whereas Wordsworth appears to be once removed from the experience, Shelley attacks the immediacy of what he feels. Wordsworth, in effect, makes a logical *comment*, and therefore creates a discourse on aspects of control; Shelley makes an intuitive *response*, and therefore can only reflect the flux of his reaction. Shelley's makes the Arve the counter-symbol for the type of flow that Wordsworth finds in the Wye. The 'sweet inland murmur' of the Wye in *Tintern Abbey* (4) seems to facilitate (or even imitate) the 'tranquillity' that Wordsworth transforms in the moment of poetic composition. Shelley's Arve, on the other hand, is like the impressions that it leaves: it is powerful, enigmatic, wild and unknowable. Shelley cannot, like Wordsworth, tame his creative response any more than he can tame the Arve. In questioning the source of the Arve's power, Shelley is thus questioning the source of his own inspiration, and that inspiration derives in an important way from his problematical response to Wordsworth. Both Shelley and Wordsworth were inspired by Nature, but whereas for Wordsworth Nature mitigates, comforts and consoles, for Shelley it agitates, challenges and intimidates.

Wordsworth and Shelley appear very different in their poetic processes. But evaluations of this difference are often made on a qualitative basis. The anti-Shelleyan argument is that Shelley never reached the heights of Wordsworth's achievement, or Shelley's outlook is that of a rather rambunctious young poet compared to the outlook nurtured by Wordsworth through his years of firm contemplation. But both of these suppositions are incorrect. First, Shelley *inherited* Wordsworth's highest achievements and attempted to build from this point. For example, as I have shown, one of Wordsworth's most dramatic endpoints, the Solitary of *The Excursion*, became the starting point for the long line of Shelley's heroes, beginning with the solitary Poet of *Alastor*. Second, remember that the Wordsworth who was the emulated precursor for Shelley was not an old man who through his maturity achieved a sounder vision than Shelley: the Wordsworth who wrote *Tintern Abbey* was just a few years older than the Shelley of *Mont Blanc*, and thus the inspiration exerted by Wordsworth's presence is more immediate than might be supposed.

Along with *Intellectual Beauty*, *Mont Blanc* is the watershed for Shelley in his rewriting of Wordsworth. *Alastor* remains Shelley's first long engagement with the authority of the Wordsworthian poet figure, and *Verses Written on a Celandine* is his most important personal consideration of Wordsworth's status. But in these other two poems Shelley for the first time explicitly expresses the difference in his approach to poetic experience. What remains as the continuation of his project is a reworking of the symbols willed down to him, to rework (un-do) the old symbols into new and potent symbols. Shelley from this angle is equally the antithesis of Wordsworth and his continuation and repetition. And remember that for Shelley this is not just a self-centred concern, or a completely personal engagement with Wordsworth; for in Shelley's gropings with influence he shows his genuine concern with the fate of the Tradition. Thus his working on Wordsworth is simultaneously his encounter with the burden of the past, his commitment to the contemporary scene and his obligation to the continuity of a particular style of poetry.

V

Mutability is one of the most active concepts in Shelley's poetry. Things are essentially unknowable and inconstant; Life, and all of its aspects, is surrounded by irreconcilable and antagonistic elements. Being so, man's world is frail, precarious. On one level man and his achievements are at the mercy of the enveloping counter-forces of Nature. *Ozymandias* (1818) is Shelley's most famous and concise expression of man's frailty and the irony of impermanence. On the other hand, man's world of ideas – politics, philosophy, religion and so on – is just as frail: values given (by being given) are bound to be taken and mistaken; power established is destined to be ursurped; all ideology is subject to contradiction. As Shelley states in his sonnet *Lift Not the Painted Veil* (1818), the path man walks down is a dangerously narrow one, bordered and defined by his 'twin Destinies' of hope and fear. The problem is to somehow work between these counter-forces and with the surrounding inconstancy and contradictions. And the poet's problem is to somehow enunciate this instability through language, itself a shifting and problematical construction. Shelley more than any of his English contemporaries poetically posed a dialectical world view. In Shelley's mind, of course, the greatest error one might commit – though the error is to some extent the most predictable of human errors – would be either to patch up or to fail to recognise the problem dialectics posed, either by a defensively patterned personal vanity or by posing artificial answers to unanswerable questions. Religion was of course Shelley's favourite example of the latter. For Shelley, then, doubt and scepticism, are, for better *and* for worse, man's lot. The former, personal and poetical vanity, may have been the error that Shelley felt Wordsworth made, where the older poet constructed a language and logic to compensate for the separation and contradictions of word/thing, subject/object, past/present, hope/fear, joy/sorrow, etc. Thus, the poet-protagonist of Shelley's *Oh! There Are Spirits* (1816) is instructed *not* to 'chase' the perfectability of relationships, and he is told that no 'hope' can be found 'On the false earth's inconstancy'. His only recourse to action is, as Shelley tells, him, to 'Be as thou art' – in other words, to go on, struggle on, regardless of the inconstancy and the denial of answers. This is the most authentic course of action.

What kind of beings are we then? *Mutability* (1816) attempts to answer the question. But as in the *Hymn* we can only note what we are by analogy, what we are *like*. 'We are,' Shelley says, like restless clouds, variously speeding and gleaming, quivering and 'Streaking the darkness radiantly!' But our radiance is inevitably subject to its antagonist, darkness, and is 'lost for ever'. We are also like disharmonious 'forgotten lyres' which give 'various response to each varying blast'. Even our daily, mundane activities are bordered by contrary yet repetitive states: 'We rest' and 'We rise'. So too are our emotional states enclosed by opposing natures: 'We feel . . . or reason, laugh or weep'; we feel 'joy or sorrow'. Shelley's conclusion is:

> Man's yesterday may ne'er be like his morrow;
> Nought may endure but Mutability.
>
> (15–16)

As opposed to Wordsworth, who formulated that man's yesterday may indeed be reformulated as his 'morrow', Shelley holds that changing and opposing forces govern the expression of our experience. But at least there were some moments when Shelley could come to positive terms with the problem: Shelley's *The Cloud* is in fact a playful tribute to mutability.

By 1821 Shelley's idea had changed very little. In another poem entitled *Mutability* he notes that

> The flower that smiles to-day
> To-morrow dies;
> All that we wish to stay
> Tempts and then flies.
> (1–4)

And in 1822 the same idea is expressed once more:

> When the lamp is shattered
> The light in the dust lies dead –
> When the cloud is scattered
> The rainbow's glory is shed.
> (1–4)

Shelley sees change as the process of breaking-up, of splitting and polarising. Here today, gone tomorrow – so the saying goes. Everything is precarious. In *When the Lamp Is Shattered* Shelley notes 'The frailty of all things here'(22). Even 'Virtue', he says in the 1821 *Mutability*, 'how frail it is!'(8). Man's most glorious work is reduced to a 'shattered visage' in *Ozymandias* (4). So too do our personal worlds crumble:

> All things that we love and cherish,
> Like ourselves must fade and perish.
> (*Death* (1820), 12–13)

So says Prometheus: 'What can hide man from mutability?' (III. iii. 25). Wordsworth too expresses the personal experience of change and the frailty of man's work, plus the lack of control the individual has; but through the project of his poetry he was able to fashion a compensating mind to fill, as it were, the gap, to pick up the pieces of shattered lamp and rekindle its flame, not in the lamp but in his mind. And in Nature Wordsworth could perceive qualities of composure and amity. Shelley questioned Wordsworth's form of idealism that could overcome such contingency.

Considering Shelley's viewpoint that has just been outlined, it might be assumed that Shelley's poetry is fraught with despair. In some of his poems this is true. The poet-heroes in many of his narrative poems die because of the failure of expression, and they die without answers, direct gain or hope. Similarly, a good number of his more lyrical poems pose unanwered or unanswerable questions, or at least end by waiting on the present moment for the next indeterminable one to arrive.

In *To a Skylark* (1820) Shelley again listens for an answer, this time, so it seems, literally. The poem's problem is to make the Skylark into something which can be listened to and understood – hence, something knowable and something to give an answer. But Shelley discovers he can only deal with the bird in his own apparently inadequate terms (his poetry) and in his own time; and so the Skylark can only remain unknowable, an intuition of feeling. Like the 'Power' in the *Hymn to Intellectual Beauty* (1–2), it too is 'unseen' (20).

Shelley takes less than a third of the poem to reach the inevitable conclusion: 'What thou art we know not' (31). Significantly, as in the 1816 *Mutability* and the *Hymn*, Shelley can only approximate a question based on metaphor: 'What is most *like* thee?' (32 [my emphasis]). Answering the question, we are told the Skylark is 'Like a Poet hidden / In the light of thought', 'Like a high-born maiden / In a palace tower', 'Like a glow-worm golden / In a dell of dew', and 'Like a rose embowered / In its own green leaves' (36ff.). But these are not, as Leavis has said, 'a mere tumbled out spate ("spontaneous overflow") of poeticalities, the place of each one of which Shelley could have filled with another without the least difficulty and without any essential difference'.[13] On the contrary, Leavis is unable to discern the common factors in each, namely, the elements of concealment and unacknowledgement. The significance of these I will point out shortly.

The problem of temporal certitude expressed in Shelley's other poems is now expanded:

> We look before and after,
> And pine for what is not.
> (86–7)

An antagonism of responses remains our only lot:

> Our sincerest laughter
> With some pain is fraught;
> Our sweetest songs are those that tell of saddest thought.
> (88–90)

Shelley hails the Skylark, notes that it is unknowable, yet wants to be taught the bird's state of knowledge so that the world will listen to his poetry. The bird is, in one important sense, the type of successful visionary poet that Shelley wants to be, an expresser of 'profuse strains of unpremeditated art'(5).[14] Thus Shelley was to write nine months later in the *Defence*:

> A Poet is a nightingale, who sits in darkness and sings to cheer its own solitude with sweet sounds; his auditors are as men entranced by the melody of an unseen musician, who feel that they are moved and softened, yet know not whence or why.

Shelley may have changed the species of bird in this passage, but not the idea. In this passage from the *Defence* Shelley is describing the ideal Poet both as a bird and as an 'unseen musician'; in the *Skylark* he is describing the 'unseen' bird as an ideal Poet – moreover as an ideal Poet on the brink of inspiring an ideal listener. The significance of the concealment and unacknowledgement metaphors which occupy a central position in the poem is now apparent. The first metaphor is the key: the Skylark is

> Like a Poet hidden
> In the light of thought,
> Singing hymns unbidden,
> Till the world is wrought
> To sympathy with hopes and fears it heeded not.
> (36–40)

Shelley here clearly anticipates the penultimate sentence in the *Defence*: 'Poets are the unacknowledged legislators of the World.' And in *To a Skylark* he has voiced both the joys and frustrations of the poet's situation, of his own situation as a poet on the brink of being heard, acknowledged.

Shelley wants to effect an impossible transference of overflowing creative power, although Poetry at least offers a moving statement of the impossible. This is how the poem ends, with Shelley listening, his ear toward a hope for a poetic future, listening for the soaring voice of inspiration. But there is no hint of any answer, only an eternal anticipation held within the framework of the poem. The Skylark thus represents the paradoxical situation of poetic creation: it is not only a symbol for spontaneous poetic aspiration ('unpremeditated art'), but also for the uncertainty of that moment of inspiration to come, which is the future's potential for hope as well as for fear, for song as well as for silence.

There is the ironic suggestion in *To a Skylark* that although Shelley is asking for poetic perfection and an altered state of experience, the latter perhaps motivated by altruism, he is not listening to the Skylark with the belief that he will actually be answered, but with the belief that waiting for an answer to the unanswerable is the only state that poet and man can experience: we 'pine for what is not'(87), yet we nevertheless pine. That is why there is pain in laughter, why 'sweetest songs' have 'saddest thoughts'. The whole point of *To a Skylark*, that is, to *be* as a skylark, is ironically undermined by Shelley:

> Yet if we could scorn
>   Hate, and pride, and fear;
> If we were things born
>   Not to shed a tear,
> I know not how thy joy we ever should come near.
> (91–5)

If we were to be unlike that which we are, then the proximity to 'joy' (which is the intended experience of the poem) could never be felt. Paradoxically, if we were as skylarks, actually *were* skylarks, then we could not experience the joy of experiencing the Skylark. Thus Shelley here acknowledges and exalts these limitations of creative and imaginative empathy, yet denies any total transformation as both illogical and poetically self-defeating. Shelley realises the former is the very limit of poetic experience, although the latter, in the face of impossibility, is what the Poet strives for. The Poet may state the impossible, but ultimately his state is impossible. The Poet's fear of success is as great as his fear of failure, perhaps greater. On the edge of Shelley's logic is this: if he could 'sing' like a skylark then he would not longer be able to write poems to a skylark.

The motivating problem behind Shelley's poetry would disappear. Just as uncertainty is a productive state, so limitations are a challenge to ingenuity. And Shelley's ingenuity is to address these limitations as poetic qualities.

Shelley's *To a Skylark* in some largely ignored but important aspects is modelled on Wordsworth's *To the Cuckoo* (1807). The most striking feature Shelley employed is the idea that the bird remains an 'unseen' yet important presence (20). In Wordsworth's poem it is an 'invisible thing', 'never seen (15, 24). Accordingly, in both poems the birds are *voices* (*Skylark*, 27; *Cuckoo*, 4, 16). Even the famous opening two lines of Shelley's poem:

> Hail to thee, blithe Spirit!
> Bird thou never wert,

can be traced to the *Cuckoo*: 'O Blithe New-comer! . . . Even yet thou art to me / No bird' (1, 14–15). But Shelley offers a revision of Wordsworth's poem. Predictably, the Cuckoo offers a way back to Wordsworth's 'schoolboy days' (17), to an ideal past, as well as to an ideal future:

> And I can listen to thee yet;
> Can lie upon the plain
> And listen, till I do beget
> That golden time again.
> (25–8)

Shelley's Skylark offers, however, a different direction, an impossible hope for inspiration: he wants the bird to teach him so that 'The world should listen then – as I am listening now' (101–5). Both birds act as teachers; but whereas Wordsworth's encounter with the Cuckoo becomes another discourse of self-reflection and discovery, as well as a hope for the recovery of the past, Shelley's Skylark holds forth an as yet unvoiced potential for Shelley to produce harmonious poetry.

When Shelly wrote his poem he knew very well that he would also be drawing attention to his poem relative to Wordsworth's poem of the same name (1807). But this obviousness had led commentators to pass over the important relationship between the two poems, and to ignore what Shelley may have had in mind when deciding to take up (take on) Wordsworth's subject. I would hold that Shelley's poem was motivated by Wordsworth's poem, in the sense that by his poem Shelley might not only align himself with the older poet, but also, that he might voice his differences and exhibit his poetic superiority. We can be assured that Shelley was as familiar with Wordsworth's *To a Skylark* as he was with some of the other poems in the 1807 volumes, notably, *I Wandered Lonely as a Cloud*, the *Intimations Ode*, *Resolution and Independence* and the Celandine poems. Either Shelley's memory of Wordsworth's *Skylark* was excellent, or else he had recently read it for the explicit purpose of composing his poem. Peacock tells us that Shelley was in fact 'fond of repeating' Wordsworth's poem.[15] The parallels in diction suggest that Shelley purposefully employed some of Wordsworth's key words in order to playfully (ironically) demonstrate his poetic mastery of the master. In Wordsworth's poem the Skylark in 'Pouring out' (24) its song is full of 'madness' (12), 'joy' (12, 25; 'Joyous': 16), and 'gladness' (29), yet it is 'scorning' and 'laughing' (17); the poet, in the end, hopes that what he learns are 'higher raptures' (31). Similarly, in Shelley's *Skylark* the bird 'Pourest' (4) its song, full of 'gladness' (101), 'joy' (15, 95; 'joyance': 76), and 'rapture' (65), and it too is a 'scorner' (100); in the end, the poet hopes that the bird's song will invoke a 'harmonious madness' (103). Wordsworth's Skylark is told 'thy song . . . is strong' (2); Shelley's bird is told 'thy voice is loud' (27). Besides these telling but relatively unimportant Wordsworthian re-usages, Shelley more significantly employed the idea of the skylark as a mode of instructor, to aid the poet in being like the bird: twice Wordsworth asks the bird, 'guide me' (6, 14); likewise Shelley asks the bird, 'Teach me' (101). But here the positive modelling ends. Wordsworth's poem finishes:

> Alas! my journey, rugged and uneven,
> Through prickly moors or dusty ways must wind;
>   But hearing thee, or others of thy kind,
> As full of gladness and as free of heaven,
> I, with my fate contended, will plod on,
> And hope for higher raptures, when life's day is done.
>   (26–31)

The Skylark here satisfies the poet's purpose to 'plod on', reminding him that there is, after all, some 'hope for higher raptures'. But the end of Shelley's poem –

> Teach me half the gladness
> That thy brain must know,
> Such harmonious madness
> From my lips would flow
> The world should listen then – as I am listening now.
> (101–5)

– prevents any further movement forward, and the poem concludes in a state of eternal expectation. There is no 'fate contented' in Shelley's poem. It is at once a more joyous and yet more despairing vision. Wordsworth's 'journey' has an end in sight, and the Skylark has a knowable voice and use that can be transferred to the poet's purpose, if only as a symbol of support. Shelley controverts this knowledge, and that singing voice remains seductively, perhaps frustratingly, just beyond the poet: he can only wait and listen with great expectations. The poem at this point becomes an act of creative suspension. For Shelley the Skylark is a symbol of aspiration, of the kind of prophet-like voice the poet strives to assume and disseminate to the world. Again, the bird can be seen as a model for the 'unacknowledged legislator'. The poet is inspired by a figure of poetic perfectibility, and in this important sense *To a Skylark* follows directly the theme set in *Alastor*. The bird, like the veiled maid, is a symbol for unattainability and the fleeting nature of poetic inspiration. The Poet of *Alastor*, had he survived the negative encounter with his veiled maid, could certainly have written *To a Skylark*.

Shelley's implicit criticism of Wordsworth is that in the older poet's work he sometimes makes emotional or temporal transformation without acknowledged or genuine appeals for inspiration, and without any aspects of empathy. This is another way of expressing the egotistical poetic constructions that Shelley (as well as Keats) felt to be flawing Wordsworth's imagination. Because Shelley intuits that Wordsworth's goal is an imaginative transformation, he is attracted to Wordsworth's poetry; but at the same time he is distracted by the means by which transformation is accomplished. In this way Shelley's affinity to Wordsworth is also his separation from him.

VI

Whatever Shelley sees, feels, or notes, he simultaneously sees, feels or notes its opposite. Likewise, and by the same logic, he realises that whatever man constructs is doomed to destruction. (This is not to say that Shelley's poetry is pessimistic: through the principle of Necessity Shelley sees forms such as evil/good and construction/ destruction as repeating stages. And Shelley's notion of perfectibility is not something which can necessarily be achieved, but is something which is continuously worked towards.) This is Shelley's way of expressing limitations – what might be called the 'boundaries' within which man exists and experiences, and within which the poet composes. This is why mutability and inconstancy are the conditions of man's world and the creation of poetry, given that contraries and opposing forces are forever redefining and reshaping those conditions. Poetic language as it works toward the impossibility of constant meaning also becomes but a nebulous formation. Man's position is not distinguished or apart from this process, although he necessarily strives for exception and distinction in order to help define what is life. The ideal man, the ideal poet, is one who can survive yet acknowledge this flux – to do so is to be as the flux; to move with it is to be influenced. As Shelley points out in *An Exhortation*, the poem that Shelley said was an 'excuse' for Wordsworth (*Letters*, II, p. 195), the ideal poet should be like a chameleon, capable of adapting not only to change, but also *with* change: that is why, he writes, 'never think it strange that poets range' (17–18). Some poets, that is. Shelley sees Wordsworth not as a chameleon, capable of progressive change and creative sympathy, but as a lizard. Shelley also expresses this in *Peter Bell the Third*, where in a note to the poem he describes Wordsworth as a victim of a 'circumscribed sensibility' – circumscribed in the sense of being creatively confined and limited. As far as Shelley was concerned, the only changing Wordsworth performed was in his diminishing poetic and revolutionary zeal.

Insecure creatures that we are, our abstract anthropological constructions, whether called history, philosophy or religion, are attempts to come to terms with our fears of forgetting, meaninglessness and death. Poets too attempt to ward off what they fear most, and their constructions, poems, are likewise attempts to create monuments of one sort or another. Wordsworth might be said to be the English poet most overtly concerned with these problems, with the construction of lasting monuments which might take his written presence into the future, whether the device within the poem is an epitaph, a leech-gatherer, or the poet's reflection in his sister's eyes.

The reconciliation of those things which he confronted in his efforts –Nature, inexplicable experience, forgetting – led him to evolve that comforting trope he called his 'mind'. His subtly expressed logic gave 'mind' priority over all else, and in this he quietly celebrated. Thus we in turn celebrate Wordsworth for naming us a way. Shelley, influenced by Wordsworth's engagement with this problem, questioned the realm of the older poet's power and this priority. What Shelley celebrates in his poetry are forms and formulations of impermanence. Wordsworth by comparison stated that his project was

> To seek in man, and in the frame of life
> Social and individual, what there is
> Desirable, affecting, good or fair,
> Of kindred permanence, the gifts divine
> And universal, the pervading grace
> That hath been, is, and shall be.
> (*The Prelude* (1805), xii. 39–44)

The last line of this passage – 'That hath been, is, and shall be' – becomes another line with the same intention in the *Intimations Ode*: 'Which having been must ever be' (186). And so we saw Shelley ironically adapt this line with opposite conclusions: 'As if it could not be, as if it had not been!' (*Intellectual Beauty*, 77).

For Shelley, Wordsworth was part of the flux of impermanence. He was part of the problem of trying to hold on to things before they change. This is what Shelley's poetry on Wordsworth is about. Wordsworth was part of the 'everlasting universe of things' that variously flowed through (influenced) Shelley's mind, that was at once an agonising trope of splendour and gloom. It is possible, as I have suggested at some points, to read most of the poems discussed in this chapter as Shelley's difficult management of influence and inspiration. I have noted in this study only the crucial factor of Wordsworth's contribution to this inflowing. I will conclude, then, with a poem that brings these images and problems of influence together.

8
The Wind of Inspiration

I

It has been argued that some of Shelley's poems are about the figure of the poet and production of poetry, and that for Shelley the production of poetry necessitates taking and combining with external forces, which for Shelley are predominantly literary forces. This claim could, perhaps, be made about any poet; but in the case of Shelley it is a claim that he himself makes, not one that we, as interpreters, are required to impose or assume. Shelley, aware of influence, writes about influence. Wordsworth, it so happens, is a singularly important part of this in-flowing.

My effort, then, has often been to show that some of Shelley's best known poetry is about influence, and directly related to the problems of creativity and inspiration. For Shelley, inspiration (that transitory moment preceding the creative act when the pervasive force of influence touches the poet) is always a problem – not just how to find inspiration, but how to maintain and retain its fleeting powers, how to translate influence into that formal creative mode known as poetry. I could be more to the point: Shelley's poetry is often about poetry coming-into-being, which is the problem of the poet coming-into-being. Shelley's poems are allegories of poetic creation. But the latter can be traced most deliberately in the solipsistic tribulations of the Poet of *Alastor*, through to the poetic distress of the Maniac in *Julian and Maddalo*, and to the liberation of creativity in *Prometheus Unbound*. The former, the subject of poetry coming-into-being, can be seen as being most forcibly presented in such poems as *Mont Blanc*, the *Hymn to Intellectual Beauty* and the ode *To a Skylark*. But again, these two concerned are one and the same: ode *To a Skylark* is as much about the poet coming-into-being as *Alastor* is about poetry coming-into-being.

Shelley's awareness of influence as an inescapable force and his ambivalence towards originality led him to both commend and condemn his precursors. Thus poems like *To Wordsworth*, *Verses Written on a Celandine* and *Peter Bell the Third*, where that precursor is Wordsworth, go in those two directions of praise and reproach. This awareness also led to Shelley's engagement with prevalent poetic ideas which were, for example, the Wordsworthian achievements of immortality, permanence and immutability. Because for Shelley the poet in the scene of influence is both an active and a passive being, the active side is always in the process of questioning and revising those ideas, sometimes complementing, sometimes correcting. Shelley reacts to the Wordsworthian poet-figure in the same way: he wants to use it, even emulate or become it; but he also wants to challenge aspects of its authority.

Shelley's awareness of influence can be traced in one of the dominating images in his poetry (and some of his prose): that of moving air, whether it be wind or breath, and often accompanied by the Aeolian harp motif of air moving through inert elements to create sound or effect.[1] It is natural moving air should be a symbol for the creation of poetry. Wind signifies movement – moreover, movement that is pervasively felt and heard, yet is unseen: it is thus akin to both a spiritual presence and magical power. Utterance is the poet's wind, and every poet is touched by the wind of other poets. Accordingly, the Latin for breath is *spiritus*: hence *inspirit(ation)*. And in Hebrew the same word is used for both wind and spirit (*ruach*). There are similar examples in other languages: *atman* (Sanskrit), *anima* (Latin), and *pneuma* (Greek). Inspiration in the creative sense, in the sense of the production of poetry, is thus metaphorically determined by the movement of air. Life and Poetry become the same thing, and, by extension, so do Death and Inarticulation. When Shelley speaks of that 'spirit of the age', he is speaking of the inspirational breath of the age, the creating wind that blows across the face of his own time. I am saying, in other words, that Shelley often uses breath/wind imagery to represent the *inspirational* circumstances of producing poetry. What I wish to pursue now is a reading of Shelley's *Ode to the West Wind* as his most important and agonising allegory of poetic influence and inspiration. The *Ode* poetically enacts Shelley's ultimate desire to be the legislating poet. But before engaging in such a reading, it will be useful to look at some of Shelley's poetry which associates wind/breath imagery with the production of inspired poetry.

II

Inspiration overlaps with influence in an important way. According to *The Concise Oxford Dictionary*, 'inspiration' is 'divine influence, especially that which is thought to prompt poets'. Shelley was aware of this usage. For example, in his *Song of Proserpine* (1820) 'Mother Earth' is asked to 'Breathe thine influence most divine' (4). More familiar is the final stanza of *Adonais*: 'The breath whose might I have invoked in song / Descends on me' (LV. 487–8). And of course there is the invocation to *Alastor*, where the Narrator waits for the 'breath' of his 'Great Parent, that my strain / May modulate with murmurs of the air' (45–6). The Poet of *Alastor* seems in some ways to be the precursor of Adonais. But whereas in the later poem Shelley takes on the task of praising the dead Adonais, for the Poet of *Alastor* no poet 'Breathed o'er his dark fate one melodious sigh' (58–9). No poet was present to breathe life into (resuscitate) the Poet, to revive or give him positive inspiration – in short, to immortalise him. But then again Shelley's poem itself fills that lack: it is *inspired* by that lack. *Alastor*, a poetic success about poetic failure, immortalises the failed Poet.

The wind/breath/Aeolian harp motif goes back at least as far as *Queen Mab* (1812–13). Queen Mab's appearance is like a 'wondrous' spell of poetry ('strain') heard by a visionary poet ('enthusiast'), and likened to both the sound of the 'west wind' and the music produced by an aeolian harp (I. 45–53). Yet this usage in *Queen Mab* is not directly tied to the notion of influence and inspiration, especially since the 'enthusiast' is left without the response we are looking for, namely the activity of writing poetry. But by the end of 1814 Shelley could write to Mary: 'I am a harp responsive to every wind' (*Letters*, I, 418). This is perhaps Shelley's first explicit description of the poet as an influenced being in these terms.

Alastor employs the device of moving air very deliberately.[2] Not only is the Narrator dependent upon the 'breath' of his 'Great Parent' to inspire his poem, but before he was inspired he describes himself 'as a long-forgotten lyre / Suspended in the solitary dome' (42–3) – the Narrator remains unproductive and motionless without the breath of poetic life. So too does the Poet, but he searches for a vision of inspiration, and he believes he has found it in his encounter with the veiled maid whose 'voice' was like the 'woven sounds of streams and breezes' (153–5). She plays on a 'strange harp', her 'breath' harmonising with the song (165–72). Suddenly 'she rose', and in the 'breath of night' he sees her 'limbs beneath the sinuous veil / Of woven wind'; and after some 'shuddering', 'gasping' and 'panting' they yield to the 'irresistible joy' and frantically intermingle (172–87).

The veiled maid can be none other than a seductive vision of poetic inspiration. She is the voice and music of the harp, and appropriately it is with her breath that the Poet so frantically desires an interchange, yet the maiden leaves the Poet 'breathless' (186) – that is, without the power of inspiration. The journey in *Alastor* allegorises a poet's quest to recapture a moment of poetic inspiration.

The Poet's search for the veiled maid is determined by the movement of air. It continues in a small sail-boat, guided urgently by the wind (309, 317, 320) until a calm spell and a 'wandering stream of wind, / Breathed from the west' (397–8). In the distance he hears a sound of a 'ghastly torrent' mingling 'its far roar, / With the breeze murmuring in the musical wood' (402–3). When the Poet begins to realise that the vision cannot be found, he foresees his death: 'my bloodless limbs shall waste / I' the passing wind' (513–14). The wind passing him by is inspiration passing him by: if a poet's life is dependent upon inspiration, then without it poetic death (silence) is imminent. It is for this reason that, as he makes his way toward this appointment with barren uncreativity, the 'green groves, with all their odorous winds / And musical motions', depart from his path (536–9).

When the Poet reaches the precipice where silence will take his life, a lone pine blasted by the wind marks the spot, while close by a river falls into an abyss, 'Scattering its waters to the passing winds' (561–70). This solitary tree images the solitary Poet. It is just able to survive, barely hanging on to the precipice of life while the unsympathetic wind rips through its boughs. Again, the winds are described as 'passing' – that is, not engaging. Yet in this scene the precipice and the pine 'were not all; – one silent nook / Was there' (571–3). The 'nook' reminds us of an open coffin, and its surroundings, with its fallen rocks', 'fissured stones', and 'Ivy', intimate an ancient or decrepit graveyard (572–86). Here too is where 'every gentle wind, whose breath can teach / The wilds to love tranquillity' comes to stay (586–8).

Finally, when death is almost upon the Poet, 'the very winds . . . / Slept, clasped in his embrace' (607–9). The Poet futilely tries to cling to life, and just before he dies he opens himself up

> To images of the majestic past,
> That paused within his passive being now,
> Like winds that bear sweet music, when they breathe
> Through some dim latticed chamber.
> (629–32)

But it is too late. *Alastor* ends with the Narrator eulogising the Poet, remembering him as a 'fragile lute, on whose harmonious strings / The breath of heaven did wander' (667–8). The Poet was both too sensitive and too inward-looking.

But why is the Poet unsuccessful in his quest for poetic inspiration? The answer is almost too simple – simple, that is, if we are aware of Shelley's idea of influence. The Poet's failing is that, in his unswerving drive for recreating the perfect poetic vision, he has fashioned *to himself* his own influence. He by-passes those necessary external forces and outside contacts (for example, the 'Arab maiden', 129–39), and thus the winds in the end either pass him by or pass through him without merging with him. Remember that Shelley believed that a successful poet must *combine* his own internal being with these external influences in order to create. This the Poet of *Alastor* does not do. The inspiration he creates (in the form of the veiled maid) is self-centred, delusional, and predictably barren of positive creative values. Shelley states as much in the Preface when he states that the Poet is no longer influenced by the 'external world'. He deceives himself into believing that it can no longer satisfy him. This is his fatal error. He forgets that 'it is not to be exhausted'. What I have claimed in this study is that this Poet who is self-centred in his inspirational life, glorifying his own created vision, owes something to Wordsworth's egotistical mode of imagination as interpreted by Shelley.

Mont Blanc continues the imagistic association of moving air and influence. In the previous chapter it was noted how the opening section of the poem is about how the mind is influenced by the 'universe of things' that 'flows' through it. Other passages take up the motif. Shelley gazes at the mountain and records what happens to him, how his 'mind . . . renders and receives fast influencings' in a continuous 'interchange' with the 'universe of things around' (34–40). This is, as Harold Bloom and others before him have noted, suggestive of the Aeolian harp which makes its fluctuating music by the inconstant movement of the wind.[3] This is how Shelley sees his own poet's mind working: it is in part passive (in the sense that it is acted upon), but it is also active in that it combines (interchanges) with the external 'influencings'.[4] For Shelley, 'The wilderness has a mysterious tongue', and the 'great Mountain' 'hast a voice' (76–83). In other words, these are presences that *speak*, that influence us.

And then there is the powerful force of water that originates from Mont Blanc. This 'River' carries its vital flowing influence ('breath') to 'distant lands', and spreads it through the atmosphere (120–6). Mont Blanc itself becomes a trope for the powerful force of influence; and it fulfils this role simply because it has inspired this poem called 'Mont Blanc'. It has breathed its voice on Shelley, and Shelley has combined with it, creating a new poem. The 'interchange' between the poem and the mountain is that each has brought the other to life. The uncertainty in the poem is not just whether the inspirational 'power' of the mountain is accessible, but whether this 'power' even exists without the poet's own powers. The poem's subject, then, is really itself. Shelley is not so much looking up to the peak of a mountain, but is writing towards that point called the poetic sublime.

In the *Hymn to Intellectual Beauty* the image continues, though not quite so pervasively as in *Mont Blanc*. The Spirit of Intellectual Beauty is said to give 'grace and truth to life's unquiet dream', like 'music by the night-wind sent / Through strings of some still instrument' (33–6). More important, at that point in the poem when Shelley describes the original moment of inspiration falling upon him (59–60), it was 'at that sweet time when winds are wooing' (56). The presence of wind is thus paired with creative ecstasy. Poetry is, strictly speaking, the manifestation of Intellectual Beauty; and Shelley's *Hymn* to it is hopeful praise of the production of successful poetry, for the ideal combination of imaginative perception ('intellectual') and aesthetics ('beauty').

The *Hymn* presents a positive use of the image, but it can also be portrayed as negative. We are, Shelley writes,

> like forgotten lyres, whose dissonant strings
> Give various response to each varying blast,
> To whose frail frame no second motion brings
> One mood or modulation like the last.

This is the 1816 *Mutability* (5–8). The frustration expressed here is similar to the 'fading coal' passage in the *Defence*, that the force of influence touches us in an inconstant and incongruous way. Being such sensitive creatures has its drawbacks as well as its advantages. For Shelley, the goal is to utilise the potential to respond to this variability of influence, to create poetry out of those unpredictable, coming-and-going moments. The dangers are twofold: the poet can be stifled by the overwhelming power of influence, or he can be unresponsive to the influence. The ideal poet, Shelley holds, must strike a balance between these two.

The Wind of Inspiration

The mastery of a particular influence is also described in these terms:

> The youth, as shadows on a grassy hill
> Outrun the winds that chase them, soon outran
> His teacher.

We recall that this is the young poet-figure of Prince Athanase going beyond the influential scope of his teacher, Zonoras (*Prince Athanase*, 176–8). But in most cases Shelley employs moving air as an image of continuous poetic inspiration, or as a description of the motivating and pervasive poetic quality. Shelley's assuming the persona of a cloud in *The Cloud* illustrates the poetic faculties of the chameleon (or unegotistical) imagination; and clouds are moved by winds, much as a skylark uses the currents of air to keep itself soaring. Shelley is more direct in his 'excuse' for Wordsworth, *An Exhortation*. Poets are to be as chameleons, but if they

> should devour
> Any food but beams and wind,
> They would grow as earthly soon
> As their brother lizards are.
> (21–4)

Shelley must be saying here that if he wants to avoid the same lizard-like fate of his brother-poet Wordsworth, he must partake of (consume) the wind's influence. Part of the poet's sustenance must be the wind.

In *Julian and Maddalo* the Maniac becomes an impressive figure of influence for Julian and Maddalo. But because the vision the Maniac describes is both pathetic and drastic, his soliloquy (composed of fragmented verses about the loss of creative powers) is appropriately preceded by an unsettling wind. The Maniac, when first seen by Julian and Maddalo, is sitting near a piano with his hair being blown by wind rushing through a window. As the Maniac delivered his words the storm 'Hissed' through the opening and unseen Julian and Maddalo stole 'his accents from the envious wind' (295–8). The external wind competes with the Maniac's own utterances. The Maniac and the wind have an antagonistic as opposed to a complementary or harmonious relationship. The wind does its best to overpower the Maniac, and succeeds to the degree that the madman's fluency obviously suffers. If somehow the wind's force might be channelled or accommodated by the Maniac, his eloquence might correspondingly improve or be restored. But he is neither co-ordinated nor correspondent with the wind. If he could somehow open up to this in-flowing he might be able to communicate better his woe. Both winds might be calmed. He is not, in other words, *combining* very well with the force of influence: without inspiration, he is a prisoner of uncreativity. In his solitude and self-centredness he has fashioned a resistance to an external or objective viewpoint. He can only create from within himself, but this is fast becoming a vacant space; soon there can be nothing left. In this way he shares the same problem as the Poet of *Alastor*: he is, like the Poet, an idealist ruined by the failure of the world to match up to his own idealism, a poetic visionary whose vision of inspiration deserts him. So like *Alastor* it is a poem revolving around the circumstance of a creative failure. Both poets empty themselves of creative life by unknowingly shutting out external influences. Without in-flowing there can be no out-flowing.

Prometheus's vision, at least when he is free from the authoritarian influence of Jupiter, is not so drastic. At that important moment when he is freed by Hercules, the Titan describes the new poetic project that will be taken up in the cave of arts: he says there will be 'heard the ever-moving air / Whispering without from tree to tree' (III. iii. 18–19); and under the new influence Prometheus promises that he and his followers will

> like lutes
> Touched by the skill of the enamoured wind,
> Weave harmonies divine, yet ever new.
> (III. iii. 36–8)

When humanity and love are asked to once more make their appearance, they are asked to 'come, sped on the charmèd winds' (III. iii. 40ff.). The touch of wind is synonymous with poetic life. The formulation of a new poetic vision depends on these winds of renewal and change. When Demogorgon arrives in the final act of the poem as the force of revitalised imagination he is told, 'Thy voice to us is wind among still woods' (IV. 548). Demogorgon, as a spirit of the times (the *Zeitgeist*), is the new voice of inspiration, the new mover.

I have passed over a number of other passages and poems which also associate the moving-air motif with the inspirational production of poetry. I have commented only on a few of those that most obviously use the device of the poet-protagonist and the theme of poetic inspiration. One more poem remains to be examined, a poem central for both Shelley and Romanticism, and in it Shelley desperately attempts to locate the poet's place in a scene where he hopes he can engage the force of influence in that moment of inspiration.

III

Shelley's *Ode to the West Wind* was written a week before writing *Peter Bell the Third*, and the day before beginning his final drafts of the *West Wind* (25 October 1819) he read Reynold's satire on Wordsworth's *Peter Bell*. During the week he also began writing a letter to the *Quarterly Review*, threatening that he might charge the reviewer of his *Revolt of Islam* with slander for the disparaging allusions made about his character and personal life (*Letters*, II, p. 130). This was the review in which it was also said that Shelley was an 'unsparing imitator' of Wordsworth. (Shelley believed that Southey had penned the piece. The letter was never completed.) The *Ode to the West Wind* can also be placed between the composition of the third and fourth acts of *Prometheus Unbound*. I mention these circumstances of composition because we can be certain that it was a time when Shelley's interests in poetry, in having himself taken seriously as a poet, were at a very high point.

The *Ode* is divided into five parts. Each part is fourteen lines long, is made up of four stanzas of *terza rima*, and ends in a couplet – a unique combination of the sonnet form with *terza rima*. The structural nature of the poem is important to note because each part acts as a unit and has its own 'tropological' logic and theme which combines with the whole. And as we will see, form and content antithetically interplay in the *Ode*: the highly-controlled structure is countered by the uncontrolled subject of the poem. Thus we can anticipate viewing the *Ode* as the poet's attempt to display and sustain his poetic powers.

In the first part of the poem the West Wind is described as an invisible mover and carrier. It is a pervasive force, and although we tend to think of the west wind as a revitalising energy, this particular wind's function in this first part is to drive dead leaves and to bear seeds to their 'dark' and 'cold' graves (4–7). The West Wind is not

'Autumn's being' but the *'breath* of Autumn's being' (1). This differentiation is important because it serves to show that it is the wind/breath element that is the moving power. The obvious connection with the 'unseen presence' is the 'unseen Power' of Intellectual Beauty (*Hymn*, 1) and the 'unseen' Skylark (*Skylark*, 20), both of which are associated with poetic inspiration. There is also the connection with the passage in the *Defence* where the Poet as an influencing force is described as an 'unseen musician'.

The West Wind joins these other invisible forces, but its importance is as an energy that will give rise to further forces. It is not an end in itself, and rather more a cause than an effect. It is both preparatory (preparing the seeds for growth) and anticipatory (anticipating the 'living' elements that will come). The role of the West Wind in this context is what makes it simultaneously a 'Destroyer and preserver' (14): in the process of preserving life for the future, the life of the past is cleared away. Old leaves make way for new buds. Moreover, decayed leaves become the humus in which the new life will begin.

The twin aspects of the West Wind continue in the second part of the poem. The Wind is both a builder and disperser of cloud formations. It signifies a beginning ('of the approaching storm', 23), and an end ('Of the dying year', 24); and the immediacy of 'this closing night' (24) marks the end of the day and the start of night. We will come to see that the poem as a whole repeats and expands this structure of end/beginning, old/new, death/birth.

The dominant image in this second section is, in fact, death, continuing some of those images in the first section of the poem. There is a connection with the dead leaves that are blown in the first section with the clouds in this second part: 'Loose clouds like earth's decaying leaves are shed' (16). Further, the 'dark' graves where those 'wingèd seeds' ('Each like a corpse', 8) were to rest becomes a larger tomb: the 'closing night' becomes 'the dome of a vast sepulchre' (24–5). But this is not a peaceful scene: on the inside of the vault, which has a roof formed by thick 'vapour', an apocalyptic scene of fire and ice brews: 'Black rain, and fire, and hail will burst' (26–8). The West Wind is a kind of angel of death and life.

The third part of the *Ode* moves to a new element: we have been taken from earth to air, and now we move to water. The West Wind's 'unseen' influence is everywhere. And it encompasses all functions: just as it puts seeds to 'bed' (6) in the 'dreaming earth' (10) it also wakes the sleeping Mediterranean from its 'summer dreams' (29).

The Wind of Inspiration

The wind that is portrayed in these first three parts of the poem is anything but the traditional west wind, the gentle *zephuros* that has become what we call a zephyr. Shelley's West Wind is not so much the complementary of its 'azure sister' (9) as its antithesis – it is a 'wild' pervasive force that drives, almost in terror, leaves, clouds and oceans before it; it is likened to 'some fierce Maenad' (21), a riotous, drunken or even orgiastic power. Even seaweeds on the ocean floor 'grow gray with fear / And tremble' on hearing the wind's voice (40–2). These scenes are hardly idyllic. But neither are they totally disharmonious or chaotic. There seems a purpose to this wind, one beyond those that have already been described. We know this because each of the first three parts have ended with the earnest appeal, 'oh, hear!' (14, 28, 42). We might assume that it is the last two sections that are to be heard. This becomes especially evident as the speaker in the fourth section directly introduces himself into the poem in an extended suppositional statement:

> If I were a dead leaf thou mightest bear;
> If I were a swift cloud to fly with thee;
> A wave to pant beneath thy power, and share
>
> The impulse of thy strength, only less free
> Than thou, O uncontrollable! If even
> I were as in my boyhood, and could be
>
> The comrade of why wandering over Heaven,
> As then, when to outstrip thy skiey speed
> Scarce seemed a vision; I would ne'er have striven
>
> As thus with thee in prayer in my sore need.
> Oh, lift me as a wave, a leaf, a cloud!
> I fall upon the thorns of life! I bleed!
>
> A heavy weight of hours has chained and bowed
> One too like thee: tameless, and swift, and proud.
> (43–56)

Suddenly the speaker has transfigured himself into the imagery of the first three sections: he must now be re-read as a dead leaf in the first section, as a swift cloud in the second and as a wave in the third. In other words, we must now, in the spirit of allegory, revise our reading and substitute the terms leaf/clould/wave for the speaker. The poem seems now to be becoming a poem about wind's influence on the speaker. He wants to share the 'strength' of the wind, to blow with it; but more important, he also wants to feel the effect of its power, in the same way a leaf, cloud or wave does. At this point, however, the speaker does not want to be the wind, although we can predict that this will be the final or ultimate transfiguration he will desire. But for the moment he wants to be more mastered (influenced) than to achieve mastery himself.

The speaker goes so far as to say that even if once again he could be as in his 'boyhood', when he could freely wander with the sky's movement, he wouldn't need to petition the wind any more strongly than he does now. The obvious allusion is to two of the most famous Wordsworthian figures: the child who is 'father of the Man' (*My Heart Leaps Up*) and the figure who 'wandered lonely as a cloud' (*I Wandered Lonely as a Cloud*). What Shelley has done in his *Ode* is to use the image of the second poem in questioning the privileging relationship in the first, namely, that the experience of childhood (the past) has more important qualities than adulthood (the present).

It is plain that the speaker is experiencing a painful lack of some kind, a 'sore need' that he hopes the Wind can satisfy. He prays to be taken upwards ('Oh, lift me'), but his movement is downwards ('I fall'). Indeed, it is a drastic fall, one that wounds and weakens him.

In the final section the speaker makes his strongest appeal:

> Make me thy lyre, even as the forest is:
> What if my leaves are falling like its own!
> The tumult of thy mighty harmonies
>
> Will take from both a deep, autumnal tone,
> Sweet though in sadness. Be thou, Spirit fierce,
> My spirit! Be thou me, impetuous one!
>
> Drive my dead thoughts over the universe
> Like withered leaves to quicken a new birth!
> And, by the incantation of this verse,
>
> Scatter, as from an unextinguished hearth
> Ashes and sparks, my words among mankind!
> Be through my lips to unawakened earth

> The trumpet of a prophecy! O, Wind,
> If Winter comes, can Spring be far behind?
>
> (57-70)

The speaker increases his demands: he moves from wanting to be struck by the Wind's force (like a 'lyre'), to desiring to be the Wind's force itself ('Be thou me'). Most important, he implores the Wind to continuously disperse his 'thoughts' and 'words' to all corners of existence. This final wish for proliferation corresponds with the appearance of the element that completes the other three: fire (in the form of 'unextinguished hearth' and 'Ashes and sparks') follows from the elements of earth, air and water that are present in the first three sections.

The *Ode* ends with a suppositional question of anticipation, of wondering if a time of poetic propagation will come. In this way it is similar to *To to a Skylark*, where at that poem's end the speaker is left waiting, listening for the bird's inspirational voice to teach him. Both poems are hopeful forms of preparation for that always-to-be moment beyond the poem. In this way they are potential prophecies.[5] The *Ode to the West Wind* is also an apostrophe;[6] it is uncertain whether or not the Wind, as the addressed subject, is present or not: in some ways it seems as if the speaker is appealing for or summoning the Wind to appear, yet in other ways it seems as if it is ever-present, and that he is just trying to channel it through himself. The poem is also a prayer in that an important request is made of the revered Wind.[7] Yet the darker and some of the more gloomy aspects of the imagery give the poem a different feeling altogether, a feeling of wonder, enchantment and black magic. In this sense the poem is as a spell and the speaker a hopeful conjurer. He wants to be like the Wind, and the Wind's magical power (in that it acts invisibly) drives leaves 'like ghosts from an enchanter fleeing'; further, the poem (as a spell) is appropriately spoken at the coming of night, with lightning and 'Black rain' soon to come; and finally, the speaker himself hopes that by the 'incantation of this verse' the Wind will come forth to him.

My reason for noting that Shelley's poem can be read as a prophecy, prayer or incantation is not to make the claim that the poem has various levels of meaning. This is obvious enough. Characteristically, Shelley combines different types of rhetorical strategies in order to fulfil his poetic aims. On the other hand, perhaps it is the case that our interpretive attempts to create and find demarcations between these types of discourses get in the way of our reading of the poem. There are obvious differences between a prayer, a prophecy and an incantation in terms of conventions, but the means and the intentions are the same: a coming-into-being through forms of utterance. Shaman, Prophet, Magician, Priest – all make invocations and claims for knowledge and power. All are, in a sense, poets. And in the *Ode to the West Wind* Shelley turns the invocation back on itself, making an invocation for a further invocation. More than anything else the poet fears silence, which is the sign of a creative lack. Shelley, we know, believed this lack to be the results of not being influenced, of not taking in those external voices and combining them with his own. I would hold that the *Ode* is Shelley's strongest and most agonising poetic expression of his desire to be influenced and influential. This is the reading of the poem I would like to come back to. But for the moment it might be useful to examine some possible origins for the *Ode* that take us in that direction. And it is now appropriate that we no longer call the voice behind the *Ode* the 'speaker', for it is clear that he is a poet, and the poem is an expression of his poetic aims.

IV

Shelley would have been acquainted with the wind as a trope for re-creative power from mythology from the story of Favonius or Zephyrus. Shelley would also of course have been aware that in the Old Testament the creation of the world itself was the result of a mighty wind or breath (or sometimes it is translated as 'spirit') blowing across the face of the earth (*Genesis*, 1:2). Throughout the Bible the wind signifies both the blessing and force of life (for example, *Ezekiel*, 37:9) as well as a curse, like the 'destroying wind' that is set against Babylon (*Jeremiah*, 51:1). Shelley also knew the west wind in Milton's *L'Allegro* ('The frolick Wind that breathes the Spring'). The same wind appears in Pope's Pastoral on *Spring* (1709): 'Here western winds on breathing roses blow'. Similarly, Shelley would have known the passage in Gray's *Ode on the Spring* (1748) where 'Zephyrs thro' the clear blue sky / Their gather'd fragrance fling' (9–10).

But much closer to Shelley, if not more familiar to him, are Coleridge's uses of the wind harp in *The Nightingale* (1798), *Dejection: An Ode* (1802) and, of course, in *The Eolian Harp* (1798) itself:

> And what if all of animated nature
> Be but organic Harps diversely fram'd,
> That tremble into thought, as o'er them sweeps
> Plastic and vast, one intellectual breeze,
> At once the Soul of each, and God of all?
>
> (44–8)

In some ways this would have been rather soft stuff for Shelley. There is a hesitance or indecisiveness in making a direct engagement with the force that moves the harp to life, and not much difficulty (at least metaphorically) connecting with it. Shelley's wind is a much more problematical energy, one that suggests the notions of both attraction and intimidation. The stance that Coleridge often takes (or at least projects) is one of passivity as opposed to engagement. In Wordsworth there are to be found more promising origins in which these paradoxical qualities are delineated.

Wordsworth's *Excursion* again offers more problematical starting points – problematical in that *The Excursion* for Shelley represents Wordsworth's poetic failure. In Book IV the Wanderer speaks to the Solitary, trying to point out that, if only he can read the right signs, the pathway towards restoration lies before him; he must note that the 'whispering air / Sends inspiration from the shadowy heights' (1170–1). The Solitary has lost the up-lifting connection with the natural world. Down on his cottage in the lonely dell the influence of natural objects has forsaken him, passed him by. The Wanderer is attempting to reconnect the Solitary with the natural flow, to point out how a recovery can be made. He says that in the 'whispering air' can be found the necessary 'inspiration'. In other words, the Wanderer wants the Solitary to be moved by the quiet utterances of the wind; he wants him to hear this utterance sent from Nature.

What Shelley condenses from this passage (IV. 1170–87) is the idea that inspiration can be felt through an interaction with the moving air. But the poet of the *Ode to the West Wind* is neither like the stoic Wanderer who apparently has no trouble in receiving the inspiration, nor like the Solitary who (we discover as the poem continues) remains unmoved by both the argument and the wind's utterances. The poet of the *Ode* moves between these two figures, but he does so without occupying a compromising position: he desires inspiration, therefore acknowledging its existence; but he is never certain that he will or can be inspired. The moving air he seeks connection with is more elusive and less containable than the Wanderer's rather more benign blowing.

In Book III of *The Excursion* there is a more direct connection with the *Ode*. This time it is the Solitary who speaks. He recalls those more 'genial times' when he could quite contentedly occupy himself with imaginative concerns, having no need of 'earthly care' (282–306). He quotes his own words of that time to illustrate how he felt:

> – 'Blow winds of autumn! – let your chilling breath
> Take the live herbage from the mead, and strip
> The shady forest of its green attire, –
> And let the bursting clouds to fury rouse
> The gentle brooks! – Your desolating sway,'
> Thus I exclaimed, 'no sadness sheds on me,
> And no disorder in your rage I find.'
>
> (307–13)

It is not difficult to recognise Shelley's text as a revision of this passage: the wind, autumn and breath which appear in the first line spoken by the Solitary all appear in the opening line of Shelley's poem: 'O wild West Wind, thou breath of Autumn's being'. Further, Shelley follows Wordsworth even in the order of the other parallel elements. For after the initial address in Wordsworth's poem, the autumn wind in the solitary woods is described as a force that strips the leaves from the trees, just as the dead leaves in the *Ode* are driven (2–3). The wind is then described as causing the clouds to storm and to burst; accordingly, in the second section of the *Ode* the Wind is the mover of clouds, preparing them to 'burst' (28). The last effect the wind has in Wordsworth's poem is that of rousing water; in the *Ode* the third section is also about how the West Wind can 'waken' the waters of the Mediterranean (29–30). But more important than these parallel elements are the respective attitudes towards the wind. In both an invitation is made to the wind to blow, but whereas the Solitary's invitation is more of a defiant gesture, a challenge even, the poet of the *Ode* goes in a different direction, encouraging yet bowing to the Wind's power. The difference is important. The Solitary sees the wind as a force separate from himself: the poet in the *Ode* wants to be one with the Wind, to channel the Wind's flow through himself.

The Solitary says that the wind has no effect on him. Neither does he find 'disorder' in the wind's turbulence, as if to say that 'disorder' in Nature is either non-existent or a negative quality. The poet of the *Ode* challenges these attitudes and observations. The *Ode* is in fact a discourse on the potentially overwhelming effect of the Wind. Concerning the notion of 'disorder' in the *Ode*, the remarkable hope of the poet is his desire to control yet be like the 'uncontrollable' (47) nature of the Wind. 'Be thou me, impetuous one!' (62) he pleads. The poet not only finds disorder in the Wind, but extols it in a remarkable gesture of desiring to be the Wind itself.

Beyond *The Excursion*, there is a further Wordsworthian influence on the *Ode*. In a letter written to *The Times Literary Supplement* on 20 June 1936 (p. 532), Frederick A. Pottle suggested that Shelley's poem must have been influenced by Wordsworth's *Composed while the Author was engaged in writing a Tract occasioned by the Convention of Cintra* (1815 – the second poem). This is Wordsworth's poem:

> I dropped my pen; and listened to the *Wind*
> That sang of trees up-torn and vessels tost –
> A midnight *harmony*; and wholly lost
> To the general sense of men *by chains confined*
> Of business, care, or pleasure; or resigned
> To timely sleep. Thought I, the impassioned strain,
> Which, without aid of numbers, I sustain,
> Like acceptation from the World will find.
> Yet some with apprehensive ear shall drink
> A *dirge* devoutly breathed o'er sorrows past;
> And to the attendant promise will give heed –
> The prophecy, – like that of this *wild blast*,
> Which, while it makes the heart with sadness shrink,
> Tells also of bright calms that shall succeed.
> [Pottle's emphasis]

Pottle proposed that these emphasised words and phrases correspond with elements to be found in Shelley's *Ode*. More important, Pottle suggested that Wordsworth's poem initiates parallel thematic concerns: (1) the wind as a symbol of influence on men's minds, and (2) the wind as both a positive and negative force.

I would hold that these two concerns are not separate but related themes: influence (as manifest in the characteristics of the wind) is a positive and negative force. It gives as much as it takes; and it necessitates passage through an uncertain period of hardship and deprivation before the possibility of success and growth. I would also be more specific than Pottle in saying that Shelley in the *Ode* is speaking of the *poet's* mind. This success and growth following uncertainty are poetic aims marking creative development. The poet must sacrifice his life for his art in order that his art sustain him. He must in that moment of inspiration give up part of his individuality, surrendering part of his poetic originality to the greater forces of influence that will consume yet support him.

All of this is recognisable as aspects of Shelley's scene of influence. In the interrogative ending to the *Ode*, the Wind, as an agent to encourage the poet to 'prophesy', is itself a potentially prophetic presence: 'O, Wind, / If Winter comes, can Spring be far behind?' The explicit hope (for Spring to come) is implicitly paired with fear (that Spring might not come). It is not a rhetorical question designed to acknowledge a foregone answer. A draft version of this last line shows very clearly that Shelley revised a rather flat statement in order to express a provocative uncertainty: 'When Winter comes Spring lags not far behind'.[8] Without the revision the *Ode* would have been an altogether different poem. It would have been an affirmation of the inevitability of a positive outcome. Shelley would have been assuring himself of poetic success. He would have been, in effect, collecting his laurels before earning them. He would have expressed a faith that looks through time.

At the end of Wordworth's poem on the Convention of Cintra we find the type of stability and assurance that Shelley would have revised or undermined. Wordsworth concludes that the wind, while making 'the heart with sadness shrink, / Tells also of bright calms that shall succeed'. In Wordsworth's mind there is no question at all about whether these 'bright calms' might come: they *will* come. And they will come as the same sober and serene future that Wordsworth attempts to fashion for himself in *Tintern Abbey* and the *Intimations Ode*. The difference between the two poets is interesting and predictable: Shelley tests the same problem as Wordsworth, and he uses the same imagery. However, the older poet's positive endorsement of a future tranquillity, of certainty and promise, are reassessed by Shelley, and become translated into problems of uncertainty, impermanence and mutability. When Wordsworth and Shelley listen to the wind, the older poet connects with it and masters it, while the younger poet can only want the connection while desiring to be mastered by the wind. Shelley reverses the priority and privileging of the poet over the wind that Wordsworth favours. At the most he can hope for an interchange, something like the one in *Mont Blanc* between the speaker's 'human mind' and 'the clear universe of things around' (37–40). The calmness that

Wordsworth looks forward to is replaced by the impetuousness or restlessness that Shelley heralds, and the uncertainty he feels.

V

The meteorological and geographical elements in the poem are incidental to the poem's meanings. This is supported by the manuscript history of the *West Wind*. The following, certainly the most important manuscript fragment of the poem, but ignored in almost all commentaries, mentions nothing at all about the landscape or conditions near the Arno that particular autumn evening, nor, for that matter, anything about the wind:[9]

> And what art thou presumptuous who profanest
>   The wreath to mighty Poets only due?
> Even whilst, like a forgotten name though wanest
>   Touch not those leaves which for the eternal few
> Who wander oer the Paradise of fame
>   In sacred dedication ever grew –
> One of the crowd thou art, – without a name
>   Ah friend 'tis the false laurel which I wear
> And though it seem like it is not the same
>   As that which bound Milton's immortal hair
> Its dew is poison, and the hopes which quicken
>   Under its chilling shade, though seeming fair
> Are flowers which die almost before they sicken
>   And that I walk thus proudly crowned withal
> Is that I know it may be thunderstriken
>   And this is my distinction, if I fall
> [Not to be huddled into the wide grave]
> I shall not creep out of the vital day
>   To common dust nor wear a common pall
> But as my hopes were fire, so my decay
>   Shall be as ashes covering them. Oh, Earth
> Oh friends, if when my [. . .] has ebbed away
>   One spark be unextinguished of that hearth
> Kindled in [. . .].

Shelley works a little over half-way towards the subject that will evolve in his final version. He questions his status as a poet relative to the 'mighty Poets'. He obviously feels overshadowed by them. The tone is negative, bordering on contempt and cynicism, and he considers his outlook as bleak. He sees himself in anonymity, as merely 'One of the crowd . . . without a name', or with a 'forgotten name'. But if he has to 'fall', he says that he will do so at least with 'distinction', and without either being pushed aside into the grave or compromising himself. This is the only way he can salvage some spark of hope or satisfaction from his feelings of poetic inadequacy.

The fact that the wind is not mentioned is singularly important in the light of the tone and mood of this fragment. Many of the other significant elements that appear in the final version of the *Ode* are already present: leaves, grave, death, decay, falling, ashes, sparks and unextinguished hearth – and most important, the desire to be a successful poet. But in order to unify these elements and to transform this mood of poetic despair into feelings of hope, one further element is needed. To put it another way, one element is conspicuously absent. Yet from this fragment Shelley moved directly to the poem as we now know it. How Shelley salvaged such despair (and transformed it into a powerful poem) is both simple and remarkable: he needed to remind himself of the pervasiveness of influence, and that what seems negative can also be seen as positive – including the crushing weight of 'mighty Poets'. Those qualities he found symbolised by the West Wind, and so that Wind becomes the fifth and most important element in the poem, the connective and combining element. In the fragment Shelley makes the mistake of fighting too hard for recognition, and of holding his self-pride too highly. He desires too much (or invests too much) in the significance of his own name. This is not the way that Shelley had learned to come to terms with influence in the prefaces to *The Revolt of Islam* and *Prometheus Unbound* and in the *Defence*. Instead of fighting for the self, one must in some ways surrender to selflessness: one must be moved or swallowed up by those greater forces of influence in order to join with them, realising that escape is not just impossible, but potentially disastrous. Thus, one must be driven like a leaf before the force of the wind, or blown like a trumpet by the wind. Once Shelley realised that the perfect symbol for this was all around him, and that it was one he had already used in other poems, he could both overcome his poetic despair and make it the subject of the very poem he was working on. In this way the West Wind became both the subject of the poem and the means by which the poem (as we know it) came into being. It is, in short, an inspired poem about its own inspiration.

The poet's invocation to the 'breath of Autumn's being' that opens the *Ode* once more draws us back to the Narrator of *Alastor* who waits for the 'breath' of his 'great Parent' for inspiration. The West Wind too is a parent of sorts, since it has the potential to bring forth a 'new birth' (64). And those 'murmurs of the air / And motions of the forests and the sea' in *Alastor* (46–7) also make a direct connection with the imagery in the *Ode*, only now in the later poem they are intensified and structured.

While carrying over some of the fatalistic tone from *Alastor*, the *Ode* has condensed many of the earlier poem's elements. I have already discussed in the opening of this chapter how moving air is functionally pervasive in *Alastor*. The unswerving movement over earth and water, the heavy atmosphere, the imagery of enclosure, the movement towards evening, are all present in both poems, and all suggest the same quest theme. Even the Poet's grave in *Alastor* –

> the charmed eddies of autumnal winds
> Built o'er his moldering bones a pyramid
> Of mouldering leaves in the waste wilderness.
> (52–4)

– seems to me to have evolved into the first section of the *Ode*, where leaves of Autumn are blown across the graves of buried seeds. In fact, those leaves in the *Ode* that are 'Yellow, and black, and pale, and hectic red' (4), remind us of the 'Red, yellow, or ethereally pale' leaves worn by 'The children of the autumnal whirlwind' in *Alastor* (583–5). And just as the Poet of *Alastor* envies the swan who can fly off (275–90), so too does the poet of the *Ode* wish he 'were a swift cloud to fly with' the Wind (44): both poets want to be swept up into the air.

The poet of the *Ode* is the Poet of *Alastor* who now has come to know the nature of inspiration, who now knows where the poetic life-force resides and how to attempt to engage it. The poet of the *Ode* wants to avoid the uncreative fate of *Alastor*'s hero in having the Wind, in his moment of need, pass him by.

Just as *Alastor* predicts and contains some of the important elements found in the *Ode to the West Wind*, so the *Ode* contains elements that are developed in the *Defence of Poetry*, written some fifteen or sixteen months later. The last section of the *Ode* alone can be read as a condensed version of some of the *Defence*'s most important passages. At the end of the *Ode* the poet implores that the Wind blow 'through my lips to unawakened earth / The trumpet of a prophecy!' The poet wants to be, with the Wind's help, the prophetic instrument inspiring the earth and mankind to stir. This idea, as well as the same image, is found in the final two sentences of the *Defence*:

> Poets are the hierophants of an unapprehended *inspiration*, the mirrors of the gigantic shadows which futurity casts upon the present, the words which express what they understand not; the *trumpets* which sing to battle, and feel not what they *inspire*: the *influence* which is moved not, but moves. Poets are the unacknowledged legislators of the World. [My emphasis]

Here the poet is both inspired and the inspiration for the future; he is, as in the passage in the *Ode*, an instrument of prophecy. We know too the famous scene of poetic production in the *Defence*:

> the mind in creation is as a fading coal which some invisible *influence*, like an inconstant *wind*, awakens to transitory brightness: this power arises from within, like the colour of a flower which fades and changes as it is developed, and the conscious portions of our natures are unprophetic either of its approach or its departure. Could this *influence* be durable in its original purity and force, it is impossible to predict the greatness of the results: but when composition begins, *inspiration* is already on the decline, and the most glorious poetry that has ever been communicated to the world is probably a feeble shadow of the original conception of the poet. [My emphasis]

As in the *Ode*, to be inspired, 'some invisible influence, like an inconstant wind', must breathe on the poet's mind. When this takes place, the poet himself becomes an influencing force, capable of illuminating others. Again, the same idea and the same imagery can be traced back to the fifth section of the *Ode*: the poet begs that the Wind

> Scatter, as from an extinguished hearth
> Ashes and sparks, my words among mankind!
> (66–7)

The coals in this hearth are portrayed as being fanned in a more constant and vigorous way. Instead of the coal merely glowing to life and giving off its light and heat (which presumably is the poem in the making), the picture is enlarged and the process is taken one step further. But it is not the case that the *Ode* represents a more positive or complete scene of influence than the *Defence*: remember that the *Ode* is describing an ideal scene – moreover, a personal and deeply felt hope – while the scene in the *Defence* is an attempt at describing a version of the poet's relationship to the forces of influence and moments of inspiration.

The opening of the fifth section predicts the first image of influence to be developed in the *Defence*. In the *Ode* the poet pleads with the Wind to 'Make me thy lyre'; he sees himself as an Aeolian harp, an instrument to be moved into sound by the creative forces that pass over him. This is precisely Shelley's description in the *Defence*: 'Man is an instrument over which a series of external and internal impressions are driven, like the alternations of an ever-changing wind over an Aeolian lyre, which move it by their motion to ever-changing melody.' Further, Shelley says in both passages that it is not enough to remain totally passive to these inflowings: one must *combine* with and *regulate* them in order to create a resulting sound that is original. (This is the exact idea developed in the Preface to *Prometheus Unbound*.) This is how, in the *Defence*, 'harmony' is created: 'by an internal adjustment of the sounds or motions thus excited to the impressions which excite them'. And this is how the poet in the *Ode* hopes that he will, by combining with the autumn Wind in the same way as the 'forest', create 'harmonies' (57–9). Recall the final stanza of *Hymn to Intellectual Beauty* where there is 'harmony / In autumn' (74–5), and think back to that important passage in *Prometheus Unbound* where the new poetic project outlined by Prometheus will be to 'Weave harmonies divine, yet ever new' (III. iii. 38).

If the first three sections of the *Ode* outline the power of the West Wind in Nature, the last two sections are increasingly desperate appeals for that power to combine with the poet, to be transferred to the writing of poetry. For there can be no doubt that this speaker is a poet speaking *as a poet*. (The draft of the *Ode* examined above – 'And what are thou' – shows clearly the initial problem of the poem began as one about the status of the struggling poet.) But he is a poet who, in the moment of his poem, wants to be moved by the Wind, just as a leaf, cloud or wave is moved. He asks of the Wind that he might 'share / The impulse of thy strength', which is to say that he desires to be carried along with the greater flow so that he might become a part of it. The painful quality of this anxious appeal is explicit in the poet's 'sore need', so much so that the only flowing he can facilitate is that of his own blood: 'I fall upon the thorns of life! I bleed!'

This last image has a possible further significance beyond acting as an indication of the poet's despair: a concern with the actual *writing* of successful poetry. The *Ode* makes use of the medieval trope which associates the thorn with the stylus.[10] We can almost make a literal translation of 'I fall upon the thorns of life! I bleed!': the poet in writing writes his life away; he puts the very meaning of his life *on the line*. For the poet, ink is his blood, the sustaining fluid to mark his presence for an eternity. Moreover, bleeding is in this context a productive state. Shelley, falling 'upon the thorns of life', is representing his bleeding as more than just a passive act of sacrifice; it is a purposeful and active response, one which he feels is the poet's duty.

In Shelley's scene of influence the poet hopes to couple his flow (his pen flowing, his fluency) with the flow of posterity that will survive him. In this way he too, in his work, will survive. But, as the *Ode* makes clear, it is not such an easily-won marriage. The sacrifice is great, and there can be no guarantee of joining the immortals. The double-bind is this: the poet must give his life (to the writing of poetry) in order to have his life preserved (by poetry's immortalising powers); only through death can the poet survive life. Even those life-giving 'sparks' in this last section are paired with 'Ashes', suggesting not only the proverbial 'spark of life', but also a cremation scene and burial: dust to dust, ashes to ashes. We have come full circle from the grave scene in the first section of the poem. Burial and death join with potential birth at both ends of the *Ode*.

The other image suggesting the motif of writing in the *Ode* is that of leaves. That is, the leaves of trees double as leaves of writing paper – moreover, as pages of poetry. (We come across this usage in the description of the pose of the Maniac in *Julian and Maddalo* – 'His lips were pressed against a folded leaf' (280) – as well as the 'leaves' in *Prometheus Unbound* on which it is written 'FOLLOW, FOLLOW!' (II. i. 138–41).) This interpretation of the leaves in the *Ode* becomes feasible in that moment when the speaker declares himself a poet who wants his poetry disseminated to all corners of the earth, 'Like withered leaves' that are driven everywhere by the West Wind.

Besides the Wind, leaves are in fact the only image to appear in all five sections of the poem (in the third part they are the 'sea blooms' and 'foliage' of the sea weed). And once more the element of death intersects our reading; for the leaves in the poem are variously described as 'leaves dead' (2), 'decaying leaves' (16), 'sapless foliage' (40), 'dead leaf' (43) and falling and 'withered leaves' (58, 64). The opening metaphor of the *Ode* can now be read as the poetry of dead poets ('ghosts') being blown before the supernatural force of influence ('an enchanter'). The poet of the poem beseeches this magical force to lift him and his poetry to sublime heights, though first he must fall and become desiccated. Yet desiccation is also a positive process in that it suggests a form of permanence through preservation. (Shelley uses this to great effect in speaking of Wordsworth as a withered flower in *Verses Written on a Celandine*.) The poet wants both to take a leaf from the book of influence, and to become himself a page in the book of influence. When the wind blows across a book the pages turn; if the pages are not bound, they are scattered. Because of this image of dissemination, the poet in the *Ode* seems to be in favour of the unbound image, of having his words dispersed throughout the earth.

Winter and Spring are the corresponding temporal marks of the Wind as 'Destroyer and preserver'. Winter destroys life yet Spring ensures that it is preserved. But Shelley means to extend the implications. These antithetical yet complementary qualities are inherent in the nature of influence. As a destroyer, the power of influence over-runs the poet, threatening to annihilate his individuality, which constitutes his poetic originality. Yet in a preserving capacity the individual poet's contribution is also open to the possibility of being perpetuated and safeguarded by combining with that greater flow in the moment of inspiration. The demands made of the poet are truly testing: he must be both humble (in bowing to the force) as well as hungry (to join the force).

Sound becomes the prevalent element in the final part of the *Ode*, balancing images of music ('lyre', 'tone', 'harmonies', 'trumpet') with those of utterance ('tumult', 'verse', 'words', 'lips'). But these images of music and utterance are brought together by the act of 'incantation', which is both a spell and a chant (*cantare* in Latin means sing). The supernatural action which the poem invites is the 'incantation of this verse', the repetition of the poem. Thus the *Ode* has its own in-built desire to be uttered over and over again, for every repetition will contain this invitation to utter it again. The *Ode*, then, goes beyond mere invocation. Its strategy for survival, which we have seen to be synonymous with being influenced and influential, is first to pray to the Wind to be moved (lifted), then to be played (as a lyre), and finally, to demand to be the West Wind: 'Be thou me, impetuous one!'

In the *Ode*, I would suggest, Shelley comes as close as he ever does to making that final sacrifice, of asking for all by giving his all. When he formulates his final question – 'Oh Wind, / If Winter comes, can Spring be far behind?' – he can in no way be certain of an answer. The questions are these: If I give my all, giving up my all and going through the worst, can I be certain that my reward will be to have my poetry survive? If I surrender to Influence now, how can I be sure that I shall later become a part of Influence's greater force? In its uncertainty the *Ode* contains both its own negation and the possibility of poetic success. It is at once a seed-bed and a cenotaph.

Implicit is the hope that the *Ode to the West Wind* will both invoke the spirit of influence and become itself an influencing element. When in the poem three times we encounter 'oh, hear!', it can mean a number of things: it can be an appeal made by the poet to the Wind to 'hear my poem'; it too can be a directive to the reader to 'hear my poem'; and it can also be a plea to the reader to 'hear the West Wind'. When these become synonymous, in that hoped-for moment of inspiration which only pretends to be beyond the poem, it will mean that Shelley is successful: he and his poem have become as the West Wind, an influence to be heard, being heard by the Wind and the reader. Spring, the season of creation, will have come.

The West Wind, in its signified sense, exists both outside of, before, and beyond the *Ode*. But the trope of the 'West Wind' also becomes a figure of the poem's reader (or hearer), not just a representation of the real wind that blows near Florence on some autumn days. Again, this is tied to the notion of repetition that the *Ode* demands: the reader is implored to read and re-read as much as the West Wind is asked to blow. The reader is next in line to be inspired. The reader is to the *Ode* as the poet is to the Wind. But the ratio does not stop there. We are asked to articulate the poem, and in doing so the saying of the poem creates its own movement of air. Shelley's desire is to be inspired, but knowing that he wants his work to become a part of the spirit of the age, in the *Ode to the West Wind* is the further desire to act as inspiration.

Shelley, drawn to the pervasive force of the 'West Wind' which is tied so closely to the production of poetry, wants to be an influential poet. He wants to be to other poets as he knows Wordsworth is to him. For when Shelley thinks about being a poet – moreover, an influential poet who represents the *spirit* of his own age – he is thinking about Wordsworth. Shelley read Wordsworth deeply and wrote about Wordsworth seriously. He both praised his older contemporary and despised him. He could allegorise Wordsworth and transfigure his poetry into new figurations. He could even kill Wordsworth, knowing that the dead always return: for Shelley, Wordsworth is the body that keeps showing up. But what he owed to Wordsworth was Wordsworth's own greatness, a greatness that he hoped would also see him through his own death.

Epilogue

'I wait thy breath Great Parent' – this is the Narrator in the invocation to *Alastor* waiting for that moment of poetic inspiration to arrive. He continued to wait, and up until his last poem, the unfinished *The Triumph of Life*, the expectation was still present, only now the obstinate question – 'Then, what is life?' – was ironically answered by Shelley's own death, a death caused, it so happens, by raging winds. And as we've seen, in those closing passages of the *Skylark* and *West Wind* he remains listening for the voice of inspiration and in anticipation of re-creative Spring's arrival. The wait (and hope) is for successful poetry, which is expressed either through the story told by a poet-narrator or the story of a poet-figure. Thus we also wait for a successful and completed outcome in *Alastor*, *The Sunset*, *Prince Athanase* and *Julian and Maddalo*, and it appears to happen in *Prometheus Unbound*, where through the freeing of Prometheus from the repressive force of Jupiter, the Titan is at last reunited with his soul-mate, Asia. What can be argued is that a great deal of Shelley's poetry is about the problem of becoming a poet, which is entangled with the problems of producing successful poetry and of 'characterising' the poet-figure. In the same way the Poet of *Alastor* seeks a vision of poetic perfectibility, Prometheus is a poet who actually achieves the goal of poetic individuation.

Shelley's search for inspiration and influence is the fundamental quest-vision making up some of his most important poems. For Shelley, inspiration is most strongly felt as that fleeting and fading moment springing from the influence of the *Zeitgeist*. The poet is always under the influence of influence. Even in that final work, *The Triumph of Life*, he has once more set the pattern we have come to know from *Alastor* through to *Julian and Maddalo*: once more a seductive female 'Shape' representing the elusiveness of inspiration is envisioned (348ff.), but even though it is 'for ever sought', it is 'for ever lost' (431). The poet within the poem (Rousseau) is led, helplessly, almost pathetically, to a confrontation with what we must conclude is a vision of his own creating. This must be emphasised, though commentators often miss the point. The poet of the poem (the narrator) envisions another poet within the poem (Rousseau) who in turn envisions the 'Shape'. What the first poet 'experiences' in *The Triumph of Life* is his own poetic scene of instruction: he has, in effect, summoned the *Zeitgeist* (in the guise of Rousseau) to come before him. *The Triumph* (or what we have of it) may be a more sophisticated poem than *Alastor*, but it is not a thematic departure.

Although *Verses Written on a Celandine* is his most important poetic response to Wordsworth, *Alastor* is Shelley's central poem in this study not just because it is his first sustained work about the problems of the production of successful poetry, but because it attempts to be a story told by a poet-narrator about a poet-figure. The effect of this is that it becomes the story about the poet-narrator. The Poet's journey in the poem is the Narrator's journey into the realm of poetry, into that delusory zone where waking and sleeping, life and death, are poetic states. The Poet never becomes a 'character', but lingers as a problem of the Narrator, of the composition of poetry, as does the Maniac, Prince Athanase and even Prometheus. The problem remains the same in such poems as the *Skylark* or *Ode to the West Wind*. The only difference is that the narrator in these poems professes to be a poet. The strategy of narration collapses into the strategy of the ode, but that object of address, whether a poet or a bird or the wind, holds the same function in both modes: it represents the poet's potential for successful poetry, for being a successful poet. All these poems express the same desire: I want to be a poet. The interesting problem has been determining the extent to which this desire originates from Wordsworth's presence and accomplishments.

What seems to be characteristic of Shelley's poetry is, somewhat paradoxically, this inspired hope for potential inspiration and completion, this waiting for the moment or event or answer that is held off by the poem's completion without resolution. There is in Shelley's poetry a future that anxiously wants to be. This future is a form of immortality, and this want-to-be is a poetic intimation. In an uncanny way many of the poems seems to be about what lies just beyond them, or they invoke what is just ahead of them. But the effect this has on us, as readers, is to draw us even more into the poem itself, in the same way a reflection draws us back to the originating image: the closer we look into the mirror, the closer we look at ourselves. In more than one sense, then, Shelley's poems are acts of self-reflection. Moreover, Shelley's poetry seems to defy the reader's normal patterns of interpretation, so much so that the reader thinks the problem is with the poetry and not with his manner of reading. This might have been the reason why the New Critics were repelled by Shelley's poetry, because it may have challenged their positivistic notions of response. It may have been impossible for them to respond in the way their principles dictated: if a poem does not fit the model, throw out the poem or discredit the poet.

Perhaps Shelley shares aspects of these characteristics with the greatest of his contemporaries. Perhaps another feature can be added to that thing called 'Romanticism'. The challenging logic in Shelley's poetry is that although the subject inspiring the poem (the poetic inspiration) is forever just beyond the moment of the poem, the poem itself is inspired. The fear of no inspiration acts as inspiration. This too is Coleridge in his 'conversation poems' having fears in darkness, silence and solitude, yet warding off those fears with the verses he composes about and in those states. The poet's death is not inarticulation, but silence. Thus it is the mystery of silence he must solve by breaking it. This too is what Keats addresses in those silent shapes on the urn, urging them to explanation by his own questionings. Ultimately they can only remain silent, yet Keats's poem joins this external silence with its own voice of truth and beauty: Keats's poetry is as fragile yet sensually enigmatic as the urn. The Romantic poet is drawn to question again and again that which he cannot answer; he is compelled to repeat that which he cannot complete. As much as this is Shelley forever waiting, Coleridge finding himself in silence and solitude once more, and Keats repeatedly testing that mysterious place between silence and articulation, sleep and death, it is Byron unable to finish off his protagonists. They cannot 'complete' themselves. Byron knew that to finish them off would be to take his own voice away.[1]

So how does Wordsworth stand as the apparent head of this clan? I would argue that Wordsworth initiated many of these qualities I have been claiming to be present in the poetry of his contemporaries. It was Wordsworth who first of all poeticised discontinuous and enigmatic tales of separation – the tale untold; who posed the problem of attempting to salvage from what might be lost a potential gain beyond the poem; who expressed fears of disability in poems which themselves display those abilities; who created a figure of himself that he could neither dispense with nor totally maintain; who invoked absence and quietude while simultaneously creating his own voiced presence; who, by addressing the silent shapes of Nature, transformed them into metaphors of his own mind; and who said that inspiration was fleeting, yet managed to formulate the poem as a monument to the momentary.

These, I would say, are some of the *styles* of problems that Wordsworth originated in his poetry and were taken up by his contemporaries. Whether or not a generalisation about Romanticism can be hazarded based on these styles is questionable, but it appears to me that a particular characteristic emerges. In much Romantic poetry there seems to be a discovery of a poetic self or place by attempting to move away from that self or place: the subject is not really the subject, and the poem's outcome undermines its own foundations and apparent aims. The paradox is tied closely to the problem we have in interpreting many Romantic poems where the literalness of the scene is called into question: Is the landscape an actual landscape? Is the subject of the poem really Nature, or is it a shifting trope for the poet attempting to situate himself in the poem? For example: Wordsworth's *Tintern Abbey* is not about revisiting a place, but is about the recollection of a memory; Coleridge's *This Lime-tree Bower* is not about a state of imprisonment, but about a sanctuary of creativity; Keats's *Ode to a Nightingale* questions not so much the ideal nature of the bird, but the transcendence of its own utterances (that is, the bird fades away into the poem, and the poem fades away into itself); Shelley's *Ode to the West Wind* does not celebrate the Wind's power, but the poet's potential for power; and Byron's *Childe Harold* is not a purposeful journey of discovery out into the world, but is an escape into a nebulous 'self' where it becomes impossible to distinguish the speaker from his protagonist. The question is ultimately one of reference and relationship. Shelley especially was capable of formulating the problem with extreme implications. In his fragment essay *On Life* he says 'The words *I*, and *you* and *they* are grammatical devices invented simply for arrangement and totally devoid of the intense and exclusive sense usually attached to them.' Shelley here is turning language back on itself, placing the signifying function of language under heavy suspicion. Although using language in very different ways, what Wordsworth and Shelley especially shared was the realisation of the importance of language: both realised that poetical language was not necessarily secondary to thought or expression, and that it is not merely a means to an end, but in some ways an end in itself.

When it is said that the Romantic poet seeks discovery of the poetic self by moving away from that self, this is the stance of solitude that he creates yet fears. The Romantic artist made the trope of solitude a prerequisite not only for the creative act, but also for the Romantic character or persona. This extends the boundaries of Romanticism beyond the British Isles, to, for example, Rousseau, Goethe and Chateaubriand. But for Shelley, more perhaps than these others, the Wordsworthian trope of solitude was often a problem, not a solution – it was an agony rather than reverie, an enslavement rather than an escape. Shelley seems to be asking an unsettling question in poem after poem: what if I cannot create a continuous figurative context to support my presence and authorial worth? The formulation of his scene of influence allowed him to at least offer an answer: My figurations draw their strength from those significant others who make up the spirit of the age; combining with them, I will join the spirit. Wordsworth, of course, was for Shelley the poetic spirit of the age. He could pay the older poet no higher compliment when in 1817 he wrote that 'Godwin has been to the present age in moral philosophy what Wordsworth is in poetry'.[2]

At bottom, there is very little difference between Keats's claims of his own selfless objectivity and his condemnation of Wordsworth's 'egotistical sublime'. In fact, the faceless or chameleon poet draws attention to his struggle with presence through his striving towards an articulate absence – it is articulate *and* conspicuous. For Shelley, the limitations that he enumerated and struggled with in his poetry likewise only serve to draw attention to those limitations, so much so that his poems often tend to become inspired statements of limitations. Keats and Shelley saw clearly the problems that Wordsworth posed, but in turn could only offer in their poetry their own brand of obstinate questions. Byron merely scorned Wordsworth's efforts, yet he could only give his poetic figures fleeter feet than the homebound Grasmere poet. Coleridge, of course, knew only too well Wordsworth's poetic powers, and he could never really separate himself from or rival Wordsworth through poetry, only through the meta-perspective that criticism offered.

But the remarkable quality of the English Romantic poets is not that there is some kind of discernable unity in their work, but that there is a difference within that unity. It is the paradox of fear and hope that the Romantics enunciated through their poetic pursuits – a search for a harmony that can never be, yet is.

Notes

Notes to the Introduction: Part I

1. F. R. Leavis, *Revaluation* (1936; Harmondsworth, Mddx: Penguin, 1978) pp. 194, 199.
2. Try though we might, we can never really forget (or forgive!) Arnold's judgement of Shelley as a 'beautiful and ineffectual angel, beating in the void his luminous wings in vain' (Matthew Arnold, Preface to *Poetry of Byron*, 1881).
3. These works are summarised by Newman I. White, 'The Beautiful Angel and his Biographers', *South Atlantic Quarterly*, xxiv (1925).
4. *The Letters of William and Dorothy Wordsworth: The Middle Years*, vol. i, ed. Ernest de Selincourt (Oxford University Press, 1937), p. 195.

Notes to Chapter 1: Shelley's Scene of Influence

1. Harold Bloom, *A Map of Misreading* (Oxford University Press, 1975) p. 10.
2. The most important study of this remains C. E. Pulos, *The Deep Truth: A Study of Shelley's Scepticism* (Lincoln, Nebr.: University of Nebraska Press, 1954).
3. Harold Bloom, *Poetry and Repression* (New Haven, Conn.: Yale University Press, 1976) p. 5.
4. André Gide, 'Concerning Influence in Literature', in *Pretexts: Reflections on Literature and Morality*, trans. Blanche A. Price (London, 1959) p. 31.
5. Quoted from *The Complete Poetical Works of Percy Bysshe Shelley*, the Julian Edition, ed. Roger Ingpen and Walter Peck (London, 1926–30; rpt 1965) vol. vii, p. 62.
6. The idea of the mind as passive, as well as the image of the mind as a string instrument, may well have been influenced by Shelley's reading of Hume's *A Treatise of Human Nature* (1739). In Book ii, Part iii, Section ix, he would have read: 'Now, if we consider the human mind, we shall find that with regard to the passions, [that it] . . . resembles a string instrument, where, after each stroke, the vibrations will retain some sound, which gradually and insensibly decays.'
7. For a more detailed but different sort of comparison of the *Preface* and the *Defence* see Bruce R. McElderry, 'Common Elements in Wordsworth's *Preface* and Shelley's *Defence of Poetry*', *Modern Language Quarterly*, v (1944) pp. 175–81.

Notes to Chapter 2: A New Presence

1. Thomas Medwin, *The Life of Percy Bysshe Shelley* (2 vols, 1847) ed. H. B. Forman (London, 1913) p. 44.
2. Ibid., pp. 147–8.
3. The best analysis of the relationship between the two poets is Kenneth Neill Cameron, 'Shelley vs. Southey: New Light on an Old Quarrel', *PMLA*, LVII (1942) pp. 489–512.
4. See James E. Barcus (ed.), *Shelley: The Critical Heritage* (London, 1975) p. 355.
5. *The Works of Thomas De Quincey* (Edinburgh, 1862) vol. v, pp. 19–20.
6. Southey wrote about Shelley in a letter dated 4 January 1812. Part of the letter appears in *The Life and Correspondence of Robert Southey*, ed. Charles Cuthbert Southey (London, 1850) vol. III, pp. 325–6. The missing passages are in *New Letters of Robert Southey*, ed. Kenneth Curry (New York: Columbia University Press, 1965) vol. II, pp. 19–20.
7. Bennett Weaver has called this poem a 'Wordsworthian imitation' in 'Shelley: The First Beginnings', *Philological Quarterly*, XXXII (1953) p. 194 – but he says no more than this. Richard Holmes says this: 'Of all Shelley's Keswick poems, easily the most striking is the long Wordsworthian "A Tale of Society as It Is". . . . It deserves to be counted as the first of Shelley's important poems' (see Holmes, *Shelley: The Pursuit* (London, 1974) p. 109).
8. The texts of Shelley's *Esdaile Notebook* poems I take from *The Esdaile Notebook*, edited and commentary by Kenneth Neill Cameron (London, 1964).
9. Ibid., p. 219.
10. Edward Dowden made a copybook of Shelley's *Esdaile Notebook*, and in it he jotted some notes opposite the poems. Beside the copy he made of *To Harriet*, Dowden noted certain parallels with *Tintern Abbey*, which I have expanded on. I would like to thank Robert Yampolsky, Bibliographer of the Carl H. Pforzheimer Library, New York, for sending me transcriptions of Dowden's notes. We can also note some further similarities between Wordsworth's poetry and this passage. Just as the progression of the argument in *Tintern Abbey* is framed by a series of 'nors' (112, 131, 147, 149) so too is *To Harriet* (32, 37, 39).
11. Cited in Neville Rogers (ed.), *The Complete Poetical Works of Percy Bysshe Shelley* (Oxford University Press, 1975) vol. II, p. 330.
12. *The Journals of Claire Clairmont*, ed. Marion Kingston Stocking (Cambridge, Mass.: Harvard University Press, 1968) pp. 47–8.
13. 'Memoirs of Percy Bysshe Shelley' in *The Works of Thomas Love Peacock*, vol. VII: *Essays, Memoirs, Letters and Unfinished Novels*, ed. H. F. B. Brett-Smith and C. E. Jones (London, 1934) p. 96.
14. Carl Dawson comments on Peacock's ambivalence as follows: 'Perhaps only Hazlitt and Coleridge quote Wordsworth more than Peacock does, however much, in Peacock's opinion, Wordsworth would have been better lost in a Cumberland bog' (*His Fine*

Wit: A Study of Thomas Love Peacock (London, 1970) p. 96).
15. Medwin, Life, pp. 147–8, and Medwin's 'Conversations of Lord Byron', ed. Ernest J. Lovell, Jr (Princeton, N.J.: Princeton University Press, 1966) p. 194.
16. The Diary of Benjamin Robert Haydon, ed. William Bissell Pope (Cambridge, Mass.: Harvard University Press, 1960–3) vol. II, p. 89; see too note, p. 558.
17. Henry Crabb Robinson on Books and Their Writers, ed. Edith J. Morley (London, 1938) vol. I, p. 212.
18. Tintern Abbey also continues to be sounded by Shelley. In his Essay on Christianity, which was probably written before 1815, Shelley quotes three lines to support his view (Shelley's Prose, ed. David Lee Clark (1954; Albuquerque, N.M.: University of New Mexico Press, 1966) p. 201). And in his review of Godwin's Mandeville, published in the 28 December 1917 Examiner, Shelley in passing quotes a line from the Intimations Ode (Clark, Prose, p. 310). As we have seen in this chapter, and as we shall see in future chapters, it is Tintern Abbey and the Intimations Ode which Shelley finds most engaging.
19. Peacock, Essays, Memoirs, ed. Brett-Smith and Jones, p. 199.

Notes to Chapter 3: 'Proteus Wordsworth'

1. Thomas Medwin, The Life of Percy Bysshe Shelley (2 vols, 1847) ed. H. B. Forman (London, 1913) p. 251.
2. The Life and Letters of Mary Wollstonecraft Shelley, vol. I, ed. Julian Marshall (London, 1889) pp. 80–1.
3. This is argued by Paul Mueschke and Earl Griggs, 'Wordsworth as the Prototype of the Poet in Shelley's Alastor', PMLA, XLIX (1934) pp. 229–45. J. C. Echeruo spends the last half of his essay on Shelley and Wordsworth also responding to Griggs and Mueschke: his conclusion is that 'Wordsworth is surely behind Alastor but not in the obvious way Griggs and Mueschke suggest' (see J. C. Echeruo, 'Shelley on Wordsworth', English Studies in Africa, IX (1966) p. 142).
4. See John Harrington Smith, 'Shelley and Claire Clairmont', PMLA, LIV (1939) pp. 797–9.
5. F. L. Jones puts this forward in 'The Inconsistency of Shelley's Alastor', ELH, XIII (1946) pp. 291–8, and 'The Vision Theme in Shelley's Alastor and Related Works', Studies in Philology, XLIV (1947) pp. 108–125 (p. 122 quoted). Raymond D. Havens in 'Shelley's Alastor', PMLA, XLV (1930) pp. 1098–15, also claims that Alastor is confusing.
6. See, for example, Evan K. Gibson, 'Alastor: A Reinterpretation', PMLA, LXII (1947) pp. 1022–46.
7. William Keach discusses how Shelley uses quotations from the Immortality Ode to frame structurally Alastor (see William Keach, 'Obstinate Questionings: The Immortality Ode and Alastor', The Wordsworth Circle, XII (Winter 1981) pp. 36–44.
8. Norman Thurston examines the relationship between the Narrator

and the Poet in *Alastor*, finding that Shelley's poem is a critical analysis of Wordsworth's poetic conditions; in this sense he finds the poem a 'negative success' (see Norman Thurston, 'Author, Narrator, and Hero in Shelley's *Alastor*', *Studies in Romanticism*, XIV (1975) pp. 119–31).

9. Following Griggs and Mueschke, the problem of Wordsworth and identification is also expressed by H. W. Piper: *Alastor* is 'an attempt to fit Wordsworth's conception of the Poet to Shelley's case – if, indeed, the Poet here be not Wordsworth himself seen through Shelley's eyes' (see H. W. Piper, *The Active Universe* (London, 1962) p. 167).

10. For this idea see Lisa M. Steinman, 'Shelley's Skepticism: Allegory in *Alastor*', *ELH*, LXV (1978) p. 260.

11. See Ronald Tetreault, 'Quest and Caution: Psychomachy in Shelley's *Alastor*', *English Studies in Canada*, III (1977) p. 291.

12. Harold Bloom, *The Anxiety of Influence: A Theory of Poetry* (Oxford University Press, 1971) p. 104.

13. Harold Bloom, *Yeats* (Oxford University Press, 1970) pp. 13–19.

14. Joseph Raben, 'Coleridge as the Prototype of the Poet in Shelley's *Alastor*', *Review of English Studies*, XVII (1966) pp. 278–92; Donald L. Maddox, 'Shelley's *Alastor* and the Legacy of Rousseau', *Studies in Romanticism*, IX (1970) pp. 82–98.

15. To quote Harold Bloom: '*Alastor* takes its theme from *The Excursion*'s Solitary, for an imaginatively inescapable reason, best expressed as the necessity to state the contrary views set forth by the Wanderer, Wordsworth's surrogate' (*Yeats*, p. 11). Earl Wasserman notes that Shelley's poem takes up the problem of solitude as left open by *The Excursion*, especially paralleling *Alastor* with the tale of Margaret from Wordsworth's poem (*Shelley: A Critical Reading* (Baltimore, Md: Johns Hopkins University Press, 1971) pp. 20–1). Also centring mainly on *The Excursion*'s significance, Yvonne M. Carothers, like Wasserman, gives a reading of *Alastor* where the Narrator of the poem is Wordsworthian and the Poet is the youthful consciousness of the Narrator. Carothers holds that through self-reflection the Narrator achieves 'correction' of his past faults – that is, *Alastor* 'corrects' Wordsworth (see Yvonne M. Carothers, '*Alastor*: Shelley Corrects Wordsworth', *Modern Language Quarterly*, XLII (1981) pp. 21–47). Further, Neil Fraistat proposes that the *Alastor* volume of poems itself is perhaps a response to *The Excursion* (see Neil Fraistat, 'Poetic Quests and Questionings in Shelley's *Alastor* Collection', *Keats–Shelley Journal*, XXXIII (1984) pp. 161–81).

16. I thank Rodney G. Dennis, Curator of Manuscripts in the Houghton Library, Harvard University, for sending me a photocopy and his transcription of Silsbee's annotation.

17. The text I am using is that of Timothy Webb (ed.), *Percy Bysshe Shelley: Selected Poems* (London, 1977).

18. *The Works of Thomas Love Peacock*, vol. VIII: *Essays, Memoirs, Letters and Unfinished Novels*, ed. H. F. B. Brett-Smith and C. E. Jones (London, 1934) p. 79.

19. Most commentators maintain that, because of the discrepant dates of publication and composition, it is unlikely Shelley could have read *Peter Bell* before writing his own poem. But J. B. Gohn, who accounts for these dates and gives other circumstantial evidence, supports the likelihood of Shelley having read *Peter Bell* (see J. B. Gohn, 'Did Shelley Know Wordsworth's *Peter Bell*?', *Keats–Shelley Journal*, xxviii (1979) pp. 20–4).
20. Richard Holmes, *Shelley: The Pursuit* (London, 1974) p. 551; Paul Foot, *Red Shelley* (London, 1980) p. 10.
21. F. R. Leavis, 'Wordsworth: The Creative Conditions', in R. A. Brower (ed.), *Twentieth-Century Literature in Retrospect*, Harvard English Studies 2 (1971) p. 325.
22. F. W. Bateson, 'Shelley on Wordsworth: Two Unpublished Stanzas from "Peter Bell the Third" ', *Essays in Criticism*, xvii (1967) pp. 125–9.
23. Geoffrey Hartman, *Wordsworth's Poetry 1787–1814* (1964; New Haven, Conn.: Yale University Press, 1977) p. 5.
24. Leavis, 'Wordsworth: The Creative Conditions', pp. 326, 329.
25. Shelley probably took Wordsworth's denial of happiness from a passage of the latter's reprinted in the *Poems in Two Volumes* (1815). It originally appeared in *The Friend*, 26 October 1809. Shelley actually misquoted the passage in a letter to John Gisborne, 10 April 1822:

> This earth,
> Which is the world of all of us, & where
> *We find our happiness or not at all.*
> (*Letters*, ii, p. 406)

Ronald Tetrault says that Shelley 'seems to have regarded the passage as typifying Wordsworth's damning flaw, the restriction of human aspiration to the natural world' (see Ronald Tetrault, 'Quest and Caution: Psychomachy in Shelley's *Alastor*', *English Studies in Canada*, iii (1977) pp. 298–9).

26. See John E. Jordan, 'Wordsworth and *The Witch of Atlas*', *ELH*, ix (1942) pp. 320–5. Jordan's argument is that the Witch is intended to 'match' Peter by being his opposite, and that Wordsworth's rather ponderous narrative, as well as the absence of any humour, are countered by Shelley in *The Witch*. The general notion that *The Witch of Atlas* is an implicit challenge to *Peter Bell* is discussed by Richard Cronin, 'Shelley's Witch of Atlas', *Keats–Shelley Journal*, xxvi (1977) pp. 88–100: 'The virtuoso sophistication of the poem's tone is itself a satire on the gauche singlemindedness of Wordsworth's tone in *Peter Bell*' (p. 100).
27. From the Bixby–Huntington Notebook no. ii, reprinted in Neville Rogers, *Shelley at Work: A Critical Inquiry* (Oxford University Press, 1956) p. 219.
28. This fragment can be found in Donald H. Reiman, *Shelley's 'The Triumph of Life'* (Urbana, Ill.: University of Illinois Press, 1965) pp. 240–2.
29. According to Franklyn Bliss Synder, *mind* actually ranks fourth in a list of Wordsworth's 'favorite words', after *love*, *heart* and *man*, and

before *life*: 'Wordsworth's Favorite Words', *Journal of English and Germanic Philology*, xxii (1923) pp. 253–6. Synder's figures indicate that, in a comparison of the favourite words of Wordsworth, Spencer, Shakespeare, Gray, Cowper, Shelley, Keats and Tennyson, twelve words appearing in Wordsworth's list also appear on the list of one of the other poets. My counting shows that in one-third of these cases it is Shelley who is the other poet sharing a favourite word (*mountain, shadow, spirit, wind*). Of eleven words that are shared by Wordsworth and two other poets, Shelley appears most often – six times (*child, cloud, deep, hope, power* and *soul*). This somewhat dispassionate approach gives us the conclusion that of Keats, Shelley and Tennyson, it is Shelley who integrates Wordsworth's vocabulary most frequently.

Interestingly and appropriately, this phrase, 'gentle mind', also appears in Shelley's translation of Guido Cavalcanti's sonnet to Dante, the 'gentle mind' ascribed to Dante before his betrayal of Cavalcanti (see p. 48 above).

30. Edward Dowden, *The Life of Percy Bysshe Shelley* (London, 1886) ii, p. 218.
31. Timothy Webb notes in *Percy Bysshe Shelley: Selected Poems* that the last line of *An Exhortation* – 'Oh, refuse the boon!' – is likely an ironic reference to Wordsworth's lamentation in *The World Is Too Much With Us* (1807) – specifically, to the line 'We have given our hearts away, a sordid boon!' (p. 211).
32. Reprinted from Rogers, *Shelley at Work*, p. 217.
33. Quotation from Sigmund Freud, 'Some Reflections on Schoolboy Psychology' (1914), in *The Standard Edition of the Complete Works of Sigmund Freud*, trans. James Strachey (London, 1955) vol. xiii, p. 243.

Notes to the Introduction: Part II

1. Judith Cherniak, 'The Figure of the Poet in Shelley', *ELH,* xxxv (1968) p. 567.
2. F. R. Leavis, *Revaluation* (1936; Harmondsworth, Mddx: Penguin, 1978) pp. 184–5.

Notes to Chapter 4: Poets, Princes and Fallen Figures

1. Bloom supports this development and change in Shelley: 'Before the winter of 1814–15, Shelley wrote badly; he was a very weak poet. After he read deeply in Wordsworth and Coleridge, particularly Wordsworth, he was able to write *Alastor* and the powerful 1816 poems' (see Harold Bloom, *Poetry and Repression* (New Haven, Conn.: Yale University Press, 1976) p. 105). H. W. Piper has said, anticipating Bloom, that 'Shelley's reading of Wordsworth was the cause of that all-important difference between *Alastor* and *Queen Mab*' (see H. W. Piper, *The Active Universe* (London, 1962) p. 150).

2. Harold Bloom, *The Anxiety of Influence: A Theory of Poetry* (Oxford University Press, 1971) pp. 70, 94.
3. Carlos Baker, *Shelley's Major Poetry: The Fabric of a Vision* (1948; Princeton, N.J.: Princeton University Press, 1966) p. 23.
4. Gerald McNiece, *Shelley and the Revolutionary Idea* (Cambridge, Mass.: Harvard University Press, 1969) p. 152.
5. A. C. Bradley, *Oxford Lectures on Poetry* (1909; London, 1920) p. 240.
6. See William Keach's essay, 'Obstinate Questionings: The Immortality Ode and *Alastor*' (*The Wordsworth Circle*, XXII (Winter 1981) pp. 36–44) on how these quotations frame *Alastor*.
7. *The Works of Thomas Love Peacock*, vol. VII: *Essays, Memoirs, Letters and Unfinished Novels*, ed. H. F. B. Brett-Smith and C. E. Jones (London, 1934) p. 100.
8. Richard Cronin in *Shelley's Poetic Thoughts* (London: Macmillan, 1981) notes that '*Alastor* is a complex series of mirror images' (pp. 89–90). Peter Butter in a discussion of the major images in *Shelley's Idols of the Cave* (Edinburgh University Press, 1954) notes that the 'image of a mirror is a favourite one in Shelley' (p. 100). But Butter's conclusion, that 'Perception of oneness is expressed . . . by the mirror image' (p. 102), is misleading: disparity and difference are also apparent in Shelley's use of aspects of the image.
9. Milton Wilson in *Shelley's Later Poetry: A Study of his Prophetic Imagination* (New York: Columbia University Press, 1959) also notes this tendency in *Alastor*: 'it has been possible to interpret the poem as mainly the story of a destructive narcissism' (p. 77). Wilson also says that the mirror images in *Alastor* are 'not worked into the poem in anything but a superficial way' (p. 77). However, as I hope the present discussion demonstrates, Shelley's use of mirror imagery is anything but superficial. It controls the Poet's quest from beginning to end, representing an important 'presence' in the poem. See, too, Edward Strickland, 'Transfigured Night: The Visionary Inversions of *Alastor*', *Keats–Shelley Journal*, XXXIII (1984) pp. 148–60: Strickland likewise points to the importance of the Narcissus-imagery in *Alastor*, although he points more to a Coleridgean source for the poem's visionary gropings.
10. Bloom, *The Anxiety of Influence*, p. 16.
11. Ibid., p. 147
12. See Earl Wasserman, *Shelley: A Critical Reading* (Baltimore, Md: Johns Hopkins University Press, 1971), especially pp. 15–21. Wasserman's observation has been very influential for many commentators on the poem (including, of course, the present author). More recently, Michael Scrivener has said: 'There is a dramatic contrast between the mediating narrator, whose nature-worship leads to imaginative humanism, and the apocalyptic Visionary [Poet], whose "natural piety" is short-circuited by repressed sexuality' (see Michael Scrivener, *Radical Shelley: The Philosophical Anarchism and Utopian Thought of Percy Bysshe Shelley* (Princeton, N.J.: Princeton University Press, 1982) p. 84). I would not, however, agree with Scrivener's rather literal reading of the Poet's (the 'Visionary') problem as having sexual

origins. Surely the Poet's failing is a *poetic* failing, otherwise the significance of the protagonist being a poet would be lost. See, too, Martyn Crucefix, 'Wordsworth, Superstition, and Shelley's *Alastor*', *Essays in Criticism*, XXXIII (1983) pp. 126–47, for a discussion of the relationship between the Narrator and the Poet as Wordsworthian presences; Crucefix holds that 'both personae are guilty of superstitious beliefs since both mistakingly claim reality for their externalised visions' (p. 133). I might also comment on Wasserman's and Scrivener's decision to call the protagonist of *Alastor* 'the Visionary'. In short, there is no reason why he should be called 'the Visionary', for throughout the Preface and the poem he is called nothing but 'the Poet'. Calling him 'the Visionary' plays down the fact that *Alastor* is about a poet and a poetic quest.

Notes to Chapter 5: The Maniac Poet

1. Ivan Roe, *Shelley: The Last Phase* (London, 1953) p. 141ff.
2. See Donald Reiman and Sharon B. Powers, *Shelley's Poetry and Prose* (New York: W. W. Norton, 1977) p. 112, n. 1.
3. Carl Grabo, *The Magic Plant* (Chapel Hill, N.C.: University of North Carolina Press, 1936) p. 268.
4. This identification seemed to be popular at the end of the nineteenth century. See Arabella Shore, 'Shelley's "Julian and Maddalo" ', *The Gentleman's Magazine*, CCLXIII, no. 1882 (October 1887) pp. 329–42; and H. S. Salt, 'Shelley's "Julian and Maddalo" ', *The Academy*, XXXI, no. 777 (26 March 1887) pp. 220–1.
5. John Harrington Smith, 'Shelley and Claire Clairmont', *PMLA*, LIV (1939) pp. 804–8.
6. This point is considered by Newman Ivey White, *Shelley* (1940; rev. edn, London, 1947) vol. II, pp. 42–50.
7. One critic believes both Maddalo and the Maniac are aspects of Byron's complex personality: J. E. Saveson, 'Shelley's *Julian and Maddalo*', *Keats–Shelley Journal*, x (1961) pp. 53–8.
8. Earl Wasserman suggests that 'Julian and Maddalo are Shelley's divided and conflicting selves skeptically confronting each other, as they do in *Alastor*; and the poem, in effect, is Shelley's debate with himself' (*Shelley: A Critical Reading* (Baltimore, Md: Johns Hopkins University Press, 1971) p. 64). William Irvine in *The Book, The Ring, and The Poet: A Biography of Robert Browning* (New York, 1974) says that the Maniac is Shelley's alter ego (p. 125). And Kenneth Neill Cameron in *Shelley: The Golden Years* (Cambridge, Mass.: Harvard University Press, 1974) concludes that 'there can be little doubt that the madman is Shelley and that this section of *Julian and Maddalo* [i.e., the Maniac's monologue] reflects an actual situation in his life' (p. 262). Because of this Cameron goes on to say that the woman the Maniac speaks of must be Mary.
9. The significance of Tasso for Shelley's poem is best discussed in Carlos Baker, *Shelley's Major Poetry* (Princeton, N.J.: Princeton

University Press, 1966) pp. 124–38.
10. Ibid., p. 125.
11. *The Works of Thomas Love Peacock*, vol. VIII: *Essays, Memoirs, Letters and Unfinished Novels*, ed. H. F. B. Brett-Smith and C. E. Jones (London, 1934) p. 79.
12. *Byron's Letters and Journals* (1814–1815), ed. Leslie A. Marchand (London, 1975) vol. IV, p. 324.
13. Byron wrote this on the sheet of the original draft for his poem 'Churchill's Grave, A Fact Literally Rendered': see *The Works of Lord Byron; Poetry*, ed. Ernest Hartley Coleridge (London, 1905) vol. IV, pp. 46–7, n.3.
14. He made this self-correction in 1816. See ibid., vol. I, p. 315, n. 3.
15. Thomas Medwin, *The Life of Percy Bysshe Shelley* (2 vols, 1847) ed. H. B. Forman (London, 1913) pp. 147–8. As Philip W. Martin writes in *Byron: A Poet before His Public* (Cambridge University Press, 1982) 'there can be little doubt that when Byron met Shelley, he met the first person (and probably the only person) in his life who was to tell him with conviction that Wordsworth was a great poet' (p. 67). This observation is singularly important in my discussion of *Julian and Maddalo*.
16. As one critic has summarised Shelley's tour of Switzerland, the 'literary ghost of the Swiss tour was Wordsworth' (Marilyn Butler, *Peacock Displayed: A Satirist in his Context* (London, 1979) p. 71).
17. From the 1831 Introduction to Mary Shelley's *Frankenstein: or The Modern Prometheus*.
18. *The Diary of Dr John Polidori*, 1816, ed. William Michael Rossetti (London, 1911) p. 121.
19. To quote James L. Hill, 'Dramatic Structure in Shelley's *Julian and Maddalo*', *ELH*, XXXV (1968): 'The Maniac, like the poets in *Alastor* and *Epipsychidion*, is a visionary whose vision fails to become a reality' (p. 91). Hill also makes two other points relevant to my thesis: (1) that Shelley's use of the infant in *Julian and Maddalo* (143ff.) is similar to Wordsworth's use of the child in the *Intimations Ode* (p. 88); (2) that 'the Maniac's ravings [are] essentially poetic' (p. 92).

Notes to Chapter 6: Shelley Unbound

1. Arthur Clutton-Brock, *Shelley: The Man and the Poet* (1909; rev. edn, London, 1923) p. 168.
2. Ibid., p. 206.
3. Anna Balakian, 'Influence and Literary Fortune: The Equivocal Junction of Two Methods', *Yearbook of Comparative and General Literature*, XI (1962) p. 29.
4. David Simpson, *Irony and Authority in Romantic Poetry* (London, 1979) p. 135.
5. In putting it like this, Shelley is echoing what Milton said about *Paradise Lost*, that 'it pursues / Things unattempted yet in Prose or Rime' (Book I. 15–16).

6. Recorded by Edward John Trelawney, *Records of Shelley, Byron and the Author* (London, 1878) vol. I, p. 118. (Originally published as *Recollections of the Last Days of Shelley and Byron*, 1858.)
7. G. M. Matthews has said that *Julian and Maddalo* 'persistently echoes or anticipates' the later poem, and he lists a large number of parallels (see G. M. Matthews, *Julian and Maddalo*: The Draft and the Meaning', *Studia Neophilologica*, XXXV (1963) pp. 73–4). Matthews says that a 'lonely, tormented, yet defiant figure stands at the centre' of both poems: Prometheus's origins are thus to be found in aspects of the Maniac, just as the Maniac's origins are to be found in the Poet of *Alastor*.
8. Harold Bloom, *The Anxiety of Influence: A Theory of Poetry* (Oxford University Press, 1971) p. 79.
9. Harold Bloom, *Shelley's Mythmaking* (1959; Ithaca, N.Y.: Cornell University Press, 1969) p. 106.
10. Allegorical interpretations of Shelley's lyrical drama proliferate. Even before the first quarter of this century N. I. White pointed this out (the title of his essay explains the point): '*Prometheus Unbound*, or Every Man His Own Allegorist', *PMLA*, XL (1925) pp. 172–84.
11. Earl Wasserman, *Shelley: A Critical Reading* (Baltimore, Md: Johns Hopkins University Press, 1971) p. 255.
12. Percy Bysshe Shelley, '*Prometheus Unbound*': A Variorum Edition (Seattle: University of Washington Press, 1959) p. 309.
13. Bloom, *Shelley's Mythmaking*, p. 95.
14. Wasserman, *Shelley: A Critical Reading*, p. 256.
15. Benjamin Kurtz, *The Pursuit of Death: A Study of Shelley's Poetry* (1933; Folcroft, Pa., 1969) p. 158.
16. William H. Hildebrand, 'On Three Prometheuses: Shelley's Two and Mary's One', *Serif*, XI (1974) p. 3.
17. See Leon Waldoff, 'The Father–Son Conflict in *Prometheus Unbound*: The Psychology of a Vision', *Psychoanalytic Review*, LXII (1975) pp. 79–96.
18. See, for example: William H. Marshall, 'The Father–Child Symbolism in *Prometheus Unbound*', *Modern Language Quarterly*, XXII (1961) pp. 41–5; James Rieger, *The Mutiny Within: The Heresies of Percy Bysshe Shelley* (New York, 1967) p. 150; Wasserman, *Shelley: A Critical Reading*, pp. 295–305; Stuart Curran, *Shelley's Annus Mirabilis* (Huntington Library, 1975) pp. 54–60; Jean Hall, *The Transforming Image: A Study of Shelley's Major Poetry* (Urbana, Ill.: University of Illinois Press, 1980) pp. 77–80; Michael G. Cooke, *Acts of Inclusion: Studies Bearing on an Elementary Theory of Romanticism* (New Haven, Conn.: Yale University Press, 1979) pp.95–8.
19. Curran, *Shelley's Annus Mirabilis*, p. 55.
20. Two important essays point to this tendency in the poem: V. A. De Luca, 'The Style of Millennial Announcement in *Prometheus Unbound*', *Keats–Shelley Journal*, XXVIII (1979) pp. 78–101; and Frederick Burwick, 'The Language of Causality in *Prometheus Unbound*', *Keats–Shelley Journal*, XXXI (1982) pp. 136–58. De Luca says that 'the form and mood of the millennium ... depend ... for their articulation upon the announcements of eloquent voices. To render the hypothesis of a

realized millennium as a convincing truth to the readers of the play, these voices must issue forth in clear, confident, and declarative utterance, as if assertive of things that are' (p. 79). Frederick Burwick takes a different angle, but presses for the same emphasis. He observes that Prometheus's 'crucial gift, as titanic mediator between divinity and humanity, is language, the *logos* as reason and word' (p. 136).

21. Daniel Hughes, 'Prometheus Made Capable Poet in Act One of *Prometheus Unbound*', *Studies in Romanticism*, xvii (1978) pp. 4, 11.
22. Ibid., pp. 6–7.
23. This struggling for a language of the sublime is the theme of Susan Hawk Brisman's ' "Unsaying His High Language": The Problem of Voice in *Prometheus Unbound*', *Studies in Romanticism*, xvi (1977) pp. 51–86.
24. See Chapter 3, note 27.
25. This same idea is suggested by William Hildebrand, who likewise notes that lips, for Shelley, are an emblem for the poet's imagination, and that the poet is portrayed as both an active and passive being: 'A Look at the Third and Fourth Spirit Songs: *Prometheus Unbound*, i', *Keats–Shelley Journal*, xx (1971) p. 95.
26. Bloom, *A Map of Misreading*, p. 19.
27. This idea is suggested by Ronald L. Lemoncelli, 'Cenci as Corrupt Dramatic Poet', *English Language Notes*, xvi (1978) pp. 103–117 (see especially pp. 104–6).
28. Bloom, *The Anxiety of Influence*, pp. 87–8.
29. See Richard Cronin, *Shelley's Poetic Thoughts* (London: Macmillan, 1981) p. 156.

Notes to Chapter 7: Righting Wordsworth

1. Wordsworth's comments on Shelley can be found in *The Critical Opinions of William Wordsworth*, ed. Markham L. Peacock, Jr (Baltimore, Md: Johns Hopkins University Press, 1950) p. 349.
2. Stuart Sperry, 'From "Tintern Abbey" to the "Intimations Ode": Wordsworth and the Function of Memory', *The Wordsworth Circle*, i (1970) p. 45.
3. The influence of Wordsworth's *Ode* on the *Hymn* has been noted by a number of commentators. For example, Harold Bloom: 'When Shelley re-wrote the "Intimations" ode as his *Hymn to Intellectual Beauty*, he underwent a *daemonization* that burdened him, morally and instinctually, with a program too intense even for his curiously tough and swift spirit to carry through' (see Bloom, *The Anxiety of Influence: A Theory of Poetry* (Oxford University Press, 1971) p. 108). Richard Cronin: 'Shelley's hymn is obviously influenced by Wordsworth's ode. The Spirit to which he refers in the poem's title as Intellectual Beauty is an intimation of immortality' (see Cronin, *Shelley's Poetic Thoughts* (London: Macmillan, 1981) pp. 224–5). And Judith Cherniak: 'Shelley's "Hymn to Intellectual Beauty" consciously recalls

Wordsworth's "Ode: Intimations of Immortality" and attempts to extend and modify its central theme. As Wordsworth's great "Ode" laments a radiance gone from the world, Shelley's "Hymn" describes the poet's perception of a beauty that is inconstant, that leaves the world "vacant and desolate", and that is yet the chief source of meaning in a world otherwise accidental, formless, purposeless' (see Judith Chernaik, *The Lyrics of Shelley* (Cleveland, Oreg.: Case Western Reserve University Press, 1972) pp. 33–4).

4. Donald Reiman believes that *Alastor*, *Mont Blanc* and the *Hymn* 'embody the high-water mark of Wordsworth's influence on Shelley', especially the influence of *Tintern Abbey* and the *Intimations Ode* (see Donald Reiman, *Percy Bysshe Shelley* (New York, 1969) pp. 45–6).

5. For example, Harold Bloom in *Shelley's Mythmaking* (1959; Ithaca, N.Y.: Cornell University Press, 1969) says that the 'natural religion' of *Tintern Abbey* is 'rejected' in Shelley's *Mont Blanc* (pp. 13, 115), yet *Mont Blanc* resembles *Tintern Abbey* 'rather more than any other poem' (p. 35). In his later study, *The Ringers in the Tower: Studies in Romantic Tradition* (Chicago, Ill.: University of Chicago Press, 1971), Bloom states that Shelley 'attacked' Wordsworth in *Mont Blanc* 'for attempting to reconcile man with nature' (p. 20). Marilyn Butler in *Romantics, Rebels, and Reactionaries* (Oxford U.P., 1981) calls *Mont Blanc* an anti-Wordsworthian poem (p. 141).

6. Jean Hall, *The Transforming Image: A Study of Shelley's Major Poetry* (Urbana, Ill.: University of Illinois Press, 1980) pp. 43–9.

7. F. R. Leavis, *Revaluation* (1936; Harmondsworth, Mddx: Penguin, 1978) p. 199.

8. W. B. Yeats, 'The Philosophy of Shelley's Poetry' (1900), in *W. B. Yeats: Selected Criticism and Prose*, ed. A Norman Jeffares (London: Macmillan, 1980) p. 71.

9. David Simpson, *Irony and Authority* (London, 1979) p. 162.

10. Bloom, *Shelley's Mythmaking*, p. 23.

11. Spencer Hall notes this parodying quality as well: 'Shelley's "Mont Blanc" ', *Studies in Philology*, LXX (1973) pp. 205–6, n. 15.

12. See Bloom, *Anxiety of Influence*, pp. 14, 49–73.

13. Leavis, *Revaluation*, p. 202.

14. The Skylark, William Empson says, 'is a very precise symbol of Shelley's view of the poet; it rises higher and higher, straight upwards, alone, always singing, always in effort, till becoming exhausted somewhere out of sight of the normal world it tumbles back in silence, and resumes a humble, isolated, and invisible existence somewhere in the middle of a field' (see William Empson, *Seven Types of Ambiguity* (1930; rev. edn, London, 1963) p. 158).

15. *The Works of Thomas Love Peacock*, vol. VIII: *Essays, Memoirs, Letters and Unfinished Novels*, ed. H. F. B. Brett-Smith and C. E. Jones (London, 1934) pp. 41–2.

Notes to Chapter 8: The Wind of Inspiration

1. M. H. Abram's well-known essay, 'The Correspondent Breeze: A Romantic Metaphor' (*Kenyon Review*, 19 (1957) pp. 113–30) made us aware that air-in-motion is both a commonplace and important trope in Romantic poetry. Although Abrams is correct in pointing out that in Romantic poems 'the rising wind was explicitly paralleled to a change in the inner state of the lyric speaker' (p. 127), I shall argue that in the case of Shelley wind or moving air is more directly related to the inspiration and the force of influence in the production of poetry.
2. The only extended analysis of wind imagery in *Alastor* is John C. Bean, 'The Poet Borne Darkly: The Dream-Voyage Allegory in Shelley's *Alastor*', *Keats–Shelley Journal*, XXIII (1974) pp. 60–76. But for the wind-harp as a symbol of harmony in *Alastor* see Glenn O'Malley, 'Shelley's "Air-Prism": The Synesthetic Scheme of *Alastor*', *Modern Philology*, LV (1958) pp. 178–87.
3. Harold Bloom, *Shelley's Mythmaking* (1959; Ithaca, N.Y.: Cornell University Press, 1969) p. 29. Bloom acknowledges his debt to I. J. Kapstein, 'The Meaning of Shelley's "Mont Blanc"', *PMLA*, LXII (1947) pp. 1046–60.
4. Shelley quite likely took the idea of the mind as a passive receptor from Hume. For Hume's influence on Shelley's thought in general, and specifically for the model of the human mind as a sort of wind instrument, see Ralph Houston, 'Shelley and the Principle of Association', *Essays in Criticism*, III (1953) pp. 45–59 (see especially p. 47).
5. Timothy Webb says that in the *Ode to the West Wind* 'Shelley wants to play the role of the biblical prophet who announces the advent of the new heaven and the new earth' (see Timothy Webb, *Shelley: A Voice Not Understood* (Manchester University Press, 1977) p. 179.
6. This observation is made by Irene H. Chayes, 'Rhetoric as Drama: An Approach to the Romantic Ode', *PMLA*, LXXIX (1964) p. 72.
7. For a discussion of the *Ode* as a prayer see Coleman O. Parsons, 'Shelley's Prayer to the West Wind', *Keats–Shelley Journal*, XI (1962) pp. 31–7.
8. Bodleian Library, MS. Shelley Adds. e.6, p. 138.
9. The text of this fragment I base on the *Notebooks of Percy Bysshe Shelley*, ed. H. Buxton Forman (1911; New York, 1968) vol. III, pp. 171–2.
10. For this idea see too Paul Fry, 'Shelley and the Celebration of Power', in *The Poet's Calling in the English Ode* (New Haven, Conn.: Yale University Press, 1980) pp. 208–10, 313–14.

Notes to the Epilogue

1. To quote Northrop Frye: '*Childe Harold* and *Don Juan* are Byron to such an extent that the poems about them can be finished only by Byron's death or boredom with the *persona*' ('The Drunken Boat: The

Revolutionary Element in Romanticism', in Northrop Frye (ed.), *Romanticism Reconsidered* (1963) p. 16).
2. From a review of Godwin's *Mandeville*, published in the *Examiner*. 28 December 1817 (see David Lee Clark (ed.), *Shelley's Prose; or The Trumpet of a Prophecy* (1954; revised edn, Albuquerque, N.M.: University of New Mexico Press, 1966) p. 309).

Index

Aeschylus, 136, 137
Arnold, Matthew, 4, 161
Augustine, St, 53

Baker, Carlos, 88, 117, 124
Balakian, Anna, 133
Beaumont, Sir George, 5
Beaumont, Lady, 14
Bloom, Harold, 4, 8, 17, 52, 87, 105, 133, 136, 137, 139, 152–3, 157, 173, 175, 180, 197
Bradley, A. C., 98
Brougham, Henry, 43
Byron, Lord, 42, 45, 54–5, 69, 113, 116, 117, 118, 119, 122, 127, 165, 223, 224, 225

Calvert, William, 27–9
Cameron, Kenneth Neill, 34
Campbell, Thomas, 40, 41
Cavalcanti, Guido, 48
Chateaubriand, François René, 225
Chatterton, Thomas, 77
Chernaik, Judith, 81
Clairmont, Claire, 41, 50, 55, 116, 120
Clutton-Brock, Arthur, 132, 134
Coleridge, Samuel Taylor, 26, 27, 28, 29, 30, 49, 52, 69, 159, 206–7, 223, 224, 225
Collins, William, 117
Correggio, Antonio, 143
Cowper, William, 117
Curran, Stuart, 143

Dante, 48, 137
Darwin, Erasmus, 40
De Quincey, Thomas, 26, 29
Dowden, Edward, 75

Eliot, T. S., 161
Esdaile, Edward Jeffries, 30

Foot, Paul, 65
Freud, Sigmund, 77

Gide, André, 17–18
Gisborne, Maria, 75
Godwin, William, 26, 30, 40, 42, 144, 225
Goethe, Johann Wolfgang von, 88, 225
Gray, Thomas, 206
Grove, Thomas, 37

Hall, Jean, 172
Hartman, Geoffrey, 68–9
Haydon, Benjamin Robert, 42
Hesiod, 142
Hildebrand, William, H., 140–1
Hitchener, Elizabeth, 26, 27, 29, 31
Hogg, Thomas Jefferson, 26, 100, 116
Holmes, Richard, 65
Hughes, Daniel, 146
Hunt, Leigh, 41, 64, 113, 114, 119
Hunt, Marianne, 43

Ingpen, Roger, 55

Keats, John, 43, 61, 64, 69, 72, 165, 190, 223, 224, 225
Kurtz, Benjamin, 140–1

Leavis, F. R., 3–4, 50, 67–8, 69, 82–3, 161, 173, 185
Lichtenberg, Georg Christoph, 159
Lind, Dr Charles, 96
Lonsdale, Lord, 43
Lovell, Robert, 27

240

Lucan, Marcus Annaeus Lucanus, 77

McNiece, Gerald, 88
Medwin, Thomas, 26, 41, 45, 46
Milton, John, 47, 88–9, 137–8, 206

Ollier, Charles, 25, 65

Peacock, Thomas Love, 18, 41, 43, 54, 55, 62, 118, 189
Peck, Walter, 55
Pilford, Captain, 144
Plato, 96
Polidori, Dr John, 119
Pope, Alexander, 206
Pottle, Frederick A., 209
Powers, Sharon B., 55

Reiman, Donald, H., 55
Reynolds, John Hamilton, 64, 66, 201
Robinson, Henry Crabb, 42
Rousseau, Jean-Jacques, 52, 74, 88–9, 221–2

Scott, Sir Walter, 40
Shakespeare, William, 32, 137
Shelley, Mary Wollstonecraft (née Godwin), 40, 45, 49, 50, 53, 55, 64, 72, 91, 116, 117, 119, 120, 195
Shelley, Percy Bysshe
  Poetry:
  A Poet of the finest water . . . (fragment), 73
  Adonais, 61, 72, 78, 87, 112, 195
  Alastor, 6–7, 29, 41, 50–4, 60, 73, 76, 77, 86, 88, 90, 91, 92–5, 98–112, 116, 121, 125–6, 127–8, 132, 134, 140, 148, 157, 172, 182, 190, 193, 195–7, 200, 213, 221, 222
  Celandine, Verses Written on a, 55–63, 64, 65, 66, 71, 75, 76, 77, 88, 110, 132, 148, 182, 193, 217, 222
  Cenci, The, 154
  Cloud, The, 184, 199

Death, 184
Epipsychidion, 77
Exhortation, An, 75–6, 191, 199
Harriet, To ('It is not blasphemy . . .'), 32–6, 39, 40
Hymn to Intellectual Beauty, 55, 90, 120, 167–71, 172, 182, 183, 185, 198, 202, 215
Jane: The Recollection, To, 82–4
Julian and Maddalo, 113–31, 132, 134, 140, 157, 193, 199–200, 216, 221
Lift Not the Painted Veil, 183
Mont Blanc, 16, 55, 109, 120, 160, 171–82, 193, 197–8, 210
Mutability (1816), 183–4, 185, 198
Mutability (1821), 63, 184
My Head is wild . . . (fragment), 74
Ode to the West Wind, 25, 65, 194, 201–19, 221, 222, 224
Oh! There Are Spirits of the Air, 49–50, 183
Ozymandias, 182, 184
Peter Bell the Third, 52–3, 63–73, 76, 77, 88, 120, 191, 193, 201
Prince Athanase, 91–8, 128, 132, 135, 140, 199, 221
Prometheus Unbound, 41, 65, 130–1, 132–58, 193, 200, 201, 215, 216; Preface to, 12–18, 22, 88, 123, 135, 212, 215
Proserpine, Song of, 195
Queen Mab, 27, 86–8, 172, 195
Retrospect, The, 36–40
Revolt of Islam, The, 120, 154, 201; Preface to, 8–12, 14, 17, 18, 171, 175, 212
Rosalind and Helen, 64
Skylark, To a, 160, 185–90, 202, 205, 221, 222
Sunset, The, 55, 91–2, 128, 140, 221
Tale of Society as It Is: From Facts, 1811, A, 31–2
Triumph of Life, The, 73, 221–2
When the Lamp is Shattered, 82, 184
Witch of Atlas, The, 71, 77
Wordsworth, To, 27, 40, 45, 46–50, 52, 54, 60, 64, 71, 76, 77, 88, 132, 193

Written on a Beautiful Day of Spring, 32

Prose:
Address to the Irish People, 30
Defence of Poetry A, 18–25, 60, 97, 103, 121, 135, 149, 161–2, 171, 175, 186, 198, 202, 212, 214–15
History of a Six Weeks' Tour, 180
On Life, 18, 224
On Love, 100
Refutation of Deism, A, 41, 177
Speculations on Metaphysics, 18
Treatise on Morals, 41

Silsbee, Edward, A., 55
Simpson, David, 133, 173
Smart, Christopher, 117
Southey, Robert, 26, 27, 28, 29, 30, 40, 42, 43, 144, 201
Sperry, Stuart, 163

Tasso, Torquator, 116
Thompson, Francis, 3–4

Voltaire, 99

Wasserman, Earl R., 138–9
Westbrook, Harriet, 26, 30, 32–7, 40, 86, 116
White, Henry Kirke, 77
Wilson, John, 26
Wordsworth, Dorothy, 138–9
Wordsworth, William
  Poetry:
  Celandine, The Small, 62, 189
  Celandine, To the Small, 43, 62–3, 189
  (Celandine), To the Same Flower, 62, 189
  Cintra, The Convention of, 209–10
  Complaint of a Forsaken Indian Woman, 31, 92
  Cuckoo, To the, 188
  Cumberland Beggar, The Old, 31
  Evening Walk, An, 74
  Excursion, The, 5, 29, 40, 42–3, 45–6, 52–4, 65, 86, 87, 88–90, 92, 96, 98–100, 107–9, 122, 124, 126, 128, 162, 165, 167, 176–7, 181–2, 207–9
  Female Vagrant, The, 31, 92
  Highland Boy, The Blind, 41
  I travelled among unknown man, 42
  I wandered lonely as a cloud, 56, 66, 98, 109, 163, 189, 204
  Is there a Power . . . , 74
  Idiot Boy, The, 31, 45, 70
  Influence of Natural Objects, 165–6
  Intimations Ode (Ode: Intimations of Immortality . . .), 36–7, 46, 48–50, 54, 61, 74, 84, 89, 99, 103, 129, 151, 163–6, 168–71, 189, 210
  Lines Left upon a Seat in a Yew-Tree, 93–6
  Lines Written at a Small Distance from My House, 43
  Mad Mother, The, 31, 41, 92
  Michael, 5, 31, 74, 92
  Milton, 47
  My Heart Leaps Up, 61, 204
  Nightingale, The, 3
  Nutting, 164–6
  Peele Castle, 74
  Peter Bell, 63–4, 71, 201
  Poet's Epitaph, A, 27–8, 29, 40
  Prelude, The, 126, 165
  Recluse, The, 90
  Resolution and Independence, 111, 124–7, 189
  Ruth, 92
  Sky-lark, To a, 188–90
  Switzerland, the Subjugation of, 43
  Thanksgiving Ode, 73
  There was a boy, 96
  Thomson's 'Castle of Indolence', Stanzas Written in . . . , 62, 118
  Thorn, The, 31, 41, 44, 92–3
  Tintern Abbey, 33–9, 41, 42, 45, 83, 101, 162–6, 169, 171–2, 177–82, 210, 224

  Prose:
  Lyrical Ballads, Preface to 8–11, 23–4, 31, 95, 114

Works:
Lyrical Ballads, 28, 31, 71, 92–3, 119, 180–1

Yeats, William Butler, 173

Zillman, Lawrence John, 139